CORPORATE RISE

CORPORATE
RISE

THE

X

PRINCIPLES OF EXTREME
PERSONAL LEADERSHIP

CURTIS J. CRAWFORD, Ph.D.

XCEO, Inc.

Santa Clara, California

Published by XCEO, Inc.
2901 Tasman Drive, Suite 222
Santa Clara, CA 95054

Publisher's Cataloging-in-Publication Data
Crawford, Curtis J.

    Corporate rise : the "X" principles of extreme personal leadership. – Santa Clara, CA
    : XCEO, Inc., 2005.

p. ; cm.
Includes bibliographical references and index.
ISBN: 0-9769019-0-0
ISBN13: 978-0-9769019-0-7

1. Leadership. 2. Management. 3. Executive ability. I. Title.

HD57.7 .C73 2005   2005930244
658.4/092—dc22

Book production and coordination by Jenkins Group, Inc. • www.bookpublishing.com
Interior production by Royce Deans
Cover design by Chris Rhoads

Printed in the United States of America
09 08 07 06 05 • 5 4 3 2 1

This work is dedicated to all of the professionals I am privileged to work with and who have contributed so much to my personal development throughout my career. Your continued support always inspires me to stay motivated and reach for the stars. When facing seemingly insurmountable challenges you always encourage me to keep my eye on the prize and never give up. When things are going well, you keep me grounded in reality, while congratulating me for making progress. But you always remind me that the "reward for doing good work ... is more good work to do!"
A special thanks to my lovely wife, Gina!

Acknowledgments

Sincere thanks go to the XCEO, Inc. research and development, and administrative teams. They include Fred Dalili, CEO of Productivity Plus; Michelle Ronco, MBA, Santa Clara University; and Richard Chen, Ph.D. student at the University of Washington; Nancy Geyer, my long-time and irreplaceable Executive Assistant; and Christina M. Pagkali-nawan, who keeps the office well coordinated and allows us to stay in touch with the real world! Your collective hard work, counsel, and commitment were critical to the success of this project. It is not possible to sufficiently recognize all the contributions that each of you made to this work. Your scholarly insight and wisdom provided a wealth of perspectives and experiences from which to draw. I thank you for your intellect and passion, and will forever be grateful to each of you. This project is a success because of your _extreme personal leadership_!

A very special acknowledgment and heartfelt thanks go to Robert Couch, a friend who once worked with me as Senior Vice President for Market Communications. Bob, thanks for your support and early engagement in preparing to write _Corporate Rise_. A few times, I admonished myself for yielding to your encouragement. But most often, I smiled and thanked you for your inspiration!

Many friends, former colleagues, and professional associates provided wisdom, keen insight, and unwavering moral support throughout this entire process. Thanks for sharing your valuable time, knowledge, and personal experiences to help make this an exhilarating journey. I will be forever thankful!

My heartfelt thanks also go to the chief executive officers and corporate board members who took time from their busy schedules to discuss their views of leadership with me. Your contributions are very much appreciated.

Very special thanks go to my editor, Judy Hardesty. I am forever thankful that you decided to come out of retirement to work with me on this project. Again, simply put, you are the absolute best! Thank you, again, for your superb support.

Contents

X-Principle One

X-Leaders have a passion for developing people. They are in constant pursuit of every employee's success.

X-Principle Two

X-Leaders find imaginative ways to inspire people. They are motivated to reach higher levels of performance by linking great ideas to exhilarating images of success.

X-Principle Three

X-Leaders cultivate creativity by looking at common things in uncommon ways. They expose old issues and develop fresh approaches to challenges.

X-Principle Four

X-Leaders are customer-centric; they realize that unless someone buys something from their company, everything they do is totally irrelevant.

X-Principle Five

X-Leaders are visionaries who anticipate the future and identify marketplace opportunities before they become trends.

X-Principle Six

X-Leaders drive their companies with decisions grounded in facts. They insist on exchanging information with all employees and customers, and they seek opportunities to tell the truth.

X-Principle Eleven
X-Leaders are role models. They lead by example.

Get Started Now!

Conclusion

The X-Principles at a Glance

In each chapter, the following outlines are provided to assist the reader in selecting specific areas of interest:

Aspiring X-Leaders

Senior Managers

Corporate Board Members

Individual Contributors

Customers

While some readers may choose to read only sections of the book that seem immediately applicable to them, all readers are strongly encouraged to read all sections. This will provide a much broader perspective on extreme personal leadership. To be a successful X-leader, it is equally as important that you develop an appreciation for the various constituents that will influence your personal behavior, ultimate performance and contributions in building shareowner value: The key to your long-term success!

Aspiring X-Leaders
Subject Guide

Senior Managers
Subject Guide

Corporate Board Memebers
Subject Guide

Professionals and Specialists
Subject Guide

Customers
Subject Guide

Preface

The X-Principles:

The Leader's Guide to Extreme Personal Leadership

I wrote *Corporate Rise* for people in the corporate world who are pursuing a great goal or who believe that they should be. These individuals are not embarrassed by their desire to lead their corporations. They want to be held responsible for delivering results. To earn the right to lead, they are willing to invest time and education, make sacrifices, and compete hard. In fact, the people who will be most helped by the information in *Corporate Rise* are those who are willing to work exceptionally hard during their long journey to the top.

If you dream big and sincerely want to be in charge, *Corporate Rise* will help you earn the opportunity to do great things in the corporate world. Following the advice contained in these pages will help you develop the skills, behaviors, and attitudes necessary to accelerate your progress to the top of the business world.

No matter what resources you draw from as you develop your own personal career plan, you can use the recommendations in this book to complement those resources. *Corporate Rise* is intended to help you reap the benefits of being an extremely successful personal leader, what I call an X-Leader.

X-Leaders have high aspirations and very positive attitudes about their futures. They are highly motivated and academically well prepared. They believe in creating their own opportunities rather than waiting in line for the next big break. They strive to do exceptional things that inspire creativity and ever-higher levels of performance. They are responsible and accountable, and they expect to deliver outstanding results. They want to win with a passion. These people feel inspired to reach for the stars!

People who already have largely achieved their leadership ambitions (such as corporate directors and senior managers) can benefit from reading *Corporate Rise*, as well. If you hold a very responsible leadership position, some kernels of my experience might be helpful to you, and reading this book will provide you with an opportunity to examine your own leadership principles and ideologies.

Corporate customers also can benefit from reading *Corporate Rise*, especially because they rely on good leadership to sustain reliable sources of supplies and keep costs down.

Of course, not everyone wants to become a great leader! Specialists (such as engineers, sales representatives, and accountants) make important individual contributions to the corporation without necessarily being leaders, and many people are just naturally followers. If you are the type of person who prefers that someone else be in charge, reading *Corporate Rise* will help you understand what your boss and many of your colleagues are up to. You'll gain a better appreciation of your supervisor's approach to exercising his or her responsibilities, and you'll gain important insights into the behaviors of many of your colleagues as they attempt to rise to the top.

The advice in *Corporate Rise* grew out of my experiences as a senior executive leader in the corporate world at IBM Corporation, AT&T, Lucent Technologies Microelectronics Group, Zilog, and Onix Microsystems, where I gained many insights into personal leadership—the school of leadership I focused on in my career and in this book.

I've been privileged to work with some of the brightest, hardest working, and most successful corporate leaders in the U.S., Europe, and Asia, and I've had the pleasure of partnering with several of the most successful international companies in the world. As a member of the board of directors at such corporations as DuPont, ITT Industries, ON Semiconductors, Agilysys, Lyondell Petrochemical and several others, I have worked very closely with many recognized world-class leaders. As I learned about personal leadership from these formidable leaders, I used what I learned to assemble a set of eleven principles that lead to the extremely successful personal leadership that I call X-Leadership. Most of *Corporate Rise* is devoted to explanations of those principles.

After several of my colleagues encouraged me to write this book, I realized that I had earned the privilege of sharing my understandings of the qualities of great leadership with a broad base of people. After many years of being passionately dedicated to teaching people how to lead, the time had come for me to record my ideas for helping people with high aspirations. Fortunately, as I contemplated the formidable task of writing *Corporate Rise*, I also entered a phase of my life in which I had the time and energy to perform the necessary research.

I believe that when a corporate leader takes on the responsibility of developing his or her company, that leader must also assume the responsibility of self-development. I also am convinced that it is very important to look at leadership from the points of view of leaders and followers at different levels. In *Corporate Rise*, as in my career, I have examined the concept of X-Leadership from the viewpoint of corporate

Many people know quite well that they have underdeveloped talents, but even those with enormous intellectual capacity often don't know how to leverage their talents into power and influence.

directors; senior leaders; specialists, such as accountants, sales representatives and engineers; and corporate customers. But, perhaps more importantly, I very thoroughly examined X-Leadership from the viewpoint of the ambitious person working to become a CEO, senior leader, or corporate director.

As you read *Corporate Rise*, you will be exposed to my beliefs about the leadership responsibilities of people at different levels of leadership, and how various types of followers can improve the quality of their leaders and thus the quality of their careers. To make using this book easy to use by the busy reader, I designed it so that each category of reader, whether corporate director, senior leader, professional contributor, or corporate customer, can easily find information applicable to his or her situation and area of interest. Corporate directors, for example, can choose to read only those sections directly addressed to corporate directors, and senior leaders can choose to read only sections devoted to their own areas of interest. However, a more valuable approach would be to read the entire book and examine the leadership concerns of various members of the corporate community. Specialists, such as engineers, administrators, and marketers, can become much more powerful by gaining insight into the motivations and responsibilities of senior leaders pursuing X-Leadership. The same is true for corporate directors and customers.

Corporate Rise is meant to be used over and over again. It explains principles that it took three decades for me to learn about and to put into practice. These principles can be applied at many stages of a person's career. If you are an ambitious leader, or want to be, referring often to *Corporate Rise* will serve your forward progress in a lasting way. I suggest that you think of this book as a tool that you can use at any point in your career to help you reflect on the different viewpoints that are affecting you.

As you read, please remember that you don't need to ask yourself whether you are a person who has potential; everyone has potential. Instead, ask yourself how to turn your talents into abilities that others see as powerful and influential. Many people know quite well that they have underdeveloped talents, but even those with enormous intellectual capacity often don't know how to leverage their talents into power and influence.

The first step in leveraging your talents is to take a good look at what you think you might be good at so that you can discover what you genuinely are good at. It is up to you to find out what your real talents are. Don't wait for other people to make the effort—it may never happen. And please don't wait for your company to look for a way to leverage your talents. Most companies won't bother. Instead, take charge and develop your own way to the top. Of course, making your way to the top will require a high degree of confidence and a willingness to learn, grow as a person, and contribute to your company each and every day. It's good to remember that the reward for doing good work always is more good work to do!

I invite you now to sit back, read, and enjoy. As you read, keep an open mind. If you practice the eleven X-Principles for Extreme Success with an honest spirit and heartfelt passion, they will prove incredibly valuable to you throughout your career!

Introduction

Experience the Higher Ground

Great leaders take exceptional actions that inspire creativity and ever-higher levels of performance. They are responsible and accountable. And they want to win with a passion. They have an attitude: a very positive one. Great leadership is something that most people recognize when they see it. Great leaders reach for the stars! I call such leadership extreme personal leadership, and I call such leaders X-Leaders.

Leading from the extreme is the practice of going far beyond the boundaries of conventional expectations. It is the pursuit of what may not seem possible from an ordinary perspective. It means setting audacious goals. X-Leaders do not want to follow, but they are willing to learn how to follow, and to do so as effectively as they lead. When X-Leaders do follow, they inspire (and respectfully demand) great leadership from their leaders. Nevertheless, an X-Leader never will be content to follow for any significant length of time. The X-Leader knows that when any leader admits that he doesn't care whether or not he leads, it is time to find a new leader.

Many researchers have tried to discover whether the ability to lead is an inborn personal trait or whether it is comprised by a set of skills that can be learned. Persuasive arguments support both views, and I see some truth in each. However, my experience tells me that leadership ability is a set of knowledge and skills that can be learned. Much of my own success as a leader is the result of what I learned from some of the best and brightest leaders and visionaries in the corporate world, together with what I gleaned from ineffective leaders who were difficult to work with. As a manager, I led some of the most highly motivated people in business, but some of my subordinates had become disillusioned and were difficult to motivate. My experiences with great leaders and highly motivated followers were courses in the best way to get things done, and my experiences with ineffective leaders and disillusioned followers were opportunities to learn how not to proceed!

No one can lead without the ability to cause change in the lives of others, and many ineffective leaders offer evidence that the power to influence change can come in the form of authority granted through political patronage or inheritance. However, the ability to cause change also can come in the form of leadership. In other words, if an individual has not been granted direct authority to make change, he or she still can cause change to take place by using any leadership skills he or she possesses. In my view, leadership is an opportunity that can be earned.

> **Although all employees should be treated fairly, they certainly should not be treated equally.**

Clearly, it takes power to become an extreme personal leader. For the X-Leader, the power source is an ability to lead that comes from within, an ability that results from the X-Leader's knowledge and experiences. The most effective way to develop the power to influence the outcome of your particular situation is to demonstrate meaningful knowledge and skills. But a person also can develop power through passion. Caring very deeply about something and effectively demonstrating that caring can earn you the power to make positive changes in your environment. An important characteristic of X-Leaders is that they are passionate about their work.

During one of my early experiences at IBM Corporation, a seasoned executive advised a subordinate: "Don't wait for me to give you a business card labeled Supervisor. Start demonstrating the attributes that a supervisor should master." That's when I learned that it is never a good idea to wait for leadership to be granted to you. Instead, find opportunities to demonstrate whatever leadership power you already have. If you want to be a leader, start playing that role today. Use the power of your own knowledge, experiences, and skill set to influence the directions taken by your company. Don't wait to be granted the authority to influence outcomes. Instead, leverage your knowledge, insight, experience, and passion to your benefit.

For an example of using personal leadership at an extreme level, we can look to Michael Jordan, former professional basketball player for the National Basketball Association (NBA) who consistently demonstrated his power to influence the outcome of any basketball game by his mere presence. Because the athletes on the court had such great respect for his talents, if Michael Jordan was in the auditorium-even if he was not playing-the athletes on the court raised their level of play. The sheer strength of his presence brought out the best in all of the players present as they tried to impress him. Similarly, in the corporate world, the mere presence of an esteemed corporate executive in a meeting can bring out the best in the performance of other senior leaders.

In any field, people respect those who are good at what they do, and we have even higher expectations for those who are great at what they do. People tend to give more power and authority to great performers than to ordinary ones, whether or not those high performers want that extra power. That is one good reason for pursuing excellence in everything you do. Try to be the best and to command the support of people who have the authority to grant you power. To be a leader, you must earn the power to influence outcomes.

Senior executives of a corporation must develop X-Leadership if they want a highly motivated, high-performance management team that increases shareowner satisfaction and corporate wealth in the long term. X-Leaders hold themselves responsible for creating a stimulating corporate environment that influences the kind of day-to-day business decisions that have a profoundly positive impact on employees and customers. This healthy environment nurtures the dynamic people and teams that get work done. One of the 10 keys to great leadership advocated by Jeff Immelt, General Electric's Chairman and CEO, is "liking people." According to Immelt:

Today, it's employment at will. Nobody's here who doesn't want to be here. So it's critical to understand people, to always be fair, and to want the best in them. And when it doesn't work, they need to know it's not personal. [i]

During one of my own executive performance reviews, Mike Quinlan, President of the IBM Data Processing Division, told me that IBM always could find managers who knew how to consistently deliver outstanding financial results and IBM always could find managers who could effectively develop people. The challenge, Mike said, was identifying leaders who could do both.

Of course, X-Leaders on the senior leadership team deliver the good short-term results that shareholders expect. And they go far beyond the delivery of short-term financial results to deliver sustainable, long-term financial success. Although these financial results are (appropriately) most often the ultimate measurement tool for calculating business success, they really are just sets of numbers frozen in time. These numbers track the hard side of the business: How many objects the corporation built and how much money it made. However, financial results seldom reveal the fundamental character of the business that led to the results and how those results were achieved. This is one reason that the influence of X-Leadership and teamwork on the bottom line seldom is appreciated. Nevertheless, sustained good financial results are not possible without an outstanding senior leadership team that delivers phenomenal products or services to the company's customers.

Good management improves financial results in the short term. However, X-Leadership improves the satisfaction of both customers and employees in the long term. To maintain improvements in the long term, most corporations need to continually improve the quality and effectiveness of

> **X-Leaders create passion and exhilaration for the mundane.**

their overall leadership. X-Leaders create environments that accomplish goals through a leadership approach that creates the energy to propel organizations to heights far beyond expectations. To become great, the corporation's pace toward becoming the company that it wants to be must be accelerated. This means changing the way managers lead.

Many glib statements purport to distinguish between managers and leaders. You have most likely heard, for example, that "managers are people who do things right, whereas leaders are people who do the right things." It is true that managers and leaders play two very different roles, and that they differ in what motivates them, how they think, and how they act. Most people prefer one role over the other, but some are comfortable in both.

Good managers are, first and foremost, problem solvers. Whether the manager's energies are directed toward goals, resources, organizational structures, or

4

people, that person's forte is solving problems. From the manager's perspective, managing is a practical effort to direct the affairs of the company. The manager fulfills his or her responsibilities by requiring that people at different levels of responsibility operate efficiently. Outstanding managers are intelligent, tough-minded, and persistent hard workers who possess analytical ability and-perhaps most importantly-tolerance and goodwill. Managers ask: What problems must be solved? How can we keep people contributing to the company's success?

X-Leadership differs substantially from managing. Whereas managers act to limit choices, X-Leaders constantly strive to develop fresh approaches to long-standing problems and to open most issues to new creative options. To be effective, X-Leaders project bold, bright ideas onto images that excite people. They make the impossible seem possible, and they build reason into the seemingly unreasonable. X-Leaders create passion and exhilaration for the mundane. They dream big and expect great things to happen. They believe that anything worth doing eventually will be done. X-Leaders recognize that what may seem extreme today will be commonplace tomorrow. For example, instead of seeing the cell phone as a handy telecommunications device for voice and data, or as a great entertainment and imaging machine, the X-Leader will see it as the 21st-century replacement for the Swiss army knife: an ultimate utility product that includes such convenience features as a flashlight, pager, TV, telephone, music box, and camera. For those of us who travel frequently and fashion ourselves as global jetsetters, it might even include a nail file!

Most ordinary leaders focus on strategy and process. However, the X-Leader focuses on creativity. To the X-Leader, a long-term vision is just as important as a good strategy. In fact, vision is a hallmark of extreme personal leadership, a lesson that was learned very well by Lou Gerstner, former IBM Chairman and CEO. When Gerstner first joined IBM, he tried to lead the information systems giant without an articulated vision. So thoroughly did he believe that IBM's problems could be solved by traditional management techniques that Gerstner openly stated that the last thing IBM needed was a grand plan. After a few months on the job, though, Gerstner held a press conference to announce to the world that IBM needed a vision. The rest is history: During his tenure as head of IBM, Lou Gerstner delivered phenomenal shareowner value.

Leading from the extreme means boldly taking (well calculated) big risks. X-Leaders learn how to work from high-risk positions and are willing to do so. Indeed, X-Leaders often are disposed by temperament to seek out risks and danger, especially where the chance of opportunity and reward appears significant. Such leaders consider mundane work to be an affliction. This characteristic separates them from managers, who value survival over the thrill of risk, a trait that permits managers to tolerate mundane, practical work.

A really strong leadership environment is characterized by extensive delegation. The ability to delegate is a logical extension of the X-Leader's constant engagement with personal awareness and development. Importantly, when X-Leaders delegate, they don't merely dump their work onto subordinates! They train and coach those subordinates and entrust them with authority commensurate to the delegated tasks. After developing their subordinates, X-Leaders give them the responsibility needed to use their developing skills for the benefit of the corporation. Giving subordinate's authority makes the X-Leader much more vulnerable, of course. However, this risk-taking leader has learned and accepted that he or she never can be the best at everything in the company.

> **Teamwork without leadership is a myth, and so is leadership without teamwork.**

X-Leaders recognize that all employees are not equally qualified. Some are smarter than others. Some work harder. Some are more motivated. Although all employees should be treated fairly, they certainly should not be treated equally. The X-Leader sets very high performance standards and maximizes each employee's opportunities. The X-Leader recognizes that he or she is privileged to work with other people and develops each of those people accordingly. In terms of respect and opportunity, the X-Leader always treats all employees as well as leadership is treated. This, a commitment to excellence, will strike terror in the heart of any competitor!

X-Leaders also know how to inflict pain. As one long- term, infamous executive once pointed out: "One's ability to lead is confirmed once one's ability to inflict pain is demonstrated!" My view of the "ability to inflict pain" is the courage to be constructively honest with all employees. This practice sometimes causes pain, but it also contains elements of compassion, because telling people the truth-even if they don't want to hear it-usually is the best and

6

most respectful course of action. Of course, telling people what they want to hear is easier than telling them what they need to hear, but when an employee's performance is less than expected, he or she should be told what is required and encouraged to improve. When an employee's performance is good, that person should be congratulated and encouraged to continue improving. When the employee's performance is superb, he or she should be told so and be encouraged to help others improve their levels of performance.

It almost goes without saying that X-Leaders are intensively competitive. They do not enjoy losing, and they definitely do not regard losing as a way to build character! Extreme leaders don't play just for the fun of it. They never want to lose: They want to win. However, losing is a fact of life, and X-Leaders recognize that no one always wins. Although the X-Leader may despise the thought of not achieving his or her goals, this leader does not fear failure. When the X-Leader does lose, he or she does so gracefully and with respect, keeping in mind that he or she has lost to a better solution, a better product, or a better team.

This attitude is possible because the X-Leader is committed to success. This leader learns from a defeat and expects to do better the next time around, along with his or her team. Although X-Leaders constantly pursue excellence, they recognize that they never will achieve perfection. And,

> **To be a leader, you must earn the power to influence outcomes.**

especially for the X-Leader, the experience of excellence is fleeting. As soon as the X-Leader achieves a higher level of performance, new expectations will be set and the bar will be raised. X-Leaders know that they always will be expected to outperform the ordinary competitor and deliver consistently better results. As I always remind my teams, the reward for doing good work is sure to be more good work to do! Being recognized as an X-Leader does not mean that you have reached the summit or that you can afford to take it easy. In the globally competitive marketplace, thinking that you have made it is an early sign of impending disaster. You certainly cannot allow that to happen! In fact, the challenge of delivering X-Leadership becomes much more difficult once you accept responsibility for advocating great leadership.

Teamwork without leadership is a myth, and so is leadership without teamwork. Achieving X-Leadership without teamwork is very difficult. X-Leaders recognize that their success is highly dependent on the achievements of others, so they surround themselves with the best people available and invest heavily in the development of those people. X-Leaders provide their subordinates with opportunities to make valuable contributions to the team. In the environment created by the X-Leader, each person becomes motivated to perform at his or her highest level.

In their pursuit of excellence, X-Leaders are audacious and, most often, guided by ambition. However, they are never blinded by aspiration. X-Leaders are not afraid to find a balance between their goals and their professional activities. When they align their professional activities with their goals, they keep in mind that too much alignment is just as imperfect as too little. The X-Leader knows that, as a general rule, the more significant the opportunity, the stronger the competition and the more difficult the task. However, significant opportunities are fewer in number than ordinary ones.

> **X-Leaders do not enjoy losing, and they definitely do not regard losing as a way to build character!**

Michael Jordan achieved fame as a man with an extreme set of skills, mastery in executing those skills, creative performance, and an acute understanding of the momentum of his game. He became famous for always demonstrating a high level of coordination, speed, and rapid decision-making. His ability to predict other people's movements and eye-hand-mind synchronizations made him a legend. He earned great respect for his belief in synergy, building for long-term success, and making money in an honorable way. However, we all know that not everyone is capable of being a Michael Jordan, just as every leader cannot be an X-Leader. Being great at what you do does not in itself make you a leader, any more than the sum of Michael Jordan's skills make him a coach. If you are not cut out to be a superstar, I advise you not to worry about it. No team wants only Michael Jordans.

However, if you have a burning desire to lead, I am here to tell you that extreme personal leadership is a combination of knowledge and skills that can be learned. And, not only can extreme personal leadership be learned, it can be improved with practice. If you have a passion to lead, you can become the X-Leader who sees realities that most people choose not to see. You can bring yourself and those around you up to a higher level of performance. *Corporate Rise* was written to help you on the path.

Endnotes

[i] Fastcompany. (2004, April). Things leaders do: GE's Jeff Immelt on the ten keys to great leadership. Fastcompany.com [On-line serial]. Retrieved May 3, 2004, from http://www.fastcompany.com/magazine/81/

X-Principle One: *X-Leaders have a passion for developing people. They are in constant pursuit of every employee's success. X-Leaders do not declare total victory until all the people around them have succeeded.*

CHAPTER 1

Extraordinary Personal Development

An important characteristic of the X-Leader is that he or she wants to energize the entire company through personal achievement. The X-Leader believes that every member of the company should be developed to his or her maximum potential. As a result, this leader extols the virtues of personal development for the benefit of the entire team. X-Leaders understand that, in the company, solo victory is impossible to achieve. Anyone aspiring to become an X-Leader certainly will need the passionate support of the equivalent of a village of people! To gain such support, X-Leaders make certain that they are as committed to the success of others as they are to their own success. X-Leaders also work very hard to be good communicators. Even when the competition is weak, the market is soft, or the economy is bad, X-Leaders are on the lookout for opportunities to build on their greatest asset: a strong set of people skills.

The Challenge of Change

Today's ever-shrinking world is characterized by the availability of a remarkable variety of talents, skills, and personalities from different places and cultures. For a company to benefit from the potential infusion of these disparate resources, it has to absorb them quickly, which means being able to make rapid changes. Also behind the need for change is the company's constant, passionate pursuit of three elusive targets: increased revenue, increased profit, and increased market share. With product cycles getting shorter and competition getting keener, competitive advantage must be regularly replenished and re-delivered. To outrun the competition, indeed, even to survive as a business entity, the company must initiate change and nurture it.

More than 50 years ago, Ronald Lippitt showed that the best starting points for change are not images of problems, but images of potential.[ii] For most businesses, the challenge is to identify opportunities early on and make choices that rapidly propel the company toward its goals, even though this often means taking calculated risks. Knowing this, the X-Leader places the company's effort to pursue opportunities on equal footing with the company's effort to solve problems.

Valuing Employee Talent

It has become obvious that assembling a successful, 21st-century corporation requires more than high technology; it requires attracting, developing, and maintaining employees of very high quality. Certainly, using new high-tech tools can drive down costs and make operations more efficient; after all, better microprocessors and other computer chips lead to faster and more powerful Information Age tools that enhance employee productivity. Moreover, advanced manufacturing techniques, such as machine reprogramming, make it possible to tailor products to each customer's needs.[iii] However, corporate success in the 21st century absolutely requires corporate leaders who can manage change and even thrive on the chaos offered by today's business climate.

In this climate, X-Leaders, not technology, will provide long-term advantage because no corporation can succeed without creative, committed, successful employees who produce profits. X-Leaders understand that anything less than optimal performance by employees results in lost market share and missed opportunities for the company and for themselves as individuals. Merely hiring the best and the brightest, X-Leaders understand, is not sufficient. Corporations also must invest-and invest heavily-in developing their people.

X-Leaders are able to make better results a reality and enrich the corporate culture beyond imagination because they make it their job to thoroughly understand their employees. X-Leaders also give recognition to employees not only for producing profit, but also for developing their individual talents. By developing their special strengths, employees become better able to make unique and valuable contributions to the company. When an X-Leader creates an environment that encourages each employee to be the best that he or she can be, that leader is helping each employee to make the most significant possible contributions to the company's overall success. A big part of helping employees succeed, of course, is creating advancement opportunities that nurture each individual's unique strengths and help them fill the gaps in their skill sets.

Clearly, valuing the intrinsic contributions of human beings is critical to a company's overall effectiveness. Despite this reality, for decades many American companies believed that investing in people development should wait until business conditions were good. In recent times, however, the distribution of American jobs around the globe (euphemistically termed *outsourcing*) has substantially reduced most companies' flexibility to rearrange their expense structures during down cycles. Corporations no longer can differentiate themselves exclusively through manufacturing costs: The opportunities to outsource are too abundant.

The trend toward increased outsourcing and job complexity makes investments in people development less discretionary. Companies wanting to differentiate themselves in today's climate must increase their intellectual capacity, and the pressure to do so has created a rush toward more highly technological and sophisticated industrial training systems. The American Society for Training and Development estimated that, by 1998, employers with 50 or more employees had increased their spending on formal training to $55 billion per year.[iv] One reason that corporations began to offer more training is that more people were entering the workforce lacking basic skills. By the mid-1990s, fully half of Fortune 500 firms were regarding themselves as the "educators of last resort."[v] Of Fortune 500 companies surveyed at that time, 91% were providing middle-management training, 75% were providing sales training, 56% were providing secretarial training, 51% executive development, and 44% technical training.[vi]

Motorola Corporation was spending an annual average of $1,350 per person to teach courses in basic skills to bring workers to a level at which they could be retrained; Polaroid Corporation was spending $700,000 at its Cambridge, Massachusetts, facility to teach its employees basic English and mathematics. [vii] By 1999, Gerald Dotson, former AT&T Technical Education Director, was reporting that American industry had undertaken "a job that education used to do—teaching the basics," at a cost of $50,000 per new employee."[viii]

Such training, although expensive, definitely is not wasted. Worker training has been shown to have significant beneficial effects. A 1995 study of 1,000 firms revealed that a 10% increase in the educational attainment of a company's workforce increased productivity by 8.6%, whereas a 10% increase in the value of capital stock (tools and buildings) increased productivity by only 3.4%.[ix] Retraining workers for new jobs has been established as more cost effective than releasing them and hiring new ones,[x] not to mention offering gains in worker morale.

The urge to develop the skills of the people who produce the company's profit might seem, at first glance, like a natural instinct for the company, but often such is not the case. Ironically, when business slows down and revenues or profits

> **Merely hiring the best and the brightest, X-Leaders understand, is not sufficient. Corporations also must invest—and invest heavily in developing their people.**

begin to decline, some corporate leaders cut back on employee development and visits to customers. These areas may represent the lines of least resistance to cut-backs, but it is totally illogical to reduce customer contact when sales decline, just as it is unreasonable to cut back on people development in hopes of producing positive consequences for the shareholders.

Finding competitive advantage is becoming increasingly difficult, and cost certainly will continue to be an important factor in maintaining or increasing market share. However, I strongly believe that the people side of business will continue to demand managers' ever-increasing attention. Corporations will invest more and more money and energy in developing people who have the creative instincts to imagine exciting new products and the competitive drive to bring these products to market.

Offering everyone who works in the company encouragement, support, and opportunities for personal development is an important way to build value for all of the company's stakeholders. If you are a senior executive, you want to develop the company's personnel to the fullest so that these workers can give their best to the company's success. If you are a board member, you owe it to your company's shareholders and other stakeholders to make sure that the company's senior leaders create a corporate environment that maximizes returns for investors. If your company is the customer of a strategic supplier, you want the personnel assigned to your account (and therefore entrusted with the responsibility of servicing your company) to be well trained. Because you want your company to be highly productive, you should be keenly interested in ensuring that the people assigned to your company's account can and will deliver world-class competitive products and services to your company. It is in your best interests that these people be fully developed by your strategic supplier. Last but not least, if you are a professional or specialist, such as an engineer, sales representative, administrator, etc., you obviously want to work for a company that acts very strongly to develop its personnel.

Different groups of stakeholders are sensitive to different areas of people development. For the convenience of readers, the advantages of X-Leadership for different types of stakeholders are discussed separately, starting with some advice for the ambitious future X-Leader.

Aspiring X-Leaders: Strive for Success

If you feel a strong desire to lead, don't be surprised. X-Leaders have a passion for leading. In fact, the results of various studies have shown that leaders and managers actually *feel* a need for power, achievement, and affiliation with the group, and effective managers seem to need these more than ineffective ones. [xi] Apparently, feeling a need for power and achievement seems to help make people good leaders.

Conversely, a leader who doesn't want to lead and doesn't value achievement cannot be effective. Sometimes people are thrust into leadership roles that they don't want to fill. For people who are not energized by leadership, the responsibility that goes with it is a heavy burden. Those who are obligated to follow an unwilling, complacent, or unprepared leader also are experiencing misfortune; such a leader is unable to provide his or her followers with the guidance and direction they need. When someone tells you, "Well, I didn't really want this position," or "I am only doing this only because I was asked; I never really had a desire to do it," I suggest that you be very, very leery of their long-term prospects! The only thing worse than having someone in charge who does not want to be in charge is having someone in charge who is not qualified to be in charge.

Having a passion to lead doesn't mean that the person who wants leadership is willing to take it at the expense of others; there is absolutely nothing inherently wrong or undesirable about wanting to lead. In fact, followers tend to be impressed by the courage of those who step up to the leadership role to provide guidance and direction for the rest of the team. Wanting to lead doesn't in itself make someone more intelligent than the people who do not share this passion. It is well for those who aspire to lead to keep in mind that a burning desire to be in charge does not give anyone the right to get there by being selfish and inconsiderate of others. On the contrary, to earn the right to be in charge, the aspiring leader must garner the support of the people who will follow. To be a great leader, you must master the skills needed to be a great follower.

The urge to develop one's own talents as an employee might seem like a natural instinct, but very often this is not the case. Nevertheless, anyone who seriously wants to achieve the highest levels of corporate responsibility must take advantage of opportunities to develop his or her skills. You cannot excel in your career unless you significantly outperform your colleagues. You must be more passionate about your job and work harder than anyone around you, and you must consistently deliver outstanding results. Generally speaking, those who perform best, have the most positive attitude, and work the hardest will go farthest in the company. Other elements also influence career advancement, such as politics and luck, which always play a role at some level. However, focusing on the areas under your direct control will help determine whether you advance a few steps or all the way to the top.

I believe that any corporate leader's success ultimately depends on the character and drive that he or she displays on the job each and every day. The act of striving for success is equally as important as absolute intellectual achievement, a lesson illustrated in an anecdote told to me by a friend. While attending his school reunion, my friend recognized a former classmate who had developed into a debonair gentleman with a distinct air of success. This classmate had obviously become a winner. My friend approached him and asked, "Listen, as I remember, you were not much of a student. To what do you attribute your success?" Mr. Success replied, "I always figured that if I bought something for $1.00 and I sold it for $4.00, I would make a nice 3% profit!" This story illustrates that pure intellect is not the only key to success.

Whatever your intellectual capacities, to be extremely successful you must be constantly committed to achievement. No matter how tough the going gets and how difficult the task, you must maintain a positive attitude. You must manage yourself effectively and establish a win-win relationship with your supervisor. You must learn how to calculate whether the risks you contemplate taking are likely to pay off. And you must maintain the highest level of integrity at all times.

You also must determine whether you are working in an environment that values people development. If you are not, your aspirations for success and leadership will be thwarted over and over again. One way to test your company's commitment to your personal development is to look around and see whether your peers are pursuing their own development; if other people in the company are as focused on their own personal development plans as they are on the corporate business plan, your organization is poised for great achievements. Linking personal development and business development creates a synergy that delivers a competitive edge in the marketplace. It's no wonder that X-Leaders have a passion for people development!

When honing your plan for becoming an X-Leader, pay careful attention to career velocity. Do not be misled: Speed is important! How fast you advance can determine how far you advance. During your career you will be assigned to a variety of positions. These jobs all will be temporary; never make the mistake of thinking that any assignment is permanent! During my 15 years at IBM, I held at least 12 different positions, several of them lateral moves, not promotions. Each of these jobs was intended to further my development.

Gaining this variety of experience is an exceptionally effective method of developing your X-Leadership skills. However, even though you must fill a variety of jobs in the firm, you need not master all of them. As long as you can master 80% of what is required to become expert in a given area, you have achieved enough to advance to broader responsibilities. In general, you should be able to reach 80% mastery of a skill in about half the time it takes to reach 100% mastery. Thus, if it takes 5 years to master a skill, you should be able to develop 80% proficiency in this skill in 2 1/2 years. Because achieving the last 20% of the knowledge needed to become an expert in the skill will require a time investment of another 2 1/2 years, it is obvious you cannot afford to become an expert in more than one or two areas in business. Allow those who elect to become experts to spend the additional time honing their skills. Don't be guided in any other direction. Your challenge as a future X-Leader is to develop a broad set of skills. To make it to the top, you must experience as many areas as possible along the way. Spend only enough time in each position to really understand and appreciate it, add value to the company, and demonstrate your competencies.

You don't have the option of staying in any position for too long because there are too many jobs that you will have to learn. Very simply put, if you need to do 10 different jobs within your career, you can afford to spend no more than 2 to 3 years in each job. And, generally speaking, 2 or 3 years is plenty of time for an exceptional performer to establish leadership in any job. Striving to reach the top is a never-ending effort requiring many sacrifices, and the price rises each and every day. If you want to play the game, you must play by its rules or else earn the authority to change the rules.

Speaking of rules, every business is guided by a set of rules, policies, and practices that you must understand. The company's *rules* govern people's behaviors in most company operations. These rules are interpreted and followed under an umbrella of practices (habits and customs) and *preferences* (priorities). The programs of action that the company adopts are called *policies*. X-Leaders focus on the intent of these policies so that they are able to understand when these policies have been effectively implemented and when they should be changed.

The X-Leader also applies ethics and morality in the corporate environment. He or she certainly does not break the company's rules or act immorally or unethically. For the X-Leader, it is not necessary to expend energy trying to break the company's rules because he or she has earned the responsibility and commensurate authority to make and change rules.

If you do choose to play the game, you will quickly find that playing the game is much more fun when you are winning. Unfortunately, losing is an experience that we all have at some time. Nevertheless, you must never develop an appreciation for losing. To the X-Leader, the only value in losing is to provide inspiration to win the next time. To reach the top, you must win most of the time. The person who wins only occasionally usually ends up with a short career.

To win consistently, you must carefully craft a long-term strategy and redefine that strategy when appropriate. Select venues that allow you to leverage your skills, always striving to be better prepared than everyone expects you to be. As legendary football coach Vince Lombardi once observed:

Winning is not a sometime thing. It is an all-the-time thing. You do not win once in a while. You do not do things right once in a while. You do them right all the time. Winning is a habit .... Unfortunately, so is losing.

To excel in X-Leadership, you must perform at the highest levels at all times. If you expect to become an X-Leader, heroic performance should become your norm. The key to heroic performance is making sure that you are creating opportunities to do great things all the time. Although crisis has accelerated many a career, don't wait for a crisis for an opportunity to differentiate yourself from your peers! X-Leaders stay in first place by delivering consistent performance; they know that second place is never more than a few steps behind!

For X-Leaders, the definition of success is very simple. They are in pursuit of the gold. X-Leaders want the opportunity to lead from the front. They want to be in charge. They choose to be responsible. They seek the level of authority and accountability needed to make the last decision. In the last second of a basketball game, it is not only Michael Jordan's teammates who want him to have the basketball in his hand. Michael Jordan wants to have the ball in his hands, too. He wants to be in charge, he wants to be the leader on the floor, and he has the confidence that he can lead the team through the most difficult times.

X-Leaders are constantly in pursuit of *everyone's* success, and they do not declare total victory until each and every one of their associates is on the path to success. This does not mean that each person defines success in the same way; of course, each person defines success differently. Although X-Leaders want the people they work with to have expectations as high as their own, they do not try to define what other's expectations should be. This sensitivity to other people's definitions of success assures the X-Leader's associates that, as they pursue their goals, they will receive the X-Leader's support.

Ambitious, determined companies are always on the lookout for people who are passionately interested in and capable of leading, because those companies need to develop future leaders to maintain a winning edge. If you truly want to achieve more than average success in your career, developing yourself for leadership will provide you with tremendous opportunity for success.

Senior Leaders: Leverage People Development into Shareowner Value

If you are a senior leader whose board of directors value X-Leadership, you are fortunate indeed because they will support you in developing high-performance people, which in turn will substantially enhance your chances of success in many ways. As the quality of the people working in your company improves, so will your chances of driving the company's long-term growth and satisfying your CEO, senior leadership team, and shareholders. Also, as your subordinates gain skill in understanding your strategies and directions, you will become more effective (and thus more valuable) as a leader. Indeed, as you work with people who are constantly nourishing their abilities, you will improve as a person.

High-performance companies deliver more value to their shareholders than their peers, enjoy longer periods of success, and attract the best talent. If you are a leader, it is up to you to consciously choose between the emotional satisfaction and personal pride of watching the people in your company reach their highest levels or to suffer the frustration and indignity of seeing them drift along producing marginal results. As I always remind my colleagues, marginal preparation and marginal efforts produce marginal performance and thus marginal creation of value for yourself and your company's shareowners.

To effectively leverage the skills of employees into shareholder value, you and your fellow senior leaders must establish an expected level of continued training and development. It is up to you to make sure that every person in the company has a documented personal development plan. That means the plans must be inspected to make sure that they get done! Each supervisor should develop a plan jointly with each employee in his or her charge. Implementing and religiously managing mandatory personal development is extremely important, not only to the company, but to you as a senior leader because, as I stated earlier, your success will be marginal if you rely on marginal people to produce results.

Moreover, you must place as much emphasis on people development as on product and service development. You and your fellow senior leaders should make sure that developing the company's people receives as much energy as building its business plans or managing its financial resources. Of course, none of these should be done at the expense of the other; X-Leaders always find a way to do everything that is required, and most things that are important. People development is not a part-time initiative nor a program du jour; it is as important as anything else done by the company and must be practiced each and every day, year in and year out. If you are a senior leader, it is extremely important to your company's success that you generate a passion for developing people. By committing to the long-term development and growth of every person in your company, you will be serving your relentless pursuit of excellence. Your company's performance is correlated directly to the quality of the people who work for

To be a great leader, you must master the skills needed to be a great follower.

your company, so you should be constantly improving the options of every person who works in the company. In the short term and in the long term, employees are a company's most valuable assets. That fact makes quality people development a hallmark of business success.

Inspired people who are excited about their work and prospects in the company produce greater returns for their investors than those who merely put in their hours in exchange for a paycheck. All of us have seen people start looking at their watches as soon as they arrive at work because they can't wait until it is time to leave. This is a sure sign that their environment is not rewarding them, and it certainly is not challenging them!

You and the rest of the senior leadership team should aim to create an environment in which each person arrives at work ready to kick the door down to get in and contribute to the company's success! This is possible if all of your company's employees enjoy their work and can earn great returns on the time and effort they invest in the company. In a productive corporate environment, people learn and grow; the company enables them to maximize their contributions to its success. In this enriched environment, people deliver greater returns to the company than most senior leadership teams would predict.

To create great companies, great people must flourish. That is why it is critically important for your senior leadership team to create the kind of environment that causes people to become inspired and to make remarkable contributions to the company's success. Some academic studies support the view that charismatic leadership can improve employee performance. In one study, people working under leaders whom they considered to be charismatic had better task performance than those working under leaders whom they considered to be merely considerate.[xii] In another study, followers changed their attitudes and improved their performances under the influence of the leader's vision and vision implementation.[xiii]

In my experience, high levels of performance can be stimulated by three fundamental motivators: fear, recognition, and good compensation. First, the environment must challenge people with a sense of urgency. Second, managers and supervisors must provide their subordinates with constructive feedback about their individual performances, and that feedback must include recognizing their great achievements and consistently celebrating their victories. Third, the company must pay people exceptionally well!

Corporate environments that bring out the best in people are not politically charged. In the X-led environment, all the company's people are measured by their accomplishments, not their skill at playing corporate politics. When performance overshadows political concerns, the team with the greatest talent has the greatest odds of winning, but when political concerns overshadow performance, talent plays a secondary role. Thus, if you want to continuously improve each employee's contribution to the company, you cannot abide a politically charged environment. By strongly focusing on people's actual contributions, you will minimize workplace politics' negative impact on productivity and, eventually, eliminate political bastions in the company.

One obvious risk of developing your people is that your competitors' recruitment efforts will target your carefully nurtured employees. After all, the median number of years that wage and salary workers had been with their current employer was 3.7 years in January 2002. Employee tenure was somewhat higher for men than for women, but the gap was smaller than it was in the 1980s.[xiv] Even during times of high unemployment, the best people are very difficult to retain because great performers are always in demand. However, you needn't fear that your company will put itself in the business of developing talent for your competitors. Even though your nurtured employees will be attractive to your company's competitors, those competitors will not necessarily be attractive to the nurtured employees! In fact, a company with an enriched environment is likely to experience both less voluntary attrition and less involuntary attrition. If you create a corporate environment that provides employees with opportunities to contribute to the company, expand their talents, grow as individuals, and share in the company's prosperity, they will be much less likely to join the competition. Although a company that expects excellence inevitably will lose some great employees (and some marginal ones), it never will be altogether lacking in great employees. However, if you don't invest in your company's employees, don't consistently recognize them for their contributions, and fail to create an encouraging environment for them, you certainly are putting your company at risk. When marginal people have become the standard in a company, the best people leave, and the company is left with a group of average workers.

I strongly believe that building the brightest, smartest, and most passionate teams creates the kind of environment that retains the workforce. In my career, I have always been fortunate to have opportunities to hire some of the best people in the industry. At IBM, AT&T, and Lucent Technologies, we knew that we would never have a lock on talent, but we always pursued the best and brightest talent available. To revive Zilog and Onix Microsystems, we tried to attract the best minds in the country. No company should ever compromise on talent.

Even as you pursue the best and the brightest people, however, you always must be careful to acquire the broadest set of talents. Consider this: When Michael Jordan was scoring 40 points per game for the Chicago Bulls, but the Bulls were losing four out of every five games, Michael Jordan was considered an excellent player. Later, when he was scoring 30 points per game, but the Bulls were winning three out of every four games, all of a sudden Michael Jordan was hailed as a star. Clearly, winning is what counts: Individual performance only is important when it is part of a winning cause. That's why X-Leaders build teams with complimentary skills. So, recruit Michael Jordan, then surround him with people whose skills accentuate his performance and accelerate their own performances.

As you pursue the best talent you can, be careful not to pack your team with all-stars. The law of diminishing returns dictates that an X-Leader cannot afford to have only superstars on the team. If you own a basketball team and are blessed with a player like Michael Jordan, the more Michael Jordan's that you add to your team, the more your returns will diminish. A player like Michael Jordan probably reaches his peak performance when he has the basketball in his hands at least 60% of the time that he is on the court. Also, he probably needs to be on the court 80% of the time. Every time you add another Michael Jordan to the team, you will reduce the amount of time that Michael Jordan can keep the basketball in his hands. Obviously, five Michael Jordan's cannot keep their hands on the ball 60% of the time. Nor can four, three, or-as a matter of fact-two.

Training employees to work effectively in a team environment is important. One of my colleagues at Lucent Technologies Microelectronics Group expressed it well: "Teamwork is what makes the dream work." When every person on the team feels gratified and valued, the whole team's performance increases. Not only do the stars shine more brightly, but marginal performers also contribute more. Any employee is much better off working with many talented people than working alone. He or she learns from the team, benefits from the team, and is responsible to the team to make a major contribution. As each of us pursues our individual development plan, we need to recognize that teamwork is what determines how well each individual will play. X-Leaders don't think, "I make the team work." Instead, they understand that the team makes them work! For a person with leadership ambitions, the team offers the opportunity to fulfill those ambitions.

The great skill of the X-Leader is creating high-performance teams. This requires that senior leaders create a high-performance environment in which people want to excel. To do so, senior leaders *must commit* the resources necessary to train and develop people. When senior leaders inspire the company to incorporate people development into the company's overall fabric (or fail to do so), they act as role models–a very powerful position that is discussed in more detail later in this book.

Your company's belief in the power of people development to drive the company to success will mean little if you don't effectively implement your development programs. Below, I have provided some solid recommendations for realizing great returns on your people development dollars.

Measure Your Returns on People Development

People development is a big responsibility for leaders. My experience in corporate America has been that things that matter to leaders get measured. If they don't matter to leaders, then they don't get measured. If they don't get measured, they usually don't get done. And, if by some chance they do get done, they don't get done very well. For this reason, X-Leaders administer people development by the numbers just like they administer product development by the numbers.

Most corporations do a fine job of evaluating their financial performances by tracking their earnings, spending, productivity, product manufacturing cycles, and sales yields. However, most companies woefully fail to track the effectiveness of their employees. Nevertheless, human resources should be tracked and measured like other critical assets in the company's competitive arsenal. Recently the largest U.S. industrial trade association, the National Association of Manufacturers (NAM),

> **Linking personal development and business development creates a synergy that delivers a competitive edge in the marketplace.**

elevated worker training to one of its top priorities.[xv] Actions like this, which move training into greater prominence as a major strategic variable, highlight the need to apply rigorous planning and evaluation to people development.

To track the performance of the company's people-development plans and efforts, senior management should follow methodologies similar to those they use to track the performance of all other business metrics. To build a great environment for people development (and thus maximize shareholder returns), businesses must treat people development as carefully as product development.

Often, companies have no idea how much money they actually spend on people development. Therefore, to start, the company should determine how much money it spends on people development and then decide how much money it is willing to invest in leader development. The senior leadership team should develop a formula that relates this amount directly to the company's annual revenue, a method no different from that used to establish other types of percentages of return, such as return on investments or research and development. I recommend that your senior leadership team spend quality time developing an overall people development strategy and plan to invest at least 2% of annual revenues in executing that strategy. Most corporations spend 2% to 4% of annual revenues on information technology. Without doubt, the people who produce the company's profits are at least as important to the company as the technology they use!

Next, you should develop procedures to measure the returns on your investments in your people. This means tracking their performance, and it is up to your senior leadership team to find effective methods for doing so. Very simply put, you should track the performance of people development in the same way that you track other major categories in the expense line. I believe very strongly that people development must be tied directly to the bottom-line performance of the company. Computing financial returns on people development should not be implemented or executed much differently than returns on invested capital or returns on sales and marketing expenses. Senior leaders' achievement in attaining people-development objectives should be measured rigorously, and you should be held accountable for achieving those objectives.

Compensation is a major element in implementing and managing personal development plans. A substantial part of your base compensation and bonus plan should be tied to your overall effectiveness in developing people. This tie to compensation should be based on a formula that utilizes measurements of development plans, efforts, and results that quantify changes in production levels and employee job satisfaction. Using such a formula will cultivate a more creative team that works to inspire employees to produce more competitive products and services.

Your company's performance will improve dramatically if the performance plans of every leader and manager in your company include mandatory and voluntary training and development. As part of this overall process, you should seek to augment the company's resources using whatever incremental skills are available to help the company deliver outstanding people-development results. Never assume that all of the answers exist within the company.

Mandate Supervised Use of Personal Development Plans

Obviously, smart, hard-working people create more shareholder value than those with fewer skills and less motivation. To produce substantially greater results, make sure that every person in the company follows a personal development plan that has been jointly developed by the employee and his or her immediate supervisor. Creating such a plan is very important to personal development, and the participation of each supervisor in this activity should not be optional. After all, increased individual performance translates into superior collective performance. This is why smart companies invest heavily in employee training and development and encourage employees to pursue their maximum capabilities.

Designing a personal development plan should not be a strictly voluntary activity for employees. Left to their own volition, many employees will not begin to invest in themselves, and thus they will deliver less value to the company than they otherwise might. Be prepared for some initial resistance to your personal development plan policy. Both employees and middle managers might have a hard time accepting the idea that every time a company employs someone who is not actively increasing his or her own skill set, that company increases its risk of losing shareholder value.

However, because most employees genuinely want to contribute to the company's success, if these employees are offered encouragement, over time many of them will develop an insatiable appetite for continued learning. The experience of many people will be similar to my own: "The more I learn, the more I realize how much there is to learn!"

Whether the company's employees and middle managers immediately accept the idea of personal development or grow into it gradually, there is no denying that active personal development is strongly correlated to good job performance. Even though everyone in the company cannot excel, it nevertheless remains true that everyone should become the best that he or she can be! Thus, every supervisor should be held responsible for ensuring that each of his or her subordinates has a personal development plan. For each employee, including senior management, no less than 60 hours of training and development should be mandatory each year. In addition, all employees should be encouraged to attend relevant educational and training programs, seminars, and symposiums, and to share what they have learned with their team members.

Senior management should insist that each employee dedicates one day per quarter to his or her own personal development. This is not a vacation day. It is not a personal day. And it is not a sick day! This is a day for employees to focus on themselves and improve their value and effectiveness.

One day out of each quarter of the year, each employee should be encouraged to take time for personal development in whatever form that person believes will maximize his or her contribution to the overall effectiveness of the company. Certainly, management can provide input and guidance to help each individual focus on areas that need improvement, but the ultimate decision on what area the person will concentrate on during this one day per quarter should be left entirely up to that individual, under the approval of his or her immediate supervisor.

However, I suggest that senior leaders not track each individual's activity. If senior leaders discourage the employee from making whatever improvements that individual thinks are important to his or her development, the employee will feel far less motivated to participate in the personal development program. Approval of the employee's plan by his or her immediate supervisor should be considered sufficient evidence that the person's work on a skill or characteristic is aligned with the company's overall success.

Although I do not recommend that senior leaders track each individual's development activities, I strongly recommend that they track overall employee participation in the program. This will help leadership develop an environment that encourages each employee to take the time to develop his or her characteristics and skills.

Track Employee Job Satisfaction

An important measure of the success of a people-development program is employee satisfaction with the company. A satisfied employee is one whose work is pleasant and includes the opportunity to contribute personally to the company's success.

To measure employee satisfaction, employee opinion surveys should be administered frequently and regularly. The employee opinion survey is a valuable measurement tool that allows leaders to keep the dialog within the company crisp and focused on important concerns. Although the opinion survey is not a cure-all, it does provide a platform from which leaders can spot problems and measure progress over a specific period of time. Some responses to the survey will reveal problems that require immediate correction; others will indicate that certain practices are working well and should be reinforced. Employee opinion surveys also offer employees chances to recommend improvements to the company's effectiveness, and they offer management opportunities to speak with employees about their concerns.

Establish Coaching and Mentoring Programs

Two important tools for people development are *coaching programs* to train employees and *mentoring programs* to pair ambitious employees with more experienced individuals who can guide them in their career development. Coaching and mentoring are quite different from supervising in that coaches and mentors provide

> **To the X-Leader, the only value in losing is to provide inspiration to win the next time.**

input that supervisors do not or should not. For example, a coach or mentor might discuss topics unrelated to the supervisor's duties or, in some instances, discuss topics that would be inappropriate for a supervisor to broach.

The coaching program should be offered as an integral part of the management process. Obviously, those who participate in the program-coaches, supervisors, and managers-should be well trained and guided by a process that ensures active employee participation in development programs.

Mentoring can be very helpful to everyone in the company, not just company leaders. A mentor is someone who can be counted on, who will listen, and who will provide candid feedback about a variety of concerns important to job performance. The opportunity to be guided by a mentor should be available to all employees, but having or being a mentor should never be mandatory. The mentoring program should link the interests of the company to the interests of employees, but the mentor need not be a member of the employee's department or even of the company. Nor need the mentor be a senior leader; instead, he or she could be an employee's supervisor or more experienced peer. The individual seeking a mentor and his or her supervisor should decide, together, who they believe would be a great mentor.

Corporate Directors: Develop the Company's Leadership

You might be wondering why corporate directors should concern themselves with the development of the company's people. The answer is threefold. First, directors ultimately are responsible for the company's leadership continuity and succession planning, which requires very strenuous development. Second, it is the board's job to ensure that the senior leadership team concentrates on people development as effectively as they concentrate on product development. Third, considering the increasing exposure and risk associated with serving on a corporate board, directors should be highly motivated to develop the best possible talent for the company they serve.

If you are a corporate director, you should make sure that the senior leadership team of the company is focused on preparing and retaining the company's future leaders. The preparation of future leaders should begin as soon as they join the company. To make sure that this is happening, every year the entire board of directors should attend (and actively participate in) a management presentation and review of the company's senior leadership continuity and succession plan. You also should make certain that the company's review of its people development is conducted with as much rigor as its review of product development. Without great people, the company never will produce great products or deliver outstanding service.

The board also bears responsibility for ensuring that personal development plans are designed for the company's senior leaders. Your own personal development plan, and that of each of your fellow directors, should include providing mentorship to one person on the senior leadership team. An added benefit of this activity is that, through this mentoring experience, you will learn much more about the company than you otherwise could.

After focusing on development of the company's future top leadership, the board should look for development practices that have proven profitable at the top and that can be deployed throughout the company. Investments in training have been shown to result in positive returns for the company, including increased employee retention. In fact, increased productivity and reduced costs of replacing employees will substantially offset a company's investments in building outstanding talent. At least twice each year, the board agenda should include an update on the company's personnel practices and development plans, which should include views of the company's employee attrition rate.

The board also is responsible for crafting personal development plans together with its individual members. You will be wise to develop an intense focus on your own development of the skills you need to help solve the company's problems and take advantage of its opportunities. By becoming the best director you can be, you will be putting yourself in the best position possible to protect yourself and the company you serve. I believe that a positive correlation exists between well developed directors and organizational success.

In keeping with the company's effort to develop its people, all new directors should participate in a formal education process to learn the basics of their individual responsibilities on the board. New directors should augment what they learn on the job with specialized training to help them become more effective in executing their responsibilities.

Moreover, every year all directors should spend at least 2 or 3 days in some kind of training that will improve their effectiveness on the board, such as attending a college program, participating in a university seminar, or independently studying materials published by a professional board-work association.

This training program must include the CEO, who, however successful as a leader, will not necessarily be a great member of the board because the skills and experience needed to be a great entrepreneur, financial expert, or lawyer are not always those needed to be effective as a corporate director. Although I would love to have Michael Jordan on my basketball team, I am not certain that I would want him to coach my team! When appropriate, directors should seek opportunities to coach the company's CEO. I am not suggesting that each board member develop a plan to become a personal mentor for the CEO, but I am recommending that each director seek an opportunity to add some value to the CEO's overall development.

Professionals and Specialists: Boldly Develop Your Career

Another important group that benefits from people development are the professionals and specialists in the company who do not have direct people management responsibilities, such as accountants, administrators, engineers, sales representatives, and marketers.

If you are such a specialist, you should be very concerned about people development, especially because you have less control over what happens in the company than the company's senior leaders, board of directors, or customers. Developing your skills will make you better at what you do, enhance your current position in the company, and provide you with opportunities to distinguish yourself.

The effort you put into your own development will be especially important to you during economic downturns and when your industry undergoes restructuring. In a downturn, the first employees to be turned out of a company usually are those with the fewest skills. These people often are the least motivated, the worst performers, and consequently the lowest paid among their peers. Obviously, an employee who is not highly motivated and is comfortable being paid less than his or her peers is not likely to advance very far in the company.

Conversely, people who are highly trained and better educated than most of their peers generally are honored with broader responsibilities, which are in fact opportunities to demonstrate the high levels of performance that ultimately lead to promotions and raises. If you have high career aspirations, your ideal situation is one in which you are getting the best training possible from a corporation that values your personal development.

It is vitally important that you understand that not all corporations practice the art of people development. Although extreme personal development is easy to subscribe to, it is very difficult to practice, and some companies that believe in people development are so poor in implementing their development ideas that they produce empty "human resource" campaigns that promise much but deliver little. Other companies believe that personal development is the employee's sole responsibility, but they will provide some support tools for the employee's development. And, of course, some companies don't believe in paying anything to develop their people.

Actually, people who are not performing at peak levels and who are uninterested in their own development are putting the company at risk every day, every month, every year. When the company fails to maximize the contribution of each of its employees, it exposes itself to its competition. As a consequence, each company has a responsibility to develop its people. It is in the interests of the company's success to seek employees who have the interest and the capacity to be continuously developed and to pursue that development jointly with those employees.

You, as an individual, should understand this fact and make sure that your company provides you with an opportunity to be the very best that you can be. If you discover that your company has no interest in helping you become your best, it may be time for you to reconsider working for that company in the long term.

If you want to advance to the top of your company and maximize your earning potential, then you need to work for a company that follows the spirit of extreme personal development. Don't allow yourself to be misled by the empty rhetoric, slogans, or human resource campaigns that some organizations use to deceive employees who would like to advance themselves. Make sure to align yourself with one of the many great companies that not only believe in maximizing the development of their people, but also are very good at developing their people.

If you want to be a successful individual contributor, then you have to develop yourself to the maximum. My suggestion to you is that you make your own personal development as important to you as anything else in your life beyond your family. If you develop yourself and actively use your skills in the most effective

> **How fast you advance can determine how far you advance.**

way you can, you enhance your opportunities for promotion and your earning potential in your company. If you make sure that your skills are portable, you also increase your earning potential outside of your company, which could come in handy if, for some reason, you are laid off (often a euphemism for *fired*) or become dissatisfied with your rate of progress in your company. An excellent performer who has developed excellent skills always has the option of finding opportunities outside the company.

If you develop yourself into an excellent performer in your field, you also are likely to enjoy higher job satisfaction. Commitment to your own personal development will enable you to contribute your maximum to your company and make you a very valuable member of your team. The more educated you become and the more skills you acquire, the more you can contribute, the better you will feel about your job, and the more likely you will be to continue to advance within the company. Because you will feel valued, you will take more pleasure in your work, which in itself will enhance your performance. Increased personal development also will provide you with a much broader perspective on the company.

To maximize your success, leverage your development opportunities by focusing on specific areas of development. Start by developing a set of development goals for yourself. Be sure to include both long-term goals and short-term goals in your plan. Over a period of two or three months, set aside some quality time to work through and develop these goals. Scrutinize them carefully to decide whether you can really live with them. Be sincere with yourself. Be intellectually honest.

Over time, of course, the conditions of your life and employment will change. Be willing to modify your goals as changes occur. However, if you find yourself frequently making major changes in direction, you are not doing a very good job of recognizing and defining your goals. In this case, please take another look at the introduction to *Corporate Rise*!

After you have put your plan together, meet with your immediate supervisor to develop your annual personal development plan. Be clear with your supervisor. Make sure that you understand and can *effectively* articulate the difference between your personal *development* plan, which is primarily about your career, and your personal *performance* plan, which is primarily about your job, even though it might include areas where you need further development of skills. Whatever you do, don't be misled into thinking that these two kinds of plans are the same.

Your *personal development plan* should define your aspirations, development needs, and time lines. Your *personal performance plan* should define what you are supposed to do and how you will be measured against the performance plan. Your career success will be determined by your own commitment to excellence and your passion for winning, and by the company's willingness to invest in you to help you create and develop the skills required for you to perform your job. Your job success (or failure) will reflect how well you succeed in performing your job responsibilities and fulfilling the specific objectives of your operation.

Again, don't be deluded into thinking that a personal performance plan and personal development plan are the same. They are clearly distinct and different. However, if you are able to inextricably link the two, the synchronization will speed up your career success. Locate any linkages between your personal development plan and your personal performance plan and, whenever possible, work on both at the same time to accomplish more with less effort.

When you examine your personal development plan and your personal performance plan, you might discover that your personal development plan is preparing you for new skills that aren't fundamental to your current job. Remain mindful that you earn the right to work on a new career plan by delivering outstanding results in your current job. Don't allow yourself to believe that you can perform at a marginal level in your current job while you are off developing new skills to move into some new career opportunity. It is one thing to increase your personal skills to perform better at your current job and another to manipulate your current employer into training you to make you a more successful candidate for other employment-that would be a disservice to the company's shareholders. Today, be the best that you can be in your current position, while you develop skills that will make you even more effective tomorrow. If, after careful consideration, you discover that you really do want to switch careers, pursue your desired career with the same vigor as you fulfill your current assignment! But clearly understand that you must earn the new opportunity by performing well in your current job.

To assess your actual performance against your planned performance, you must meet at least quarterly with your supervisor. Meeting with your supervisor every few months will keep you well connected in terms of expectations for your performance. Creating *shared expectations*, that is, making sure that each party knows what to expect from the other, is critical to communication and success. Knowing how well you are doing in your job certainly is important and, in some situations, it is even more important that your supervisor knows how well you are performing your job. Don't presume that the important people in your operation are aware of your good performance! Make sure to schedule periodic reviews to discuss your performance with your boss.

I am not at all suggesting that every day you ask your supervisor how well you are doing. However, you do want to eliminate the possibility of an unpleasant surprise when you see your performance evaluation, which is not likely when you and your manager track your performance throughout your performance period. Then, when you meet your supervisor for your annual review, a direct correlation will exist between your expectations and your supervisor's expectations.

Because your career development plan probably has a longer time horizon than your job development plan, you and your supervisor should meet at least twice a year to review your personal development plan. Make sure to meet with your immediate supervisor at least twice a year to ask him or her to assess your progress. Share with your manager where you believe you are in your career. Discuss your concerns and redirect them as appropriate.

Each employee should be bold in letting his or her aspirations be known. There is no shame in being ambitious! Not everybody aspires to become the company's CEO, but I suggest that you definitely shoot for the top of your profession! If you desire to be the top engineer in your company, I advise you to raise the bar and aspire to become the best engineer in your *field*. Shoot for that goal, even though you know that it is a very lofty one. Be audacious and reach for the stars. In a constructive way, let your supervisor and colleagues know that you aspire to be the best. While you are doing this, don't be overly aggressive and certainly not obnoxious! But don't hesitate to let your supervisor and colleagues know that you want to learn. Let them know that you want to take on more responsibilities and that you want their support in maximizing your contributions to the company. Believe in your heart that you have the capacity to do great things. Disclose that you have a passionate interest in becoming your best.

> **Although crisis has accelerated many a career, don't wait for a crisis for an opportunity to differentiate yourself from your peers!**

Become a student of the company. That means understanding the company's organizational chart and where the influence and power are located. Make sure you know how things get done. Find out how people are developed. Learn the rules of the game and, if you don't like them, work to earn yourself a position from which you can influence or change those rules. In the interim, you must understand how the company works and how you can use your knowledge to leverage your own personal characteristics into attributes of success.

Don't be fooled into believing that people in positions that are similar to yours (that is, competitive to yours) are eager to see you advance. Some employees of your company really do not care whether you advance at all. Be acutely aware of this! It is vital to your development that you are aware that you will have to navigate a way around the will of people who don't care if you succeed, or who don't want you to succeed.

Learn where the successful people in your company gained their experiences. If you are in your company's accounting division and you want to become the chief financial officer (CFO), learn what key jobs the present CFO had before he or she ascended to that position. While you are at it, find out what positions the controller previously held. In your own way, track the career paths of the successful individuals that you are interested in mirroring.

No matter what your environment, focus your energy on the positives and decide how you can best make a constructive contribution to the company. Partner with your teammates and partner with management. Establish yourself as a positive influence for the overall organization.

In your process of personal self-development, decide whether you want to be mentored. Participating in mentorship is not a prerequisite to becoming extremely successful. However, every person deserves the opportunity to have a mentor, an experienced person who can help someone with less experience deal with broad career concerns. If you decide that you would like to be mentored, make sure that you select a mentor who has the time, the interest, and the capacity to be effective. Providing mentorship is a difficult task, and many people who want to mentor are not qualified to do so. A good mentor will candidly tell you things that you don't want to hear, for example, your weaknesses as he or she sees them. A good mentor will boldly tell you his or her views of your preparation, performance and, accordingly, your career opportunities. A good mentor will listen to you, tell you about your strengths, empathize with you, and understand your efforts. Considering what is at stake, when you choose your mentor, be very selective.

Not every employee needs a mentor, but every employee does need a coach. The role of the coach is to help an individual improve his or her job performance. Most often, the employee's coach also is the employee's supervisor. Employees should demand that their relationships with their immediate supervisors include coaching. X-Leaders know how to supervise and develop people, but some good supervisors are not effective coaches. Don't allow your supervisor to fail at his or her job by not providing effective coaching and guidance to you: Set high expectations and work with your boss to make him or her a better coach!

In addition, it is critically important to your career that you establish a working relationship with your supervisor's boss. You should always seek at least two levels of support within the company. This will provide you with broader reward opportunities. The greater number of senior people that you know, the more opportunities you will have to learn and to make your achievements visible to senior management. Remember, however, the reverse is also true: The more people that are exposed to your work, the more risk you take if you fail to perform as expected!

Watch out! If your supervisor is confident and competent, he or she will encourage you to have a constructive relationship with him and an appropriate working relationship with his immediate supervisor. However, if your immediate supervisor is a marginal manager or an insecure one, he or she might be extremely paranoid when confronted with the prospect that a subordinate might get to know his or her boss or other senior management! If your supervisor sorely lacks confidence, he or she will not facilitate any process that will help you expose your skills to influential people in the company. Obviously, any immediate supervisor who is threatened by your desire to have a working relationship with his boss is a weak supervisor, and the sooner you know that, the better off you will be!

To be extremely successful in your company, your support team should not include just your immediate supervisor and his boss. Build effective relationships with your colleagues and learn from them all. Maximizing your own personal development means contributing to your colleague's projects and being a team worker.

Professionals and specialists who work for a company must make people development their own responsibility as well as the company's. Be bold, take the initiative, get out front, and build a great career by developing extreme leadership skills.

Corporate Customers

If your company's strategic suppliers take a keen interest in developing their people and have excellent people development programs, they are likely to have very talented people interested in delivering world-class products and services to your company. If you receive outstanding service and products from your suppliers, your company will be in a more competitive position to deliver outstanding services and products to your customers. That's why leading companies want to buy from leading suppliers, and why X-Leaders believe that their suppliers must have a passion for developing great people.

Your company, as a customer, should take a keen interest in the people who deliver products and services to it. You want your company's strategic suppliers to assign their most highly motivated, talented, and inspired people to servicing your account, and you want them to partner with other suppliers who are staffed by great people who do great things. You will partner with a marginal player only when your company cannot partner with a leader.

To maximize the effectiveness of your communications with your suppliers (and thereby reduce your costs), make a commitment to welcome your strategic suppliers as partners, teach them what is important to you, and design the communications path between you to be as minimal as possible. To maximize your supplier-development efforts, you can take a few important steps.

First, include your strategic suppliers' people in your own corporate training programs. Your company should train them to do business with you in ways that make sense to your business. In fact, your company should require that any person servicing your account participate in your corporate training program. For this training, select only those people who have a direct relationship with your company.

Second, clearly communicate to your strategic suppliers' senior leaders that you have high expectations of the talent and skills of the people who service your account. Demand that your suppliers assign their best people to support your business. Even if you don't get the very best people, your suppliers' management will develop a keen interest in making sure that you have excellent people working for you. Do not accept any marginal player who, in the long term, will be bad for your company and for the supplier. If you refuse to accept marginal players, your suppliers will be motivated to sharpen the skills of all of the people who provide service to your account.

Third, serve as a mentor or coach to a strategic supplier's representative and suggest that other people in your company do the same. If you are very careful in setting up such a mentorship program and selecting which people to mentor, you will open the door to very effective relationships between your company and your strategic suppliers.

People development is so important that smart companies develop everyone who can make important contributions to the company, even if those people are not paid directly by the company.

X-Leaders understand that, in a corporation, success is not a solo achievement. X-Leaders need a village of people supporting them, and they are as committed to the success of others as they are to themselves. They leverage their success through the success of their team.

Three Steps to Getting Started

1. Get prepared both mentally and physically! Leadership is a long journey! Stay intellectually sharp, look good, and feel great!

2. Establish a working relationship with a trusted mentor and a partnership with your spouse or a valued friend. The route to the top often is lonely! Success is meaningless, and often elusive, unless you have someone important to share it with!

3. Get emotionally engaged in developing a definitive short-term plan and an audacious long-term plan. If you do not care where you are going, then any road will take you there! If you have a specific destination (such as the top of your company) it is best to have a plan.

Endnotes

ii Lippitt, R. (1949). *Training in community relations: A research exploration toward new group skills.* New York: Harper.

iii Wall, T. D., Jackson, P. R., Mullarky, S., & Parker, S. K. (1996). The demand-control model of job-strain: A more specific test. *Journal of Occupational & Organizational Psychology,* 69, 153-167.

iv Bassi, L. J. & Van Buren, M. E. (1998). The 1998 ASTD State of the Industry Report. *Training and Development,* 52(1), January, 21-43. In its state-of-the-industry report of 1998. This estimate was based on a survey of a random sample of 340 organizations with 50 or more employees--Human Performance Practices Survey (HPPS).

v Goldstein, I. L., & Ford, J. K. (2002). Training in organizations (4th ed.) Belmont, CA: Wadsworth Group; Drucker, P. F., 1995, as cited by Goldstein & Ford, 2002.

vi Ralphs, L. T., & Stephan, E. (1986). HRD in the Fortune 500. *Training and Development Journal,* 40, 69-76.

vii Ibid.

viii Baker, M. (1999). GWEC: A white paper. *The Global Wireless Education Consortium overview document.* Retrieved April 27, 2004, from the GWEC Web site: http://www.gwec.org/about4.cfm; see also, Global Wireless Education Consortium. (2004). Stronger wireless curriculum for higher education. [Brochure]. Available from 1501 Lee Highway, Suite 110, Arlington, VA 22209-1109.

ix The National Center for the Educational Quality of the Workforce. The other shoe: Education's contribution to the productivity of establishments. 1995, EQW, RE02, p. 2. Note: Productivity is measured by output.

x Cascio, W. F. 1994, as cited in Goldstein & Ford, 2002.

xi Stahl, M. J. (1986). Managerial and technical motivation: Assessing needs for achievement, power, and affiliation. p. 211. New York: Praeger.

xii Howell, J. M., & Frost, P. J. 1989. A laboratory study of charismatic leadership. *Organizational Behavior and Human Decision Process,* 43, 243-269.

xiii The core components studied were vision, vision implementation through task cues, and communication style. See Kirkpatrick, S. A., & Locke, E. A. (1996). Direct and indirect effects of three core charismatic leadership components on performance and attitudes. *Journal of Applied Psychology*, 81(1), 36-61.

xiv U.S. Department of Labor. *Employee Tenure* in 2002. September 19, 2002. Retrieved January 15, 2005 from the USDL Web site: ftp://ftp.bls.gov/pub/news.release/History/tenure.09192002.news

xv Carnevale, Anthony P. (1991). *America and the New Economy*. San Francisco, CA: Jossey-Bass; Marshall, R. (1994). Organizations and Learning Systems for a High Wage Economy. In Clark Kerr and Paul D. Stadohar (eds.) *Labor Economics and Industrial Relations*. Cambridge, MA: Harvard University Press; Bassi, L. J. et al. (1997). Position Yourself for the Future: *The Top Ten Trends*. Alexandria, VA: American Society for Training and Development.

Principle Two: X-Leaders find imaginative ways to inspire people to transform themselves for the better. They motivate themselves and others to reach higher levels of performance by linking great ideas to exhilarating images of success.

CHAPTER 2

Excite Breakthrough Thinking

For decades, researchers have attempted to discover how leaders motivate their followers. In the 1970s, one influential researcher, James McGregor Burns, theorized that leadership behaviors fall into one of two broad categories, which he called transactional and transformational.[xvi] *Transactional leaders*, Burns argued, influence people by appealing to their self-interest.[xvii] They offer people something in exchange for the desired performance, such as wages, status, or favors.[xviii] Often, they also offer punishments in exchange for non-performance or poor performance.[xix] *Transformational leaders* influence people by empowering and elevating them. They believe that leaders and followers can raise each other to higher levels of motivation and morality; as a result, they influence not only their followers, but also their peers and even their own leaders.[xx] By appealing to powerful ideas and moral values, transformational leaders (who are also known as charismatic leaders) go beyond mere exchanges with other people and actually *transform* other people's values, needs, beliefs and attitudes.

X-Leaders ascend to the next higher level of leadership. They move transformational leadership to a broader platform by identifying visions and then articulating those visions. Every X-Leader discovers justifiable reasons to maintain a positive attitude about the future of the company and also encourages his or her colleagues to dream up innovative approaches to accelerate the company's performance. X-Leaders do more than encourage individuals to elevate themselves; they encourage entire groups to accept their visions and to work toward the goals demanded by those visions. To propel themselves and other people to act in ways that elevate, X-Leaders link great ideas to inspiring images of success.

When we think about high-performance companies, some corporations immediately spring to mind. For example, IBM (large-scale computers), Sony (entertainment products), Intel (Pentium microprocessors), ITT (night vision technology), and DuPont (engineered polymers and Corian surface materials). Their customers consistently reward these corporations, and no wonder! By regularly delivering competitive new products and great service, these corporations help their customers stay on the leading edge of their own markets. By constantly innovating, they create the benchmarks against which their competitors measure success.

Customers recognize that the high performance they appreciate results from the type of leadership at the helm, which, in my experience, is likely to be what I term X-Leadership. High-performance companies know how to develop world-class innovations, and their leaders know how to develop world-class innovators. If it is true that chance favors the prepared mind, then it certainly also is true that innovative solutions favor the prepared company.

> X-Leaders do more than encourage individuals to elevate themselves; they encourage entire groups to accept their visions and to work toward the goals demanded by those visions.

A company valued for its innovations develops more intellectual property than its competitors, including more patents with more applications. That company's leaders obviously have prepared their people to develop valuable intellectual property. They did so by creating corporate environments that are grounded in reality, yet charged with the excitement that results when employees enjoy many opportunities to explore their thinking.

In environments where new ideas meet with encouragement instead of criticism, creative people feel safe presenting their ideas and working to develop them into product and service improvements. Where effort is acknowledged and financially compensated, people feel motivated to produce profitable innovations. Such environments certainly are recognized by their people as great places to work!

> **High-performance companies know how to develop world-class innovations, and their leaders know how to develop world-class innovators.**

Clearly, the people who develop the innovations that drive high-performance companies work in environments that reward bold originality. The energy released in these environments is undeniable. You can feel it just passing through the halls: Foot traffic is speedier, conversations quicker, interactions more numerous, and meetings more tense than those of less successful companies. As employees create new products and services, they simultaneously are creating new opportunities for advancement for themselves and the other people in the company. X-Leaders know that environments in which people are encouraged to become their best mean long-term success for the company.

Aspiring X-Leaders: Try New Ideas

If you want to rise to the top in an X-led company, you will have to differentiate yourself from many talented people. Obviously, you cannot become a senior X-Leader until you first become a good manager, but you must do much more to distinguish yourself from your peers and competitors. Being average will not win new customers or propel the people around you to new heights. Except in rare instances of extraordinary luck or political advantage, an average performer will not make it to the top.

Even if you are a *very* good manager who organizes and directs people extremely well, to be an X-Leader you must inspire people to perform at much higher levels than they otherwise might. No matter how highly motivated and creative your co-workers may be, they will hesitate to expose their ideas if they expect those ideas to meet with unhelpful criticism. Even the most courageous among us do better when truly inspired. That is why it is of prime importance that you do your best each step of the way to create an environment that inspires you and your co-workers to passionately pursue peak performance.

To create an environment that perpetually inspires learning and high performance, you must think in ways that excite people. The X-Leader takes his or her company to a level that can be reached only by a radical departure from traditional thinking. If you aim to be an X-Leader, you must try new ideas and exercise your imagination. Start by making a list of

> **X-Leaders know that environments in which people are encouraged to become their best mean long-term success for the company.**

justifiable reasons to maintain a positive attitude about the future of your company. To really break the mold, as you must if you want to lead a successful company, you must be very bold in your thinking. When you follow up your bold thinking with bold action, sometimes you will fail, particularly in the short term. When you do, admit your mistakes and correct them. People who have that kind of courage are the people who have what it takes to make the company *really* work. Your company's top executives are responsible for understanding the boundaries within which they will encourage people to take risks, and it would be good for your own development to learn what those boundaries are and why they were developed.

Be ambitious, be bold, but always be careful to operate exclusively within the confines of what is legal. Let your creativity and inspiration be guided by personal honesty and a highly visible set of values and ethics. It will not be difficult for you to find powerful new ideas that will work within that set of values and ethics, provided that you bring everyone you work with into the creative-thinking process.

Obviously, to an X-Leader planning to win in today's competitive environment, good performance is never good enough. The X-Leader thinks performance should start with excellence and move up from there. He or she is mindful that any less-than-excellent product development or service delivery chips away at market share and market opportunity; at some point such performance will eventually deteriorate the value of the company. In an X-Leader's view, employees should feel that their own jobs ultimately are at risk unless they adopt excellent performance as their starting point. Of course, I am not suggesting that you or any leader threaten employees by suggesting that their performance levels will determine whether or not the company survives. But I am stating that you as a future X-Leader should regard anything less than peak performance as exposing the organization to the risk of losing shareowner value.

Senior Leaders: Inspire High-Performance

X-Leaders develop insights capable of driving their companies to new heights, and then they tie these insights to exciting images of success. One way X-Leaders gain powerful insights is by visualizing ways to turn difficulties into opportunities. Another way is by developing lines of communication within their companies that bring into view powerful employee experiences and insights.

In less successful companies, senior managers might acquire their positions because they have reputations as *turn-around experts*, that is, specialists in restructuring businesses. This is unfortunate. Every senior leader should have (as a minimal core competency) the ability to reorganize a company that is in trouble. Before being considered for the great responsibility of senior leadership, candidates should have proven themselves to be audacious in their efforts to gain competitive edge.

One way of gaining competitive edge is to put *X-Principle Two* into action. The following recommendations can help you, as a senior leader, to utilize imaginative vision to enrich your company.

Boldly Explore All Available Options

When I challenge you, as a senior leader, to think boldly, I am challenging you to go far beyond imagining ways to help your company succeed. After you develop your own ideas about what will help your company prosper, make yourself aware of the competing ideas developed by other people. Make sure you understand these ideas and thoroughly explore them.

When you are presented with a potential solution to a problem facing the company, you and the rest of the senior leadership team *always* should carefully examine that solution for clarity, thoroughness, and objectivity. Find out whether the problem-solver explored all of the alternative solutions, given the time available. Find out why the problem-solver chose the proffered solution as the one most likely to deliver the desired results within the limitations of the company resources that can be allocated to the problem.

A solid knowledge of all the available ideas for serving your customers and building market share will give you a strong competitive advantage. The value of examining all kinds of alternative scenarios was illustrated for me by a developer of more than 300 patents. He explained that he followed a policy of developing not only the patents that he regarded as key to his company's success, but also the patents that he thought would deliver inferior solutions. By exploring, as well as possible, all the potential ways of satisfying his customers' needs, he got a reasonably objective look at the various solutions and, very importantly, also gained great insights into approaches the competition might pursue.

Draw Talented People to Your Company

As I discussed in Chapter One, talented people will rise to the top, whether times are hard or easy. The best people are so desirable that senior leaders never have an easy time attracting them. In the eyes of the outstandingly talented person deciding which job offer to accept, whether your company offers an inspiring and encouraging environment is very important because that individual will want to reach his or her highest potential. For talented people, every step you take to create an inspiring environment will help differentiate your company from your competitors in a very positive way.

Motivate Your Sales Force

Whenever you gain a corporate customer, you can be sure that you have gained a customer who is looking for a strategic supplier committed to excellence. That customer wants the representatives who service their account to be excited to have the opportunity to do great things for their company. If you build an enthusiastic and motivated sales force and back them up with a great support team, your corporate customers are much more likely to become your engaged partners, and you will earn larger shares of their business. However, if you neglect your sales force, if your company's representatives serve your corporate customers only half-heartedly, and if those representatives have poor back-up from a lukewarm support team, your corporate customers will soon be thinking (correctly) that choosing your company to supply their needs was a bad decision.

Communicate and Make Sure Others Communicate

How can you and the other senior leaders of your company find the imaginative linkages between ideas and success that will inspire your company's people to transform themselves for the better? Part of feeling good about the future of your company is recognizing that many of the great ideas and visions that your company needs already exist somewhere in your company. The most efficient way to capture those great ideas and visions is to make sure that they flow directly to your office. You can regulate that creative idea flow by establishing specific communication policies in your company. Once you have captured promising ideas and visions, you again will be dependent on established communication policies—this time to help the company turn ideas into products and services.

X-Leaders understand that good communication policies pump valuable (and inspiring) information throughout the entire company, and that establishing such policies is an important way to maximize people's individual contributions to the company. Organized communication events leverage personal development into company development by giving individuals the opportunity and encouragement to share knowledge. For this reason, the senior leadership team should establish policies that facilitate group meetings throughout the company. These meetings will give you and other managers vital opportunities to listen to, hear, and understand the recommendations of your company's people, as well as their needs and wants. Make sure that all meeting attendees are encouraged to dream up innovative approaches to accelerate your company's performance. In fact, your company's program of group meetings held regularly throughout the company should include brainstorming sessions.

As a senior leader, it is important for you to remember that good communication in the company-wide learning environment you hope to achieve will help you to learn most of what you need to know to help your company succeed. Start by listening, really hearing, and then making sure you understand what you hear. A large part of the fun of communication comes from the fact that it is a two-way street. To teach (that is, to convey your vision and other vital messages), you must articulate what you have learned and are thinking. Until you have developed good communication skills, you will be unable to inspire exceptional levels of performance in other people.

The (smart) X-Leader, who understands that a vigorous flow of learning throughout the entire company is of vital importance to the company's bottom line, will make sure that you and all other employees are urged to participate actively in group information sharing.[xxi] Of course, leveraging the information gleaned by individuals into the company's broad base of knowledge demands good articulation of ideas and good listening by a number of people. For you as a senior leader, leveraging the personal growth of individuals into growth for your entire company will require that you develop a strong understanding of *group dynamics*, that is, the phenomena that occur in groups based on their interactions and interrelations. The X-Leader knows how to enable group discussions to promote constructive engagement, while minimizing the potentially negative effects of group dynamics.

Ray Stata, the former Chairman and CEO of Analog Devices, in Boston, believes that the values and culture of an organization have a significant impact on the learning process and on how effectively a company can adapt and change. "In fact," he said, "I would argue that the rate at which individuals and organizations learn may become the only sustainable competitive advantage, especially in knowledge-intensive industries."[xxii]

The X-leader understands and appreciates the diverse composition of people in a group, individual and group characteristics, and how their personal energies come together as a team. Group dynamics is essential to organizational learning. And organizational learning is a fundamental driver of management innovation!

Corporate Directors:
Inspire Senior Leaders to Become Great Motivators

Today's board of directors operates in a business environment that demands unceasing response to a constantly changing market. As a result, every successful company is in a constant state of transition, which means that the board always is facing difficult major challenges, such as job outsourcing, asset acquisition, and asset disposal.

A board that effectively answers these challenges will be one that believes in the company's future success and helps the company's senior leadership team motivate others to act boldly to ensure that success. This board will fully engage the team in planning the company's business continuity and leadership succession. Its members will constructively challenge the strategic directions chosen by the senior management team, including customer value propositions and choices of competitive products and offerings.

To enhance the company's potential for success, the board should set the leadership tone for the entire senior leadership team. The board should ensure that the senior leaders inspire their people to perform their best, and directors should consistently encourage the company's senior leaders to dream up innovative approaches to increasing the company's profits and market share.

Research has shown that corporate employees look to the examples given by senior leaders as a way of generating their own motivation. That's a very compelling reason for the board to select the right chief executive officer and then make certain that person selects the right senior leadership team. The directors must make sure that the company has the kind of senior leadership team that is ready, willing, and able to build the kind of corporate environment that will attract the most talented people and ultimately help retain them. This team should want to inspire the company to achieve extreme levels of performance, have the skills to motivate people, and possess the courage to lead. Each member of the team must not merely possess an ability to turn-around or reorganize a weak company, but also be able to contribute new insights that will drive the company to new and higher levels of performance.

The board's responsibility to govern is accompanied by the opportunity to add value to the senior leadership team. If the board is unimaginative and shuns this opportunity to lead, it will act as a dead weight suppressing the healthy tendencies of any team to be inspired! Fortunately, if the board chooses X-Leadership, it will set a tone that inspires the company's senior leaders.

Professionals and Specialists:
Help Your Company Energize You for Success

If you are one of your company's professional accountants, engineers, administrators, and other individual contributors to the company's success, you know that you become energized when you truly believe that your manager wants you to succeed.

Your manager might have excellent reasons for wanting you to succeed. One of these is self-interest. Another reason, closely related, is profit motive. For-profit corporations exist primarily to create value for their shareholders. Their investments make it possible for the company to offer both your manager and you gainful employment. To justify shareowners' continued investment, your manager and the people he or she manages must create shareholder value. Understandably enough, shareowners expect great returns on their investments.

Employees with strong skills make strong contributions to the companies that provide their jobs. As the company becomes more competitive, so do the people who work in it. This means that employees who keep their skills sharp by working in a learning environment also keep their competitive edge, enhancing their opportunities for continued and increasingly lucrative employment.

It obviously is in your own best interests to expect, and even demand, that your company be a perpetual learning environment. Your personal success depends on it, and so does your company's success! Ask yourself how you, as a professional or specialist working in a corporation, can ensure that your working environment truly inspires employees and adds to the fundamental and distinctive character of your company.

Here are some suggestions for you. First, check to see whether your personal aspirations are truly aligned with that of the company's leadership. It will be helpful if you can make a list of justifiable reasons to maintain a positive attitude about the future of your company. If you are working for a company that does not inspire employees toward extraordinary performance, you will have a much harder time becoming successful in your profession, and you may never reach your full potential. On the brighter side, working in a lackluster environment does present you with many opportunities to lead the charge toward creating an inspiring environment.

To accelerate your own promotional opportunities, you can hardly do better than practicing inspirational leadership skills yourself. But first, you must determine whether you want to take a leadership role in the company. If you do, make sure that getting training in inspirational leadership skills is part of your personal development plan. Do not wait for senior leaders to increase your responsibilities. Instead, be bold in your thinking and do things that excite people to learn more or perform better. Regularly seek opportunities to take on more responsibility.

Establish a pattern of volunteering to participate in company-sponsored task forces. To find out where the opportunities are, get in front of the issues. Take the lead. Also look for ways to participate in programs (such as seminars) designed specifically to help you think in ways that can help you transform your company.

Don't keep it a secret that you are focused on generating maximum return to the shareholders and on earning opportunities for your own advancement. Make sure that your company's senior leaders know that you are seeking opportunities to help lead the organization in transformational thinking. Find imaginative ways to bring your leadership talents to the attention of your colleagues and customers as well. Use your contributions to let it be known within the company and among your customers that you are working very hard to earn the opportunity to take a leadership role in your company. Let it show that you are passionately interested in being part of the process that takes your company to the highest level.

Do not wait for management to inspire you. Instead, create an environment that inspires management to want you to be engaged. If necessary, inspire management to create a great working environment that improves your performance. Let your ideas for contributing to the overall success of the company be known. Tell the leadership team, and particularly your own managers, what would help you become excited about creating a great company.

Energize yourself for success by doing your job with enthusiasm. Your attitude is important, and, please remember, your attitude is the only thing in life that you ever will control. You determine whether the glass is half full or half empty. You determine whether you will be happy or sad. You determine, each and every day, whether you are going to be in a good mood or a bad mood.

Always keep in mind that your success is directly linked to the success of your team! Consequently, one of the most effective ways for you to build an effective career is through teamwork. Partnering with your colleagues to pursue excellence is not only necessary, it provides irreplaceable competitive advantage against the competition and your peers. So, make teamwork an important objective. Encourage your colleagues to dream up innovative approaches to accelerate the organization's performance.

Like communication, inspiration is a two-way street. X-Leaders inspire their teams, but they also are inspired by the support their teams give them. To become your best, merely being a team player and allowing teamwork to happen isn't quite enough. Build a plan to encourage and foster teamwork. Inspire your colleagues to partner with you! Teamwork does not stop at the engagement level, it is very important throughout an entire process; always share praise and success with your colleagues.

Tell others why you are inspired to work for your company. As you spread your spirit of enthusiasm, you will inspire others and benefit from the growing enthusiasm in your company!

Corporate Customers: Inspire Your Strategic Suppliers

Be assured that, as a corporate customer, you can help create environments that inspire improved products and service. Naturally enough, you will want to start by linking your company to strategic suppliers that have bright futures. When choosing a strategic supplier, have justifiable reasons to believe in its future success. Only as an absolute last resort should you consider building a business relationship with a supplier whose survival is questionable, or who lacks passion for generating great products and services.

How can you recognize the probability of a strategic supplier's future success? Look at that company's leadership. If it is led by X-Leaders, you have good reason for feeling confident in its future; that company very likely will keep delivering imaginative products and services that enhance your company's competitiveness in the marketplace. Your supplier's representative is likely to be inspired by high aspirations, which means that he or she will be striving to offer your company the kind of products and services that excite you and can

60

help you grow your business. Furthermore, you can expect to learn from-and even be inspired by-the X-led supplier. If you cannot learn much from a strategic supplier, you should find a new one!

Great strategic suppliers also are great sources of talent for your company. Keep in mind that working with your suppliers creates opportunities to partner with some of their most talented individuals. At some point in time, these people could become employees of your company. However, far better than recruiting talent away from your strategic suppliers is developing your own!

If you are a corporate customer, you should treat your best and most valuable strategic suppliers as integral parts of your team. Share your best practices with your most valuable suppliers. Boldly tell them what you expect. Together, build a set of great expectations. Include them in the early stages of your strategic planning processes. Encourage them to dream up innovative approaches to serve your company. Do your best to benefit from their experience helping customers develop inspirational products and services. Last, reward them when they deliver great things. Create a most preferred supplier status to recognize their senior managers for demonstrating inspirational leadership. Tell your valued strategic suppliers that you expected great things from their company and that your expectations were fulfilled!

X-Leaders never allow someone else to dispirit their dreams! They know that if a dream can be imagined and is worth pursuing, it eventually will be achieved. They think big; they are intense; they are committed to delivering exceptional results. In fact, one way they discourage their competition is by consistently pursuing excellence.

Two Quick Ways to Add Points to Your Inspiration Quotient!

1. Awaken your passion for exploration! Make a list of justifiable reasons to maintain a positive attitude about the future of your company.

2. Create your own personal think tank! Encourage your colleagues to dream up innovative approaches to accelerate your company's performance.

Endnotes

xvi Burns, J. M. (1978). *Leadership*, p. 226. New York: Harper & Row.

xvii weLEAD, Inc. (2003, January). Leadership tip of the month, January, 2003. leadingtoday.org. Retrieved February 21, 2005 from http://www.leadingtoday.org/Onmag/jan03/transaction12003.html

xviii Ibid.

xix Burns, 1978, *Leadership*, p. 226.

xx weLEAD, Inc. (2003, February). Leadership tip of the month, February, 2003. *leadingtoday.org*. Retrieved February 21, 2005 from http://www.leadingtoday.org/Onmag/feb03/transform22003.html

xxi Evidence that encouraging innovative thinking is a meaningful behavior is provided by studies involving factor analysis of questionnaires on transformational leadership. See Bass, B. M., & Avolio, B. J. (1990). *The implications of transactional and transformational leadership for individuals, teams, and organizational development.* JAI Press; Yukl, G., Gordon, A., and Taber, T. (2002). A hierarchical taxonomy of leadership behavior: Integrating a half century of behavior research. *Journal of Leadership and Organizational Studies*, 9(1), 15-31.

xxii Stata, R. (1989). Organizational learning: The key to management innovation. *Sloan Management Review*, 30(3) 63-74.

X-Principle Three: *X-Leaders cultivate creativity by looking at common things in uncommon ways. They expose old issues to new options and develop fresh approaches to long-standing problems.*

CHAPTER 3

Exceptional Idea Generation

These days, companies must continually improve just to stay even with the competition. The pursuit of innovations has become a journey, a perpetual process of challenging old ideas to discover whether they still lead to the best solutions. One of the key features of the innovative company is a corporate culture that fosters *creativity*. Innovation is critical not just for the sake of your corporation or mine, but also for the sake of our national competitiveness. As observed by Professor Michael E. Porter of Harvard University, a leading authority on strategy, "national prosperity is created, not inherited."[xxiii]

The only way a company can develop an enduring, broad-based competitive position is by effectively applying knowledge. However, before knowledge can be applied, it must first be captured and, as the human knowledge base expands at an unprecedented rate, capturing the needed knowledge becomes ever more difficult. Moreover, in the face of shrinking life-cycles of products and services, even assessing customer desires and needs must be done in shorter and shorter periods of time,[xxiv] not to mention developing answers to those needs and desires. The widespread acceptance of outsourcing has made maintaining market differentiation more difficult as well. Innovation clearly is the path to survival, but today's pressures demand creativity on a scale undreamed of in the past.

Continual learning has become a fundamental imperative for high-performance, a fact of life that X-Leaders understand. X-Leaders are able to point the way to extraordinary success because they extricate their people from pedestrian attitudes and thinking. X-Leaders place high value on good preparation, and they prepare the way for creative solutions by means of the creative process. They examine ordinary situations for extraordinary opportunities. As *X-Principle Three* states, they expose old issues to new options and develop fresh approaches to long-standing problems. They experiment. They take carefully calculated risks. However, the solutions X-Leaders seek need not be complex. The most creative solutions are often elegant in their simplicity. (One very simple solution that became wildly successful is the Sony Walkman.)

Innovation on the scale required can occur in only one way: by capitalizing on the creative potential of the workforce. For both corporations and nations, the building blocks for organizational innovation are the products of the individual creativity of many unique human beings.[xxv] Because creativity is the path to a strong competitive position, a corporation needs the guidance of a strong internal supply of creative thinkers. X-Leaders don't waste time on piecemeal approaches, so it follows that when an X-Leader fosters creativity, that leader fosters creativity throughout the entire company, often in a way that sets benchmarks for the entire industry. X-Leaders consider the ability to innovate to be a necessary core competency for every employee in the company. X-Leaders make sure that employees with access to promising new ideas are encouraged to bring them to the attention of upper management, even if that means stopping a senior executive—the CEO if necessary—in the hallway (and later following up with the senior executive to find out whether the idea is being addressed in a timely fashion). In fact, as the often-cited Modesto Maidique of Stanford and Robert H. Hayes of Harvard have pointed out, "the CEOs of successful high-technology firms are usually so actively involved in the innovation process that they are often accused of meddling."[xxvi] When researchers examined the creative process of 12 leading-edge global corporations, they found that their leaders demonstrated in every decision, action, and communication that innovation propels profitability.[xxvii] All 12 of these companies had established creativity "safe havens" to ensure that highly experimental work was not neglected.[xxvii]

X-Leaders, who are courageous innovators themselves, understand that gutsy innovators often surprise their companies in very pleasant ways.

When an X-led company benefits from a new idea, so do the individuals who captured the idea, pursued it, and developed it. These rewards are not the result of trickle down. X-Leaders consistently recognize and reward new ideas and developments, and the employees who take part in making them happen.

Building high levels of internal creativity within a company goes a long way toward increasing confidence in that company among its investors and other stakeholders. These folks will regard the company as boldly inventive only if it addresses market opportunities in uncommon ways that create real value for its customers. To succeed in this momentous task, corporate leaders must motivate themselves and their people to find ways to create substantial value for the company's shareholders. Fortunately, as is discussed below, clear steps can be taken to do just that.

Aspiring X-Leaders: Cultivate Creativity in Yourself!

Not everyone can be expected to become a source of breakthrough ideas. Nature dictates that some people will be better than others at thinking up new ideas, processes, and products. However, creativity does involve certain skills that can be taught, as has been confirmed by behavioral research. You can learn skills to improve your ability to solve problems, and you can also improve another ability crucial to your future success–the ability to recognize and accept the creative breakthroughs made by other people.

Traditionally, a person's creativity has been thought to spring from a source beyond one's control, such as God, nature, or genetic heritage. However, an alternative, and very helpful, view holds that creativity is, in large part, the result of a conscious decision to interact with ideas in specific ways. [xxix] According to one theory, called the *investment theory*, creative people invest in ideas in much the same way that good investors invest in stocks, by "buying low" and "selling high." [xxx] The creative person generates a "low-value" idea that is unusual, defies the crowd, and often is viewed as bizarre by his or her colleagues, and then attempts to raise the value of that idea by convincing other people that the idea has value. When the creative person has convinced other people of the idea's value, he or she moves on to generating a new unusual idea, much like a good investor who doesn't hold onto a block of shares forever, but sells the shares at a profit and then purchases more shares in a different company.[xxxi]

Working with other creative people in a company that offers you challenging work will offer you many opportunities to learn creativity skills and formulate new ideas. Make it a point to constructively probe the solutions that you and others arrive at to see whether they can be improved. Enrich your ideas by seeking out different points of view from people with different backgrounds and areas of expertise. Get creativity training, on the job if possible, and make continuing creativity training part of your regular routine.

> **X-Leaders place high value on good preparation, and they prepare the way for creative solutions by means of the creative process.**

More discussion about these methods can be found in another section of this chapter, *Professionals and Specialists: Develop Creativity and Reap Rewards*.

Put the skills you learn from others into practice, but start today to bolster the creative skills you already possess. If you want to become more creative, I suggest that you give up doing more of what you *already* are doing and set aside time to reflect on new ways to be more creative and effective. Concentrate on breaking the mold! Contemplate ways you could make things better, perhaps by developing a new procedure to improve customer service, or by making a product more exciting to customers. Get things moving by initiating one bold action a month. Occasionally, do something creative that pleasantly surprises your team.

When you come up with a good idea, it's very important to develop some scenarios that will help you get it into the physical world. Taking a valuable new idea from conception to invention to innovation requires dedicated focus and attention, plus significant time and effort. A lot of the things you already are doing too much of are bound to get in the way, so make sure the scenarios you develop include ways of protecting your new idea. Anticipating and planning for disruptions is one of the best ways to keep your new idea from getting lost in your daily workflow.

Senior Leaders: Take Charge of Change

In today's business climate of certain, unremitting, turbulent change, creative thinking can make a significant difference in whether your company leads the changes that are occurring, or falls victim to them. The more creative your organization becomes, the better your chances will be to lead the changes taking place in your industry.[xxxii] *X-Principle Three* embodies my contention that the ability to look at common things in uncommon ways adds substantial value to a company. For your company to perform extremely well, you and your fellow leaders must cultivate deep creativity throughout the entire company.

If you are willing to confront long-standing challenges with new approaches and stimulate other people who work in your company to think outside the box, I've supplied some straightforward suggestions that will help you and your company discover new paths to success.

Give Your People Chances to Innovate

Once you accept that individual creativity is a building block for organizational innovation,[xxxiii] as a senior leader you must ask yourself: How can I lead other people to innovate? Leading toward innovation is largely a matter of perspective. If you carry with you the realization that doing things exactly as you've always done them will not produce innovations, you will be well on your way. In the view of the X-Leader who looks at leadership as a means of benefiting the company, the whole point of leadership is to give people chances to change and produce changes.[xxxiv]

Today, even the most mundane and pedestrian business requires at least some creative thinking, and even a small measure of creative thinking in a company will cause the people who work in it to see things differently and to behave differently. As a senior leader, you can decide whether you want to guide your people in the changes they make in outlook and behavior, or whether you want to leave the ball in someone else's court. If you want to take charge of the change, make sure your company hires the best talent in the industry to lead the changes that are coming. Successful companies can be depended on to develop and hire the most talented people they can find for that vital task. As part of the process of change, good leaders can increase the job satisfaction and even the routine productivity of the people who work in the company.

Of course, the best and the brightest people always are more difficult to recruit and maintain than average people. Obviously, talented people want to join high-performance companies that reward talent. They want to work in environments that provide them with the freedom to break new ground using the full spectrum of their abilities. Talented people search for activities that utilize their creative abilities. If you give your people the chance to do things in new ways, you will not only be building more creativity within your company, you will be attracting innovators from outside the company.

Train, Train, Train Your Workforce

Generally speaking, doing things in new ways feels very rewarding to people. However, for the sake of your company, it is not enough that your people become creative; they must become creative in ways that produce the desired results. As a senior leader, it is up to you to channel your people's natural energies into innovations that contribute to the company's bottom line.

Multiple studies have shown that, in corporate settings, people's ability to creatively produce desired results is directly related to how capable they feel on the job. To effectively use their creativity, employees must first feel a sense of job mastery.[xxxv] When you and your fellow senior leaders ensure that your company's employees are getting the training and experience they need to develop a sense of job mastery, you are building a foundation for their subsequent creative work.[xxxvi]

People's need for creative work also affects their job commitment. Companies used to be able to depend on the so-called "economic contract" between employer and employee to attract, motivate, and hold their workers, but that contract has been eroded.[xxxvii] College graduates (who are being churned out faster than our industrial base can create jobs requiring higher education) are increasingly dissatisfied with conventionally designed jobs and less willing to obey orders without question.[xxxviii] In industrial settings, worker commitment has been ground down by unchallenging specialized jobs, poor communication of goals, and increasing centralization of control systems. As soon as workers feel relatively secure in their survival and jobs, their desires rapidly expand to encompass freedom, self-esteem, personal growth, and self-realization.[xxxix]

As a senior leader, you can harness this dissatisfaction for the benefit of your entire company by making sure that your company offers creativity workshops for all employees.

Creativity workshops introduce the participants to the importance of creative thinking and provide opportunities for groups to develop effective, innovative approaches to solving ongoing problems. The workshop sessions usually are structured to allow all participants ample time to experience the value of innovative thought. They are trained to use specific problem solving techniques, which often include abstraction, conceptual combination, and analogical transfer. After participating in these workshops, the participants are expected to return to their work environments more energized and engaged in their work. They should be ready to "kick the darn door down!"

Researchers have confirmed what many X-Leaders (and other creative people from the beginning of time) have intuitively understood all along: If you want people to be highly creative, you must give them creative tasks that they enjoy under the supervision of someone who also enjoys those tasks.[xl] When employees enjoy their creative tasks, they produce high levels of creative output and, when their supervisors are motivated by the intrinsic enjoyment of the task, employees' creative performance seems to be enhanced.[xli] Creativity workshops are a good way to start or enhance this process.

Regard All Efforts as Work in Progress

If you want to keep innovative solutions flowing through your company, an important rule of thumb is to regard every product and every procedure as a work in progress. As a work in progress, a product or procedure is open to constant improvement; each solution is viewed as temporary when people recognize that these solutions are based on whatever limited information and experience were available at the time each solution was implemented. Good answers for yesterday's problems don't necessarily constitute good answers for today's problems; nor do today's solutions promise the best answers for tomorrow's problems. Never regard any solution as the answer for all time. If you do, you will allow what exists today to get in the way of what could exist tomorrow.

Ask Questions

Another very important rule of thumb for keeping innovative solutions flowing through your company is to ask questions that impel yourself and your colleagues to investigate ideas more deeply, a process that leads to better answers and thus better solutions. Throughout history, great questions have led to the discovery of breakthrough innovations, but what you, as a senior leader, may need to know is whether your questioning style probes and encourages, rather than impedes and discourages. If your questions push on boundaries to make a solution even more efficient and more effective, then they encourage and are probably being viewed as helpful. If your questions condemn solutions that are working today, or that look promising for the future, then they are discouraging, and may even be making you seem arrogant.

Choose the Right People

The celebrated CEO of General Electric, Jack Welch, once explained his job duties as follows:

> Look. I only have three things to do. I have to choose the right people,
> allocate the right number of dollars, and transmit ideas from one division to
> another with the speed of light. [xlii]

These three tasks, which are familiar to most people involved in large-scale creative collaboration, are essential to the healthy functioning and creative accomplishment of any company.

Even if you are not highly creative yourself, as a senior leader you can be indispensable to the creative process in your company by choosing the right people.[xliv] How can you recognize the people most likely to make creative contributions to your company? X-Leaders know to look for the best tip-off of all: Interest bordering on obsession. It takes a person genuinely in love with a branch of work to push beyond what is known and beyond where it is safe.

Tap Into Your Company's Reservoir of Ideas

A great idea normally results from an intersection of shared ideas. When a team gathers to solve a problem, each team member brings to the table a different view of the problem that is based on his or her unique history. This variety is a rich source of new outlooks that can be combined to produce uncommon potential solutions. Encourage your people to take advantage of the variety of unique views present in your company to uncover fresh approaches to problems both old and new.

For tapping into a company's large reservoir of talent and ideas, few tools compare to a comprehensive, company-wide suggestion program. Corporate suggestion programs are designed to encourage all employees to aggressively look for new ways and opportunities to improve the effectiveness and efficiency of the company.

X-Leaders consider the ability to innovate to be a necessary core competency for every employee in the company.

When properly implemented, each team's entire membership is included in decision-making. When a team is fully engaged in a corporate suggestion program, their morale goes up, while the company's operating cost goes down. Likewise, some of the suggested solutions result in increased revenue from existing and new customers. Effective suggestion programs reward employees for their creativity. These rewards may be gift items, such as cash, company stock, business trips, or other tangible prizes. However, most importantly, employees usually place equal value on team, peer, and management recognition.

Unfortunately, suggestion programs are viewed with suspicion in many corporations because they are either poorly designed, not effectively implemented, or not highly valued and supported by senior leaders. Like other efforts that can be exceptionally important to your company, the results of your comprehensive employee suggestion program should be tracked and reported.

Reward Innovators and Recognize Achievements

Any company that needs to focus on creativity must recognize and reward it. By all means, you and your fellow senior leaders should set the bar high, but you should never neglect to celebrate people's successes when they achieve or surpass the company's goals. Creativity requires continuous nourishment. If you and other senior leaders want to perpetuate your company's creativity, you must recognize and value it.

Establishing a quarterly recognition program for highlighting significant innovators and their innovations is of vital importance. However, your company shouldn't honor only your star innovators at the expense of the feelings and hard work of others whose successes contributed less to the company, but were, nevertheless, collectively valuable to the shareholders. Make sure that your company holds an annual program to recognize *all* of the people who participated in its creative development process.

You can accelerate your company's success process by using your suggestion program as a tool to reward innovators. Lavishly praise all individuals who strive for creative new ways to improve the overall success of the company. Reward the authors of ideas that generate substantial income for the company with shares of that generated income. Similarly, reward authors of ideas that save the company significant amounts of money with a share of those savings. Cash rewards motivate employees to dig deeper for the kinds of new ideas that create incremental value for shareholders. One model company that uses innovation as a major driver for advancing their business, 3M Corporation, has found it helpful to make innovation a key ingredient of their compensation program.

As highly innovative companies realize, creative people need more than monetary rewards, so don't neglect to use your company's suggestion program as a tool for personal recognition of achievements, including increased independence and visibility and the opportunity to play a leading role in the next big project. These recognitions all are necessary to motivate and retain innovation champions

Your suggestion program also can function as a broader recognition system that motivates the less creative people in your company to accept and participate in new approaches. For example, in addition to celebrating an individual who originated a substantial cost-reduction breakthrough, a department might also celebrate the people who participated in the cost reduction. Including as many people as possible in the celebration of a success helps news of the success (and the company's rewards for that success) to spread throughout the company.

Allocate Time for Innovating

Innovation is so vital to corporate success that each employee's efforts to envision competitive changes should be appraised as part of their performance. As you know, doing things differently takes time and resources, and it is up to you and your fellow senior leaders to dedicate time and resources for your people to work on their innovations. Each employee's innovation project (or projects) should be included in his or her personal performance plan, and the employee's work on the desired innovation should be monitored to ensure that the employee is following that performance plan.

These steps will help your employees defeat one of the chief barriers to growing fragile new ideas into vigorous new products or services: disruptions. To keep the development of your employees' innovative ideas from getting blocked by their daily workflow, it is imperative that your company allocates 5% to 10% of the non-management workday to creative thinking. (3M allows people to spend 15% of their work time on self-defined innovations.) Allocate a higher percentage, 15% to 20%, of a manager's workday to creative thinking, and at least 25% of your time as a senior executive.

Today's investors are driving senior leadership teams to be much more creative. Motorola Corporation responded to investor demand by pioneering the Six Sigma programs to foster creative thinking among its employees, and these programs were successfully implemented by hundreds of other companies, including DuPont Corporation and ITT Industries, where these programs have proven to be great drivers of creative thinking.

In a simple context, Six Sigma is a measure of quality that strives for near perfection. It is a disciplined, data-driven methodology for eliminating defects (driving towards six standard deviations between the mean and the nearest specification limit) in any process—from manufacturing to transactional, and from product to service.[xlvi] Motorola learned about Six Sigma as a direct result of losing market share in the 1970s. According to Thomas Pyzdek, an author and Six Sigma consultant, when a Japanese firm took over a Motorola factory that manufactured television sets in the United States, the factory soon was producing TV sets with 1/20th the number of defects than before. In short, Six Sigma is much more than a modification of the old engineering idea of three sigma quality levels; it is an effective method for managing companies.[xlvii]

Several manufacturing companies, such as Ford Motor Company, Motorola, and Toyota Motor Company, have implemented the concept of total quality management (TQM). TQM is a philosophy of perpetual improvement in which quality must be managed and, processes, not people, usually are the problem. In the TQM value system, every employee is responsible for quality, and problems must be measured and prevented, not merely fixed. The quality standard is "defect free," and companies must plan and organize for quality improvement. TQM has been used to improve customer service performance, reduce manufacturing development cycle times, and improve administrative systems training.

Other approaches, such as continuous improvement process management, also can be used to place emphasis on quality. Whatever approach your company takes will work as long as you and the rest of your company's senior leaders place major emphasis on quality and use an accurate quantification system to measure your company's progress in attaining and improving the quality of products and services.

Corporate Directors:
Drive the Company's Creativity Engine

Boards that seek high company performance must oversee the utilization of *all* shareholder assets. If you are a corporate director, you are well aware that this is no easy task, particularly in light of today's complex intertwining of companies, customers, partners, and competitors. This task calls for fresh, innovative approaches to oversight.

The board sets the tone for the entire company, and board members must expect creative, value-added solutions for customers. Because the company's senior leaders are responsible for driving the company's creative engine, you and the company's other directors are responsible for cultivating creativity among the senior leaders. You cannot set the right tone unless you study the company thoroughly and then test whether breakthrough thinking is being encouraged and is occurring in the company. After you and your fellow directors encourage senior leaders to foster creativity in themselves and others, it is essential that you support their efforts to recognize the company's most creative leaders.

As a director, you are responsible for constructively challenging the way the company is being managed. During the board's annual review of the company's strategic plans, directors should do much more than discuss what the company will be doing in the future. It is very important that the entire board *partner* with the entire senior leadership team to deeply and constructively drive the company to develop bold new creative approaches that maximize shareholder value. It also is important that, on a regular basis, your board look for ways to weed out under-performing business operations.

Much of what the board needs to do will be effective only when done regularly. To influence the company's creative efforts, the board will need to schedule its reviews and structure its support. In doing so, the board must anticipate and plan for disruptions, so that they don't push the vital details of establishing the creative environment into the margins of the board's efforts.

Professionals and Specialists: Develop Creativity and Reap Rewards

What if you aren't a manager, but instead are one of the experts your company depends on for some expert service, such as accounting, administration, engineering, marketing, or selling? How can you ensure that you'll have opportunities to learn how to increase your creative powers? The following suggestions can take your far.

Work for a Creative Company

Creative thinking not only generates the ideas that lead to new products and services but also carries them through development and into delivery to the marketplace. Thus, whether your company wins or loses in the marketplace might very well depend on how creatively you and your co-workers solve problems. Of course, any successful product or service will be of high quality, be competitively priced, and be operationally efficient. But it is the creative thinking of a lot of people that underlies that quality, price, and operation.

No matter what role you play in your company, you are likely to become as creative as your employer will encourage you to be, or, lacking encouragement, as creative as your company *permits* you to be. That's why working for a creative company is a cornerstone of career advancement. If you choose to work for a company that cultivates the creativity of its employees, you are very likely to find that your workplace offers you exciting, challenging, and engaging work. In other words, your workplace will be a fun place to be. Although that might sound inconceivable to some people, given the nature of work, you certainly will be more effective at your job if you and your co-workers enjoy what you do, than if you despise what you do. In fact, a substantial body of research strongly suggests that, if your company offers you enough training to feel competent in your job, your ability to creatively produce what is wanted will naturally rise.[xlix] As your job competency, confidence, and creativity grow, so will your ability to deliver value to your company's shareholders. That is very important because the quality (and perhaps even existence) of your job is tied directly to your company's creative ability to build shareholder value.[1]

Any company that wants to survive the long haul must give people like you opportunities to build skills. Obviously, companies that help their employees provide customers with world-class services and innovative products are the ones most likely to thrive. It's a rising cycle. Your company helps you develop skills that gradually enrich both you and the company. In this thriving company, you will enjoy opportunities to increase your skills, which will place you in higher demand in the job marketplace. That, in turn, will make you even more valuable to your current employer, which will raise your earning power. These are excellent reasons for you to seek employment by a corporation that believes in growth.

Answer Questions With Other Questions

X-Leaders ask probing questions to push the envelope of what people imagine can be done. Your personal style should include answering probing questions with other questions that open up the discussion for more ideas and options. Never accept the first answer as necessarily being the last answer, nor the best answer. Find a constructive and energizing way to push for a better solution all the time. Do this with a spirit and style that makes others feel good about your level of interest in the topic, instead of feeling bad because they perceive you as thinking you have the best answer. Desiring excellence can easily be viewed as arrogance, so always approach the creative process in a spirit of helpfulness and always be willing to accept other people's solutions when they are better than your own.

Become a Student of Creativity

It is not easy to look at everyday things in novel ways; in fact, when you first try it you might feel uneasy. However, to differentiate yourself from your competition, you must learn how to push ideas into new areas where there is a possibility that they will get translated into new, exciting products and services that generate shareholder value. To enjoy success, you must prepare for it, just as you prepare for the other events, small and large, in your life. In any pursuit, preparation is the foundation of success.

To prepare for creative success, you must become a student of creativity. Start regarding creative thinking as a valuable skill that you must master. You will never run out of creative ideas if you keep reading and learning, so develop an insatiable appetite for these pursuits. The more you learn, the more you will know; the more you know, the more creative you can be. Eventually, creative thinking will become an almost effortless automatic response that will feel fun and exciting.

Above all, in your preparations for success be willing and even eager to consider and try new things. Never allow yourself to get comfortable with the status quo.

Seek Different Points of View

Ideas for creative innovations often occur when two different points of view intersect. People who hold different jobs, work in different fields, and were raised in different places naturally see things in different ways. To learn more and learn faster, spend time with people whose points of view are different than yours. Talking with people who look at things differently will drive you to inspired ideas. You'll know you've made great progress in developing creativity when you feel quite comfortable with people who constructively disagree with you.

Get Creativity Training

Starting today, make creative thinking one of your competitive business tools. To make more sales, find ways to deliver services that are more valuable to your customers. To differentiate a product from your competitor's product, add value and functionality.

Research suggests that people who feel competent in their jobs find it much easier to find creative solutions than people who don't feel competent. [lii] Creativity workshops should be a part of your training curriculum and, if they are not, you should ask for them because they can help you and your co-workers develop new ideas and take a fresh look at long-standing problems. Because creativity must be one of your company's mainline themes, creativity training should be a mainline part of your training, not an appendage tagged onto other programs. Nor should it be a once-in-a-while event. You and your co-workers need continuing creativity training because what works today isn't always what worked yesterday, and you and your co-workers should have as much exposure as possible to new options.

Explore other creativity development tools as well. Creativity workshops offer important tools that can provide your team with opportunities to develop innovative approaches to solving ongoing problems. Some of the tools you can learn to use to generate creative ideas include creative writing, visual arts, and brainstorming techniques.

The sharper your company's focus on creativity, the greater the likelihood that you and your co-workers will develop products and services that increase shareholder value and keep people working.

Share Your Ideas

As you become more creative in your thinking, you should also become more audacious in sharing your ideas. Don't spend time worrying that your best ideas might be taken by someone else. In fact, when this does happen, your best course of action might be to give that other person the credit for your idea! Remember, teamwork really does make the dream work.

Resolve to initiate one of your best ideas every month. From time to time, use your creativity to bring a pleasant smile to the faces of your teammates. Don't let your daily responsibilities get in the way! To forestall disruptions, create some scenarios to protect your ideas and put them in place. When you share your great ideas throughout your company, you and everyone else in the company ultimately will benefit.

Corporate Customers:
Choose Creative Suppliers and Work With Them

Everything else being equal, your company will enjoy better results if your strategic suppliers are always looking for better ways to serve your company. You should buy from suppliers who focus hard on developing solutions that will help differentiate your company's products and services in the marketplace. Creativity on this scale depends on trust.

As a customer, you can help develop that trust by letting go of some of your uncertainties about dealing with creative strategic suppliers. Creative suppliers do provoke some uncertainties because they *always* challenge their customers' thinking! Take advantage of your strategic suppliers' creativity in such a way that your company acquires better products and services. Their efforts to do things differently can produce positive effects far

Building high levels of internal creativity within a company goes a long way toward increasing confidence in that company among its investors.

beyond improving their relationship with your company. Creative suppliers will work with your company to lower entry barriers into new markets and to shorten your company's product development cycles.

You can drive a supplier's creativity by demanding that the supplier's best talent handle your account. Meet with the senior leadership team, ask them about the backgrounds of the people that are going to be assigned to your account, and insist that these people's qualifications meet the criteria needed to service your account effectively.

Next, make sure that the supplier's sales representatives are students of their company. You want the people working on your account to be capable of leveraging their company's resources to serve your company. If they don't have a thorough understanding of their own company, they won't be able to offer you the service deserved by an important customer. If a supplier's people don't meet your company's needs, request that the supplier retrain or replace them. If that doesn't happen, you should replace your supplier.

Your strategic supplier's people should be experts in the service and value that they are creating for you, which means that they should be able to deliver better solutions than the ones you suggest. Don't let your supplier's account manager and sales representatives deliver what amounts to a regurgitation of solutions that you suggest. Drive them to improve on your original idea. If they do not perform at the high level that you expect, then you should meet with their management and suggest that they receive appropriate further training or be replaced.

Consider your supplier's account managers and sales representatives to be integral members of your team. Require them to attend your strategic planning sessions, and hold them accountable for understanding your needs and for delivering solutions to meet them. Include your strategic suppliers in joint development activities.

To keep the creativity flowing, about once a month introduce a new idea to your supplier's team. Occasionally do something creative that brings a pleasant smile to their faces. Recognize that, like you, your supplier's team will experience disruptions that get in the way of their service to you. Work out scenarios to minimize these disruptions and put them into place.

Make sure that you and your suppliers have shared expectations. Meet with them frequently; make sure that they understand what you expect of them; and make sure that you understand what they expect of you. Shared expectations are critical to driving creativity, and creativity is critical to creating shareholder value for the long term.

X-Leaders' thinking may be unconventional, but it also is appropriate and effective. Creativity is the power source X-Leaders use to connect the seemingly unconnected. X-Leaders are willing to tackle compelling problems with solutions that others don't dare to perceive! When the problem is solved, their competitors ask: Why didn't we think of that?

Three Tips for Generating Creative Excitement in Your Workspace

1. Initiate one bold action a month! Come what may, do something courageous and exciting in your workspace at least once a month.

2. Surprise your team! Occasionally, do something unexpected that earns a positive reaction from your colleagues.

3. Anticipate disruption! Plan scenarios to ward off the pedestrian elements of your daily workflow.

Endnotes

xxiii Porter, M. E. (1990). *The competitiveness of nations*, p. 73. New York: Free Press.

xxiv Tierney, P., Farmer, S. M., & Graen, G. B. (1999). An examination of leadership and employee creativity: The relevance of traits and relations. *Personnel Psychology*, 52, 591-620.

xxv Amabile, T. M. (1988). A model of creativity and innovation in organizations. In L. L. Cummings and B. M. Staw (Eds.), *Research in Organizational Behavior*, 10, 123-167; Tierney, Farmer, & Graen, 1999, An examination of leadership.

xxvi Maidique, M. A., & Hayes, R. H. (1984). The art of high-technology management. *Sloan Management Review*, 25(2)(Winter), 29.

xxvii Zien, K. A., & Buckler, S. A. (1997). From experience dreams to market: Crafting a culture of innovation. *Journal of Product Innovation Management*, 14, 274–287.

xxviii Ibid.

xxix Sternberg, R. J. (1999). The theory of successful intelligence. *Review of General Psychology*, 3, 292-316.

xxx Sternberg, R. J., & Lubart, T. I. (1995). *Defying the crowd: Cultivating creativity in a culture of conformity*. New York: Free Press.

xxxi Ibid.

xxxii Tierney, Farmer, & Graen, 1999, An examination of leadership.

xxxiii Amabile, T. M., 1988, A model of creativity; Tierney, Farmer, & Graen, 1999, An examination of leadership.

xxxiv Uhl-Bien, M., & Graen, G. B. (1992). Self-management and team-making in cross-functional work teams: Discovering the keys to becoming an integrated team. *Journal of High Technology Management Research*, 3(2), 228.

xxxv Tierney, P., & Farmer, S. M. (2002). Creative self-efficacy: Its potential antecedents and relationship to creative performance. *Academy of Management Journal*, 45, 1137-1148; Chartier, C. T. (1998). *Strategic leadership: Product and technology innovation in high-technology companies*. Unpublished doctoral dissertation, Alliant International University.

xxxvi Ibid.

xxxvii Basadur, M. (1964). Organizational development interventions for enhancing creativity in the workplace. [Working Paper #43]. Available from Management of Innovation and New Technology (MINT) Research Centre, Michael G. DeGroote School of Business, McMaster University, Ontario, Canada.

xxxviii Sternberg, R. J. (2000). Identifying and developing creative giftedness. *Roeper Review*, 23(2), 60-64; Schneider, S. M. (1997). Learning to be creative [A response to Sternberg et al., 1996]. *American Psychologist*, 52, 745; Dauphinais, G. W., & Price, C. (1999). *Straight from the CEO: The world's top business leaders reveal ideas that every manager can use.* New York: Simon & Schuster; Albrecht, K. (1983). *Organizational development: A total systems approach to a positive change in any business organization.* New Jersey: Prentice Hall.

xxxvix Basadur, M., 1964, Organizational development interventions; Herzberg, F. (1966). *Work and the nature of man.* Cleveland: World; Maslow, A. H. (1954). *Motivation and personality.* New York: Harper.

xl Tierney, Farmer, & Graen, 1999, An examination of leadership.

xli Ibid.

xlii As quoted in Bennis, W., & Beiderman, P. I. (1997). *Organizing genius: The secrets of creative collaboration,* p. 26. Boston: Addison-Wesley.

xliii Bennis & Beiderman, 1997, *Organizing genius,* p. 26.

xliv Dauphinais, G. W., & Price, C. (1999). *Straight from the CEO;* Csikszent-mihalyi, M. (1996). *Creativity: Flow and the psychology of discovery and invention.* New York: HarperCollins.

xlv McClelland, D. C., & Boyatzis, R. E. (1982). Leadership motive pattern and long-term success in management. *Journal of Applied Psychology,* 67:737-743; Amabile, T. M. (1993). Motivational synergy: Toward new conceptualizations of intrinsic and extrinsic motivation in the workforce. *Human Resource Management Review,* 3, 185-201.

xlvi Pyzdek, T. (2003). *The Six Sigma handbook, revised and expanded: The complete guide for greenbelts, blackbelts, and managers at all levels.* New York: McGraw Hill.

xlvii Ibid.

Hansen, D. A. Total Quality Management *(TQM) Tutorial/Help Page.* Retrieved May 4, 2005, at http://home.att.net/~iso9kl/tqm/tqm.html - Principles%20of%20TQM)

xlix Tierney & Farmer, 2002, Creative self-efficacy; Chartier, 1998, *Strategic leadership.*

[l] Ibid. See also, Tierney, Farmer, & Graen, 1999. An examination of leadership; Chartier, 1998, *Strategic leadership.*

[li] De Dreu, C. K. W., & Van de Vliert, E. (Eds.). (1997). *Using conflict in organizations.* London: Sage.

[lii] Gist, M. E., & Mitchell, T. R. (1992). Self-efficacy: A theoretical analysis of its determinants and malleability. *Academy of Management Review,* 17(2), 183-211; cf. Bandura, A. (1977). *Social learning theory.* Englewood Cliffs, NJ: Prentice Hall.

[liii] Basadur, M., 1995, Organizational development interventions.

X-Principle Four: *X-Leaders are customer-centric; they
realize that unless someone buys something from their
company, everything they do is totally irrelevant.*

CHAPTER 4

Excess is Not Possible

Customers are so thoroughly the lifeblood of any company that a CEO's reputation is nothing more than the reflection of how successful that leader has been in serving customers and promoting their success. X-Leaders understand clearly that it is much easier to create shareholder value when the company does what customers expect them to do. No matter how many linkages the company has with intermediaries and partners, the X-Leader is quite aware that cash flows out of the corporation through these relationships. Generally, cash flows *into* the corporation through only one linkage: the one with customers. That's why X-Leaders become their customers' servants and also why X-Leaders are very respectful of the work of the sales team, those who support the sales team, and those who seek the guidance and assistance of the sales team. In other words, the X-Leader is customer-centric.

X-Leaders are highly sensitive to the reality that any damage done to a customer relationship will result in loss of market share and loss of shareholder value. Any such damage, X-Leaders know, is very difficult to repair. Keeping old customers is much easier, and much more profitable, than finding new ones. Research conducted by Fred Reichheld and Christine Detrick of Bain & Company showed that customers of a wide range of businesses generate increasing profits each year they stay with a company. For example, in financial services, a 5% increase in customer retention produces more than a 25% increase in profit.[liv]

One reason that finding new corporate customers is expensive is that potential corporate customers are getting scarcer. In many industries, company mergers and closures are reducing the size of the customer base. For example, banks and insurance companies are steadily combining, and a very difficult climate in the airline industry is reducing the number of significant airline companies. Any company looking for new corporate customers in one of these industries will be competing with corporate relationships that have already been formed. Moreover, many knowledgeable customers are trimming down their costs of doing business by diligently reducing the number of suppliers with which they do business. It has become the job of the supplier company's senior management to make sure that their company is the customer's preferred supplier.

An X-Leader works with the company's senior leaders to rouse employees to develop appropriate working relationships with customers. At any point in time, numerous employees of the company are in contact with the company's precious customers: Receptionists are receiving calls from distraught customers; salespeople are responding to customer inquiries; accounts receivable clerks are following up on unpaid invoices; engineers are talking with customers about new designs. These interactions provide opportunities for the development of great relationships with customers. Unfortunately, they also provide opportunities for destroying relationships with customers. Because so many employees throughout the company engage with customers, it is extremely important that a customer-centric attitude be achieved throughout the company.

When given a choice, customers will do business with people they have confidence in, and will avoid doing business with people they don't like or trust. Because, as discussed in Chapter Two, pure product differentiation no longer is sufficient to keep revenue generation consistent; being customer-centric could be a corporate supplier's most distinguishing characteristic. This reality makes building a customer-centric environment critically important to every type of corporation.

Whether you are an aspiring X-Leader, a successful senior manager, a corporate director, a professional contributing services to a company, or a decision-maker for a corporate customer, this chapter offers suggestions for improving relationships between corporations and their customers.

Aspiring X-Leaders: Treat Your Customers Like Royalty

Serving customers is the primary way to bring cash into your company, so I suggest that you start today treating your customers like royalty! Wake up every morning with gratitude that you have customers to serve, and be willing to do whatever is necessary to accommodate them, as long as that accommodation is legal, morally acceptable to you, ethically correct, and in the best interest of maximizing shareholder value. Many customers choose to do business with the people and companies that most appreciate their business. If you treat your customers like reigning monarchs, they will reward you with loyalty that will cost your competitors market share.

Don't be like most managers, who have failed to come to grips with how their customer portfolio determines the value of their company. Believe it or not, according to Geoffrey Colvin of Fortune Magazine and Larry Selden of Columbia University, just 20% of a company's customers typically generate a huge portion of its share price—in some cases, all of it. The trouble is, the worst 20% might destroy a huge percentage of that value, with the middle 60% making up the difference. According to Colvin and Selden, until a company starts managing its highly diverse customer portfolio, it cannot hope to maximize shareholder value.[lv]

Colvin and Selden's thesis seems likely, but if you are an X-Leader in training, it is critical that you focus on 100% of your customers! Achieving extraordinarily high levels of customer satisfaction demands a mix of obsession to please the customer and the personal discipline needed to act on the customer's behalf, so make your customers the center of your attention. Concentrate on your customers as if your survival depends on them, and make sure that your highly energized commitment to them is grounded in correct information about their needs and desires. To serve your customers extraordinarily well, you need to understand a lot about their businesses.

Your own managers already possess a good deal of information from experience, customer surveys, and personal contacts that can help you provide better service to your customers. Tap into that resource. It is important that you seek the guidance and assistance of your company's sales team when establishing relationships with customers to make sure those relationships are appropriate, work well, and promote the goals of both the customer's company and your company. Meet with your counterparts in customer companies and make yourself aware of hot topics and major changes in those companies. Keep track of shifts in your customers' industry by establishing as many relationships as is reasonable with people in that industry.

Consider your contacts in the customer's company your team members. Provide your managers and team members with candid (and timely) reports about your customer's views and concerns. Do what you can to initiate or participate in joint strategic planning between your department and the customer. *Always* be constructive in your comments to your managers and to your customers, and *never* compromise the confidentiality of either your company or the customer company.

No matter how intently you and your company study your customers, only rarely will you be able to understand the customer's business better than the customer does. If you find yourself in that extraordinary situation, beware! That customer is not going to be around very long to buy your products and services. Find another customer, fast.

Make outstanding customer service a habit by establishing a structure for delivering great service. Start every meeting with a reminder of the high priority of customer service. Focus on the issues that enhance your ability to serve your customers. Ask questions that push the envelope of what can be done to improve the products and services that your company sells to your customers.

> **Generally, cash flows *into* the corporation through only one linkage: the one with customers.**

At the end of this chapter, you will find a *Customer Relationship Checklist*. A customer-centric company will be meeting at least seven of the ten customer-service criteria on this list. Perform this simple test: Select a valued customer of your company, and evaluate your company's relationship with that customer based on this checklist. You will find the results of this comparison enlightening. Depending on your current status in the company, you may be able to use those results to contribute to your company's deployment of some of the activities listed on the checklist. If you implement improvements to your employer's customer service, you will earn a special place in your organization.

Senior Leaders:
Make Your Customers the Center of Your Universe

It's very easy to say that the customer comes first, but treating your customers like the center of your universe is far from easy, and it is even more difficult to inspire your entire company to do the same! However, if you succeed in this difficult mission, you will strike terror into the hearts of your competitors, who will recognize that the customer loyalty you are building is costing them market share.

You will know you have succeeded in becoming a customer-centric leader when your customers include you in their thinking, seek your advice about their strategic plans, and want to form long-term partnerships with you. Customers will tell you what results they expect from your company, and they will work with you to build those results.

You will know you have succeeded in building a customer-centric company when your company's employees consider their experiences of serving customers to be delightful and valuable, instead of stressful and intrusive, and when customers rely on your company for partnerships and award you with most of their regular business.

Below are some tips to help keep you and your company on track.

Focus on the Customer at Every Meeting

As a senior manager, it is up to you to continually stress the importance of focusing on the customer. One very effective way to remind yourself and your team members that the customer is the center of your universe is to start every meeting, every day, with a focus on the customer. While I was president of Lucent Technology Microelectronics Group, I would start each meeting with a discussion about our customers. If the meetings were not directly related to customers, then they were not worth having. To show how much I meant that our activities should relate directly to our customers, I placed a life-sized cardboard cutout of a customer in the lead chair at my conference room table. This was a very effective way of reminding myself and my colleagues that our intent was to do what was necessary to serve our customers as effectively as we could.

Build a Training Engine to Drive
Customer-Centricity Throughout Your Company

Everyone in your company should understand that everything they do is meant to serve customers so well that your company earns the lion's share of their revenues. Of course, everyone employed by your company doesn't wake up with the goal of putting the customer first. Putting consistent customer-centricity into practice throughout your entire company requires on-going, company-wide training that constantly reminds employees of the importance of customer service, trains them in good customer-service methods, and reinforces that training.

Link Sales Plans to Strategic Direction

Another very important step in mastering customer-centricity is to make certain that your company develops (and regularly reviews) documented sales plans that are inextricably linked to your overall strategic direction. Then make sure that these documented sales plans drive the sales organization! Connect with the sales team. With their guidance and assistance, seek opportunities to establish appropriate working relationships with your company's strategic customers. To learn how to think like one of your major customers, you must include that customer in your strategic planning process. Regularly visiting with your company's significant customers will yield you important information and also set an example for others in the company.

Find Out What Your Customers Need

To understand your customer's needs, you must develop an appreciation for their thinking processes, which is a continuing process that requires a high level of engagement between you and your customer. To gain a robust understanding of a customer's particular needs, be very clear, concise, and engaging with that customer. Foster interactions between your company and that customer to establish a set of well-defined, shared expectations. When your company and your customers share expectations, very little room for ambiguity remains.

Your customers also have emotional needs that you ignore at your peril. Show a genuine interest in each customer's values and history by asking thoughtful questions; then listen intently! Gaining a sense of a customer's values and history will help you understand how to engage in a successful working relationship with that customer, and you must be willing to contemplate the customer's emotional needs at any time. Never underestimate the power of the customer's emotional needs.

Help the Customer Come Up With the Right Answer

Serving your customers does not mean always agreeing with them. Quite the contrary. By contributing perspectives that you gained from your vantage point, you might help your customers develop better solutions and thus bring value to your customer relationships. Like the old maxim advises, the customer is *always* right, but as a senior manager you are responsible for helping the customer come up with that right answer. Always accept opportunities to help, and never assume that you have the only solution for the customer.

Tell Your Customers What You Expect From Them

To sustain your relationships with customers, clearly articulate to them how much of their business you expect to earn. It is very important for your customers to understand your business expectations! They should know how much of their business you are willing to compete for and how aggressively you will serve their needs. By sharing your revenue expectations with your customers, you can take your relationship with them to new heights! Set clear, audacious goals, expressed in both dollar amounts and as a percentage of their total business. Your customers will expect your company to do what is necessary to earn that

> X-Leaders are highly sensitive to the reality that any damage done to a customer relationship will result in loss of market share and loss of shareholder value.

business, so strive to become the benchmark by which your competitors will be measured.

Each year, while I was CEO of the Lucent Technologies Microelectronics Group, during my CEO reviews I would express my desire to earn a significant amount of business from my major customers. During one of my visits with Lou Platt when he was Chairman and CEO of Hewlett-Packard, he told me, "Curt, you do not earn enough of my business to earn this much of my time." Lou said, "In order for you to continue to earn this amount of my time, you better find a way to earn significantly more of my business." Lou's statement was music to my ears because it provided me with an opportunity to regroup my team and ensure that we acted boldly and creatively to earn a larger share of Hewlett-Packard's business.

Appoint a Customer Relationships Manager

To serve your customers well, your company should appoint a high-level executive customer-relationship manager. This executive will build on the idea of shared expectations with the customer.

Build CEO Partnership Programs

In addition, I strongly suggest that you build CEO partnership programs with the strategic customers that you expect to supply your company with significant amounts of revenue. This program should be an annual event that brings together your CEO and executive team with the strategic customer's CEO and executive team to review the progress made in the prior year and to lay out plans for the current year and future years. These meetings should center on open and constructive discussions about how your company expects to improve its service to the customer and how the customer can help your company attain that goal.

I personally conducted this kind of CEO review with several of our largest customers during my tenure as CEO of Lucent Microelectronics Group. I had sessions with Lou Platt when he was Chairman and CEO of Hewlett-Packard and also met with Scott McNealy, Chairman and CEO of Sun Microsystems, Inc. I conducted CEO reviews with the chairmen and CEOs of NEC, Fujitsu, Mitsubishi, Nokia, Eriksson, and several other large customers located in the

United States, Europe, and Asia. Each of these meetings helped my executive team improve our understandings of our customers' expectations of our company. These meetings also gave me the opportunity to share my revenue expectations with these customers, which provided a great platform for leaders of both companies to discuss leading-edge projects for collaboration.

Track Your Company's Performance With Scorecards

To make the CEO partnership program work well, you must develop a "score card" survey system that customers use to candidly (and regularly) grade your company's performance. These are regular customer surveys that assess the company's performance against the expectations of customers. The scorecard system will perform as a channel through which your company receives information and perspectives from your customers. You can use this information to strengthen the foundation for a long, prosperous business relationship that you are building. Use the results of these evaluations to measure your company's overall effectiveness and to develop a baseline for tracking your company's performance. If your senior leadership team is savvy, you will develop a "score card" set of metrics to measure your company's performance against the customer's expectations.

Turn Your Customers Into Industry Heroes

Find ways to deliver products and services that will help your customers distance themselves from their competitors. Your customers will value their relationships with you much more if they believe that your company is working to improve their businesses. Customers want to partner with suppliers who have audacious goals. So be bold and set very aggressive targets, but be realistic in building your expense structure to deliver these audacious goals.

Have Multiple Contact Points With Each Customer

Senior management must establish a broad relationship with the customer that includes multiple contact points throughout the customer's company. Maintaining multiple relationships will help you gain deeper insight into the customer's organization. Multiple contact points are very important because individuals in the customer's organization will move from one position to another, providing you with opportunities, when these changes do occur, to learn more about their needs. Always work diligently to build a broad-based network of relationships within the customer organization!

Develop Listening Posts in Your Customers' Industries

X-Leaders remain alert for new ways to read the customer's organization and to improve their service to that customer. To get feedback on a customer's performance and to monitor activities in their industries, develop customer listening posts, including personal contacts, meetings, and strategic planning sessions.

Show Your Customers Appreciation

Customer recognition does not have to be elaborate to be effective, but you are well advised to acknowledge to your customers the value you gain from the opportunity to serve them. Whether you send elegant greeting cards to the customer (on a regular basis) or invite the customer to lunch, your gesture of thanks is important. Whatever customer-appreciation events you hold, they should culminate in an annual review to thank each strategic customer for their business. Together with the rest of the senior leadership team, dedicate at least one day every year to spend with each strategic customer to gain deeper insight into the customer's organizational culture. You will gain a better understanding of how the customer thinks and works, and you can use what you learn in your strategic planning process.

Keep Your Prices Competitive

Lavishing care on your customers will produce substantial benefits to your company for years into the future, but doing so will not create the opportunity to become a high-cost supplier. Neither must you provide the customer with the lowest price. Your products and services must be superior in quality and functionality to those of your most challenging competitors, and the cost of the relationship between you and your customer must remain competitive to what is achievable by those competitors.

Check Up on Your Customer Relationships

At the end of this chapter, I've provided a *Customer Relationship Checklist* that itemizes 10 indicators that a company is doing its best to focus on the needs of the strategic customers that account for a high percentage of its earnings. Take a few moments to review this list and determine how much energy your company is giving to its best customers.

Corporate Directors: Set the Tone for Customer Service

Enlightened corporate directors realize that their responsibility extends beyond creating a company that is good for shareholders; the company should produce *maximum return* to shareholders. This means creating a customer-centric company. Customer-centric companies generate more sales, and they groom future leaders to possess skills that match the needs of the marketplace.

A board of directors can and should expect senior managers to promote and achieve customer-centricity throughout the company

Pure product differentiation no longer is sufficient to keep revenue generation consistent; being customer-centric could be a corporate supplier's most distinguishing characteristic.

and soundly assist these managers in improving the company's relationships with its customers.

A very simple way of supporting the sales effort is to buy the consumer oriented products and services supplied by the company you serve. As a director, it is important that you consume the company's offerings so that you can offer senior managers feedback about your own experiences with these offerings. Next, connect with the sales team's enormous experience with identifying what customers want from the company you serve. As part of this effort, twice a year you (in concert with the full board) should review the customer-related metrics gathered by the company.

You and your fellow directors should allocate plenty of time to understand the company's plans for serving their customers and growing their business. For a concise idea of how the customer-centric company maintains contact with its strategic customers, take a look at the *Customer Relationship Checklist* at the end of this chapter. You can use this checklist to determine how the company you serve stacks up when it comes to demonstrating a desire to serve important customers.

Once you are familiar with the company and its offerings, it is time for you to advocate for the company. If you don't believe strongly enough in the company and its offerings to evangelize for them, you should not be on the company's board. Meet with people that you know in the customer's industry to discuss that industry and to articulate the advantages of your company's products and services. Visit significant customers of the company, perhaps bringing along one of the company's senior managers. Wherever you go, share your enthusiasm for the company, its corporate culture, and its offerings.

Professionals and Specialists: Make the Most of Customer Contacts

If you are one of the many people who provide your company with non-managerial services, such as accounting, administration, engineering, marketing, or sales, you can enhance your career prospects by becoming customer-centric in your job. This is true even if the people that you serve (your customers) are also employees of your company. Remember, without customers for your services, your work is superfluous.

Whatever your field of endeavor, if your job brings you into communication with customers, that job links you with customers in crucial ways. Often, you are the first to hear the truth from a customer (or at least what the customer thinks is the truth). You hear what customers want, which puts you in a great position to understand their needs and desires. You also hear what customers are dissatisfied with, which makes you your company's essential first line of defense. In either case, you are well positioned to create opportunities for your company to engage with your customers and to leverage these opportunities for your company's success and for your own well-being.

Thus, any direct customer experience that you have definitely gains you competitive advantage within your company, particularly if you are a customer-centric individual working in a customer-centric company. Under customer-centric circumstances, both you and your company face a high probability of success and, the more successful your company becomes, the more successful you are likely to become.

As a customer-centric employee, you enhance the odds that your company will survive and that you will continue in your company's employ. However, no matter what course your career takes, it always is good practice to establish as many working relationships within your industry as is reasonable. Not only will these relationships provide you with "listening posts" for assessing the needs of your customers and your industry, but, if something should go wrong for you (in a restructuring perhaps) and leaving your current employment becomes necessary, your great relationships with customers will constitute a broad foundation for surfacing into your next position. Your

If you treat your customers like reigning monarchs, they will reward you with loyalty that will cost your competitors market share.

search for a new job is likely to be much more fruitful when you have great relationships with the customers you have been serving.

No matter how eager you are to serve your customers, you will be hampered in your efforts if you aren't in personal contact with them. Make sure that your supervisor understands that you must communicate with your customers to be aware of their needs. Staying in contact with your customers will serve you well in the long run, so don't permit anyone to convince you that you should not be engaged with the customer.

Once you establish contact with your customers, listen to them, make sure they get quick answers to their questions, and keep your company informed about what they are saying. When you speak with your customers, keep alert to indications of ways that you and your company can add value to the products or services that you provide. After careful listening, select a customer whose products or services could be made more valuable through a professional relationship with you, and then proceed to build a relationship with your counterparts in that customer's organization. Be willing to share information and best practices with them, but be careful to honor your employer's and your customer's confidentiality. Never violate that trust.

Don't just converse with your customers on the phone and through the Internet; personally visit with them too. Justify a customer luncheon at least once each year. If your company is unwilling to invest a few dollars for you to take your customer to lunch, then pay for it out of your own pocket. However, if your company does not see value in this small act of customer recognition, you should consider it an indicator (though not the sole indicator) of the level of your company's customer-centricity. What if your customer is unwilling to have lunch with you? It isn't the sole measure of your customer's commitment to do business with your company, but it does send a message to you that you should discuss with your supervisor!

Provide your managers and team members with candid (and timely) summaries of the feedback you get from your customers. Again, always respect the confidentiality of all parties in these exchanges, and always be constructive in your remarks. Don't neglect to seek out and take advantage of the information your managers already possess that can guide you toward improved service to your customers. However, be willing to "push the envelope" to constantly improve customer-service solutions.

To deliver outstanding service, you must develop the habit of treating your customers like the center of your universe, establish a practice that offers you a structure for doing so, and make a long-term commitment to doing so. If becoming customer-centric to all your customers seems too daunting a task to undertake, start with one customer and build from there. By implementing improvements to customer service, you will earn a special place in your company.

Corporate Customers:
Make the Most of Your Strategic Suppliers

Given the opportunity, your company always will select strategic suppliers that provide the most competitive products and services. When your company is spending money, you want it to be the center of the universe! That is why your company should be developing strategic relationships with customer-centric suppliers.

A supplier that knows your company's needs and is willing to work to fill them is much more likely to meet your company's needs than the company that is apathetic about earning your business. Customer-centric suppliers are the companies that are willing to commit the time and resources to listen to your concerns and learn about your business. A customer-centric supplier will work to develop a better understanding of your corporate culture and expectations and will find more creative solutions to your company's problems than its competitors.

A customer-centric supplier also will be more committed than its competitors to your company's long-term success, which that company will demonstrate through their willingness to work with you, on a day-to-day basis, when conditions are good and when they are not so good. If your company embraces your customer-centric suppliers as members of your team, you and your company can learn much from those suppliers, who often will share information with you that other customers may not have given them the opportunity to share.

With this kind of corporate attitude, it is reasonable to expect customer-centric suppliers to earn high revenue and to be engaged in interesting work that attracts talented employees, indicating future success for that supplier as well. Your company is quite likely to conclude that doing business with a customer-centric supplier is strategically important to your company's longer-term success.

How can your company become a great customer that builds excellent relationships with your strategic suppliers? First, expect the quality of their products and service to be extremely high, and establish those expectations within your company. Next, tell your suppliers what you expect. Be honest. In fact, seek opportunities to tell your suppliers the truth, such as, for example, exactly what delivery dates you want. Don't fudge! Fudging usually results in increased costs and lesser quality, with no significant improvement in time delivery. If fudging is the only way to get your supplier to perform at your expected level, and they refuse to get trained, get a new supplier!

After you share your company's expectations with your strategic suppliers, track their progress in meeting those expectations. As you work with each strategic supplier, jointly develop report cards that assess their performance in serving your company. To get a good idea of what the customer-centric supplier is willing to do to earn your business, take a look at the *Customer Relationship*

Checklist at the end of this chapter. When you work to improve your relationships with suppliers, these methods present some goals for you to reach for.

Get your suppliers emotionally involved, too. Don't forget to thank and reward companies and people who give you outstanding service. In fact, develop awards and programs that recognize their excellence! And, most important of all, award your most customer-centric suppliers with most of your company's business. When your suppliers become passionate about your company, you will see tremendous results.

CUSTOMER RELATIONSHIP CHECKLIST

	Met With Top Customer Executives During the Last Quarter.
	Aware of Major Changes in the Customer's Business.
	Conducted Regularly Scheduled Reviews With Customer.
	Know the Current Three "Hot Buttons" of Key Decision Makers.
	Conducted a Joint Strategic Planning Session.
	Established/Maintained a Formal Customer Business Team.
	Engaged in Joint Product/Technology Development.
	Established (or Tracking) Joint Business Improvement Metrics
	Brokered Meeting With Customer Executives.
	Received Supplier Award or Achieved Preferred Supplier Status.

Suppliers seeking an outstanding relationship with a customer should meet at least seven of the ten criteria on this list.

X-Leaders wake up every morning with the attitude that every customer is worth dying for! They are always at least willing to "break a leg" to demonstrate their passion to earn 100% of their customers' business!

Celebrate the Good Fortune of Having Customers to Serve!

1. Connect with the Sales Team! When seeking opportunities to establish an appropriate working relationship with a customer of your company, always seek the guidance and assistance of your company's sales team.

2. Adopt a Customer! Evaluate your relationship against the customer relationship checklist on the previous page. Ask yourself what you can do to improve that relationship.

Endnotes

[liv] Reichheld, F., & Detrick, C. (2002, September 19). Want to know how to keep expenses low? Think loyalty. *American Banker*.

[lv] Colvin, G., & Selden, L. (2002, November). Profitable customers: Organizing your company around them. Discussion conducted at the meeting of the Fortune Global Forum, The Power of Leadership: Mastering the New Realities, Washington, DC.

X-Principle Five: *X-Leaders are visionaries who anticipate the future and identify marketplace opportunities before they become trends. X-Leaders often know what customers will need before the customers do.*

CHAPTER 5

Exploring With a Passion

Visionary leaders create visionary companies. X-leaders seem to possess a mysterious ability to see around corners to glimpse future trends. They are pioneers who expand the frontiers of the marketplace and continually reinvent their companies to generate exceptional shareholder value.

When it comes to developing a vision, a company's X-Leader is so far ahead of the rest of the leadership team that his or her vision becomes the company's baseline motivating inspiration. X-Leaders don't content themselves with identifying opportunities during times of prosperity; they seek out opportunities in times of despair, too, and they are able to find those opportunities because they have inspired their companies to become creative enough to anticipate customers' future needs. Like Ronald Lippitt, X-Leaders understand that companies are not so much motivated to change by the difficulties they encounter as by the images of potential that they see.[lvi] X-Leaders create images that make people feel bold and want to do new things. These images go far beyond "merely inventing the new" because X-Leaders understand the difference between creating something new and doing the "development, manufacturing, and marketing necessary for it to have a real impact."[lvii]

As Lippitt pointed out, this kind of entrepreneurial vision is needed to anticipate market needs and get to the market first. Getting to the market first is very important because, unless an innovation is highly protected by intellectual property, most of its market value will be captured within 6 months to a year of its introduction.[lviii] Of course, the X-Leader, who is a champion of preparation, has already protected the company's strategic intent by acquiring the intellectual property and know-how that competitors will regard as barriers to entering the X-led company's markets. The immense value of this foresight begins to become evident when competitors incorporate their hesitation to enter the X-led company's markets into their own strategic plans.

The process through which an X-Leader shares his or her vision is very important, perhaps more important than the fact that the vision comes from the leader.[lix] Nevertheless, the success of this vision puts the X-Leader in the position of spokesperson for his or her industry. This positive attention reflects onto many of the company's employees, who then become industry luminaries whose opinions are sought by market analysts.

You may believe that the ability to envision the future in your industry is strictly a matter of genius that is not accessible to you or your company, but the fact remains that many companies have learned how to develop a vision and then bring that vision into the world. For example, ITT Industries found ways to clean water without chemicals, and return it to the earth without harming the ecosystem. ITT Industries is helping the world and its people manage one of its most precious resources more wisely.[lx] Along with Massachusetts Institute of Technology, DuPont is a founding partner of the Institute for Soldier Nanotechnologies, which aims to revolutionize uniforms and gear so that soldiers will have greater protection, combined with a much lighter gear load in the field.[lxi] By working closely with global regulatory agencies and their initiatives, such as the U.S. Environmental Protection Agency's Energy Star program, China's CECP and the European Commission Blue Angel standard, On Semiconductor offers timely, cost-effective, energy-compliant power supply components.[lxii]

Intel envisioned mass use of ever-increasing computing power and then delivered computing tools that make their customers more productive. Whether you are an X-Leader or aspire to become one, by following the recommendations outlined below, you can learn to spot the trends of the future and understand what your customers will need before they do!

Aspiring X-Leaders: Start Envisioning the Future

If you want to become an X-Leader, you should be aware that your industry's new leaders will surface from among its latest crop of visionary executives. You can enrich your career by helping your company be ready with the products and services that customers will be wanting. There are steps you can take to help you do so.

Start by taking a serious interest in current thinking about developing vision. The key to becoming able to see things in ways that other people don't is to learn how to think outside many of the boundaries that people accept early in our lives. You can experience a simple illustration of the limiting effect of accepting unnecessary boundaries by attempting to solve the well-known "nine dots puzzle," which makes it clear that accepting common assumptions can inhibit a person's ability to solve simple problems. Avail yourself of some of the many books, courses, and workshops that teach basic techniques for thinking "outside the box." To make the techniques that you learn accessible to your usual thinking processes, practice using them to produce a real-life practical improvement of a product or service in your realm of endeavor.

As you do so, it soon will become obvious to you that, to move from imagination into the real world, your visions must be grounded in facts. To lead change, you must inform your thinking with a great deal of factual informa-

> **X-leaders seem to possess a mysterious ability to see around corners to glimpse future trends.**

tion. The more facts about your company and your industry that you have at your command, the better you will understand your industry and your company's place in it. Actively pursue knowledge about your company and industry, and give your learning an extra boost by remaining aware that not all accepted "knowledge" is grounded in fact. Work to uncover the real facts (if any) underlying the information you encounter by asking questions that explore and challenge that information. Allow yourself to be fascinated by what you learn. You will get a much richer picture of a situation if you examine it using all of your senses and your emotions. You will improve your analytical abilities enormously if you develop a habit of analyzing situations from the point of view of a smart competitor, so remember to ask questions that probe what your competitors might want to know.

Whenever you encounter an idea, explanation, or position that affects your company's plans, keep probing that information until you understand what ideas and feelings that information was constructed from. Ask yourself: How much of this information is based on facts, how much on hypotheses, and how much on emotion? All of these can motivate human behavior, but when directing your own thinking or analyzing the thinking of others, you should be aware of whether you or others are using proven or unproven ideas, or are relying purely on emotions.

As you learn, keep alert for ways to create shareholder value that align with the needs and desires of your customer base. Pay attention to the important differences between invention and innovation pointed out by Ethernet inventor Bob Metcalfe and columnist Michael Shrage (and others), especially the difference between "merely creating a great new thing and doing the development, manufacturing, and marketing necessary for it to have a real impact" (as discussed by Robert Buderi, 2004). [lxiii]

Use the facts you gather to develop various market scenarios and imagine how you and your company might influence their outcomes. These scenarios will help you perceive probable future trends and will be wonderfully informative as you work on the development of new products and services. In fact, scenario planning is so important to developing effective visions that you should use this method as a foundation of your visionary thinking.

Peter Schwartz, founder and chairman of the board of Global Business Network (GBN), provided some of his expertise in scenario planning during my tenure as CEO of Lucent Technology Microelectronics Group and President of the Intellectual Property Division. Schwartz defined *scenario planning* as:

> ... *a tool for ordering one's perceptions about alternative future environments in which one's decisions might be played out. Alternatively, scenario planning is a set of organized ways for us to dream effectively about our own future. Concretely, they resemble a set of stories, either written out or often spoken and built around carefully crafted bold plots.*"[lxiv]

As your vision takes shape, start communicating it to other people. If you desire to become an X-Leader, you shouldn't be sitting back and waiting for someone else to invent the future. Your quest to communicate your vision will be greatly aided if you have been developing a good relationship with your supervisor and have been reviewing with that person what you have learned about visionary thinking in your reading, classes, and workshops. Get your supervisor's approval to share your developing vision with your teammates and managers. Hopefully, your colleagues will offer you critiques of your ideas. When this happens, don't take offense. Remain comfortable. Their critiques will help you improve your vision.

The more you attempt to share your vision, the more necessary you will find it to sharpen your communication skills. Take advantage of classes and workshops that focus on speaking skills, and volunteer for assignments that will afford

> **Successful companies are determined as much by their vision as by their products and services.**

you opportunities to discuss your vision with other people. Serving on planning committees and industry panels and speaking at industry engagements will help your career by increasing your visibility among your colleagues and industry leaders and by focusing positive attention on your company.

Senior Managers: Build a Coherent Vision

Your corporation always will face visionary competitors. Even when a competitor's performance is not as good as yours, if that company uses their vision to create excitement, they will earn time with your customers, putting your share of the market at risk. Successful companies are determined as much by their vision as by their products and services.

Your company may not be a leader in your industry; in fact, you and your company's other senior leaders may be quite content to let your company follow. This is not unusual; certainly, many companies are followers. You may believe, like some management theorists, that creating a corporate vision is not the responsibility of senior leaders, but of the entire company. However, neither of these views reduces your company's need for a coherent corporate vision to put your company in the lead. Given a choice, companies that are followers don't partner with suppliers that are followers. Today, your corporate customers may be asking you for products that fulfill the leading-edge visions of their own markets. Tomorrow, they will be demanding such products. To win their business, you and your fellow senior leaders must discern what they will be wanting down the road, and you must make yourself able to follow that vision with on-time delivery of competitively priced products and services.

By trying the recommendations that I have outlined below in this section, you can improve your vision of what your industry's future is likely to hold and help your company take advantage of that future. By doing so, you can simultaneously enrich your own prospects. Leaders who can identify marketplace opportunities before they become trends have a lot more fun on the job, enjoy better performance, and, naturally enough, are more in demand than those who can respond only to present trends. This, of course, means that they will enjoy more positive recognition, get more frequent calls from executive recruiters, and earn more money. If you have a very strong vision that can be supported by results and also possess strong people development skills, you will be an attractive candidate for senior executive and CEO positions at a broad range of companies. Leaders who anticipate the future create a bright future for themselves.

> **Leaders who anticipate the future create a bright future for themselves.**

Because preparation is crucially important to the success of any endeavor, you should begin building your vision by doing some basic study and research. As you gather data to design, support, or modify your vision, use all your senses and your emotions. In all your efforts, surround yourself with knowledgeable, creative people who have confidence and courage. The people who are most likely to be able to help you build your vision are those who have learned to challenge every decision that they make.

Penetrate Illusory Boundaries

If you aren't already a visionary thinker (and even if you are), you can learn techniques for improving your ability to envision future trends by taking some courses in visionary thinking. Such courses are intended to help you reach beyond illusory boundaries. The techniques you learn will help you find surprising new solutions that will seem obvious once you free yourself from some of the common mental restrictions most of us accept early in life. Keeping abreast of the latest research in visionary leadership also is very useful, so it is important to read books and articles on the topic. You will benefit greatly from reading at least one book each year regarding some form of visionary thinking, which will sharpen your thinking skills and help keep you up to date on thinking about visionary leadership.

Analyze Future Markets

Wayne Gretsky, called the "Great One," was one of the best hockey players ever to lace up a pair of ice skates. When asked how he managed to deliver consistently outstanding performance, he responded, "Most of my competitors skate to where the hockey puck is .... I skate to where I think the hockey puck will be."

Think like the Great One. Don't target your product and service development to today's market. And don't merely analyze your current competition, analyze who your competition is likely to be in the future. Allocate time, effort, energy, and money too, so that you can be where the market is going. A very useful exercise for matching your company's resources and capabilities to its competitive environment is the SWOT analysis, which is used to look at your company's strengths, weaknesses, opportunities, and threats.

Develop a Corporate Strategic Intent

Every corporation should develop a compelling strategic intent that guides all of the company's thinking. Make scenario planning a foundation of your thinking. First, construct a variety of market development scenarios and then work out strategies for influencing the outcome of each of the scenarios. When developing these scenarios, don't accept the obvious answers or the supplied answers as the only answers. Imagine what could happen if you were not limited

117

by the past. Use the strategies you develop as guidelines when developing new products and services.

Don't try to cram time to develop a corporate strategy into the already busy schedules of the members of your company's leadership team. See to it that your company hires a world-class strategy officer, a deep thinker who has the capacity, interest, and ability to create a vision that motivates and inspires your company to pursue greatness. Then work with that person.

Run Experiments in the Margin

You can feed your company's vision by continually experimenting with new opportunities. As discussed by Peter Senge, author of *The Fifth Discipline*, a study by Arie de Geus and his colleagues at Shell Corporation revealed that a third of the Fortune 500 industrials listed in 1970 had vanished by 1983.[lxv] By 1990, the largest industrial enterprises had experienced an average lifespan less than half that of the people who worked in them. However, a small number of companies that de Geus and his colleagues studied did manage to survive for 75 years or longer. The key to their survival was their ability to run "experiments in the margin," that is, to continually explore new businesses and opportunities that created potential new sources of growth.[lxvi]

As you devote resources to experimental inquiries, remember that creating a great new thing is only part of the job; that new thing will need the "development, manufacturing, and marketing necessary for it to have a real impact" (as discussed by Robert Buderi, 2004).[lxvii]

Balance Fear With Reward

Fear is a strong motivator, and it can sharply focus a person's efforts for a short period of time. I believe that most people can be strongly motivated by a fear of failing to achieve what is expected of them. As a senior leader, you must instill throughout your company a fear, not of losing one's job, but of losing to the competition, of not meeting the expectations of shareholders. This kind of motivation has worked very well for Intel and some other companies.

The idea is to spend some time thinking like a wounded competitor, thinking as though "the bridge is burning." Imagine what actions you would take if your company's competitive position were at risk. If those actions are reasonable, don't wait—take those actions right away as defensive measures.

Although it is a good idea to practice motivation through paranoia from time to time, remember that fear only can be a short-term motivator. Over the long term, people are motivated by anticipation of recognition and compensation. To galvanize your company for great achievements, you must combine fear of failure with anticipation of reward.

Corporate Directors: Imagine a Visionary Company

If you are a corporate director, should you concern yourself with the level of visionary thinking demonstrated by the company's CEO and senior leadership team? Yes! If you are committed to taking the company to a higher level of performance, it is your duty to evaluate the vision and strategic intent of the company you serve.

Visionary thinking enhances the company's growth opportunities and increases the odds that the return to shareholders will be maximized. In fact, visionary thinking followed by effective execution is valuable to all company stakeholders.

> **Although it is a good idea to practice motivation through paranoia from time to time, remember that fear only can be a short-term motivator.**

Practicing the art of visionary thinking will broaden your conception of what is possible for the company you serve. Having an informed idea of what the future is likely to hold will help you analyze the company's current practices and reorient the company's strategic direction. When you develop scenarios that contain the invention of new technologies, products, or services, make sure you also anticipate what will be necessary to develop and market those inventions. [lxviii] Make certain that the company you serve hires a world-class strategy officer to create a vision that will inspire the company to maximize shareholder value. Work with and learn from that officer.

To add real value to the company, I suggest that you become a "hair shirt" director who confronts the status quo and challenges the CEO and leadership team to raise their performance to the next higher level. One great question is worth more than many good answers, so make sure your questions are pertinent to the issue. Carefully examine the answers you receive using all of your senses, including your eyes and your emotions. Your approach must be entirely helpful and inspiring so that the CEO readily encourages you and other directors to pose those challenges.

You can help the CEO and leadership team crystallize their strategy by thinking like a competitor and formulating your challenges based on that outlook. You can help them reach beyond their experience by thinking like the company's partners and telling the leadership team what your expectations would be. Inspire them by reflecting on your own relevant experiences. Always demand and accept nothing less than constant pursuit of excellence.

Professionals and Specialists: Build a More Rewarding Future

The new leaders in your industry, your field, and your company will be visionaries who can transform their visions into material reality. By demonstrating some level of visionary thinking in the building of new products, the delivery of new services, the reduction of costs, or some other area, you can build a more rewarding professional future for yourself. If you are viewed as a visionary within your company, you will get more opportunities to present your ideas and strategies to other people, including your company's leadership team.

To develop a visionary idea, you must understand what is happening in the market that you serve and anticipate the direction of your own company. Keep in mind that your idea must not only be new, but it must eventually be developed sufficiently to get into the market. To gain the knowledge to achieve your vision, you must become so inquisitive about various aspects of your field that eventually you will be considered an expert in it.

Approach new ideas in your field with fascination. Keep in mind that one great question is worth more than many good answers, so ask penetrating questions and then listen carefully to the answers that you receive. Read articles and books about visionary thinking, and take courses on this topic as well. The more techniques and tools for envisioning future trends that you have at your disposal, the more you will be able to anticipate potential developments in your field and how those might affect your customers. This knowledge also will come in handy when senior leaders test you to see if you have any notion of what the future is likely to hold.

An effective vision is grounded in facts. To gather facts you must learn to recognize them, which often means that you must determine whether the information you are receiving is based on facts, unproven concepts, or emotion. Check information presented to you in company forums to make sure it is supported by factual data. Learn to attack subject matter from a competitor's perspective without, of course, ever attacking the person who is presenting the material. When gathering information, use all your senses. Listen carefully, but also use your eyes, which capture more information much faster than your ears. Pay attention to emotions, too. If you discover that the information you are receiving is not grounded in factual data, but on abstract ideas or emotion, keep in mind that these factors can

> **To galvanize your company for great achievements, you must combine fear of failure with anticipation of reward.**

be quite valuable as you develop a new approach to a market. However, it is important that you recognize the differences among them.

Once you begin developing a vision, you will need to communicate it to other people. Start by asking your supervisor to support your "out-of-the-box" thinking by permitting you to share your ideas with your colleagues during team meetings. When developing new ideas, you don't need to have all the answers to whatever issues or concerns are raised in the discussion. A visionary thinker trying to find the right answer is comfortable keeping some ideas open for critique.

Your aspirations to build a piece of the future go hand-in-hand with leadership, so look for opportunities to lead. Leading projects will feel more rewarding than merely doing what you are told and will provide you with opportunities to demonstrate your visionary thinking. Expect to work harder than your teammates. If you take responsibility early in your career, you will reap huge dividends later.

An excellent way to start is by focusing on a company and industry that you work with. Volunteer for the "working committee" assignments of that company. Look for opportunities to serve on panels and to speak at functions in that industry. These events are platforms from which you can articulate your vision and your ideas about the future. Become associated with that company and industry in such a way that you gain an opportunity to fully engage in the planning processes that move them forward. Serving in industry venues increases your visibility among your peers and industry leaders and also provides good visibility for your company. To communicate your vision effectively, especially in public, you will need to develop a good communication style. By communicating your vision with passion and clarity, you will generate excitement about your ideas.

> **Visionary companies do not merely respond to markets, they build markets.**

If you develop a really good visionary idea, your company is likely to see the potential in it, provided, of course, that you are well positioned in a company that wants to move from success to greatness by creating future opportunities. Visionary companies do not merely respond to markets, they build markets.

A word of advice about timing: It usually will be more profitable for you and your company to become involved early in the market cycle, rather than later on in the cycle, particularly if you know when to get in and when to get out. If you get in early, you usually can get out early. However, if you get in late, you will never have the opportunity to get out early.

Corporate Customers:
Synchronize Your Vision With Your Supplier's Vision

In today's marketplace, business is occurring at the speed of light, and often, only a fine line exists between winning and losing: Victories often occur in days or weeks, rather than in months or years. The time available to respond to marketplace changes is shrinking due to Moore's Law, the laws of economics, and the sheer strength of the competitive landscape. Technologies are being produced at an ever more rapid pace, and this speeding up of innovation is lowering the bars of entry for competitors.

Getting a product or service to the market first may be difficult, but the rewards are great. If your company is like most, you are actively looking for ways to beat your competition to the marketplace and to sustain your company's competitive advantage for a reasonable period of time. In this case, your company will benefit from working with strategic suppliers who are able to work in today's time-compressed market environment, to anticipate future needs in your marketplace, and to help your company be the first to meet those needs. At the same time, your company probably is cutting costs by actively reducing its number of strategic suppliers. With your company's success becoming inextricably linked to your choice of strategic suppliers, you need to give your company's business to companies with demonstrated staying power. These companies are likely to be the ones relying on X-Leadership to help customers like you build the added value necessary to win in the marketplace.

Breakthrough thinking, new designs, and new services are the important characteristics that you should be looking for in your strategic suppliers, because these are the characteristics that differentiate the best suppliers from the marginal ones. The only constant in business is change, so you should look for suppliers whose leaders drive change. A visionary supplier will broaden your perspective as you search for more competitive solutions.

To gain maximum leverage and return from your strategic suppliers, you must require them to clearly and concisely communicate their visions to you. This is vital because your company will need to synchronize your corporate vision with the corporate vision and capabilities of your suppliers.

To be a true X-Leader in your company, let others do a lot of your thinking for you. Explore the thinking of all the best minds in your industry, and allow their intellects, investments, and perspectives help you shape your future. First, measure the visions of your company and of your strategic supplier against the industry standard. Then let your strategic suppliers know that you expect them to create benchmarks, not follow what others do. Next, measure your company's collective vision against the perspectives of the future articulated by academics and industry luminaries.

Having a vision is essential, but you must link that vision to concise performance objectives and measure the progress of your vision against those objectives. Your company should quantify and consistently measure your strategic supplier's progress toward your vision.

However, planning is not a surrogate for outstanding performance. Neither your company nor your strategic suppliers should ever lose touch with the reality of today's performance requirements. Be careful not to allow a strategic supplier's visionary pursuits to justify a failure to deliver today! The ability to deliver today is what earns a company the reputation of being visionary. Expect your strategic partners to think about tomorrow, while they deliver for today.

When you appraise your strategic supplier's past and current performance, you also should appraise that company's vision of where the market is going and how it plans to lead the way. Compare your company's expectations to your strategic supplier's vision. To do so, you must include a "visionary measurement" in your supplier-performance model. You should also appraise the delivery, along the way, of all the components of that vision. A visionary supplier that really thinks outside of the box will substantially shorten and enrich the development cycle of your company's product and extend your company's competitive reach.

Be a great customer! Always set high expectations for your strategic suppliers. If you practice X-Leadership, you usually will get what you expect!

X-Leaders develop a clairvoyant view of the marketplace. By focusing on what is possible, they heighten the slope of their industry's creativity curve.

Four Ways to See Around Corners!

1. Use all of your senses. Sharpen your listening skills. Use your eyes, which capture more information much faster than your ears. Pay attention to emotions, and learn to emotionally feel your way around your environment.

2. Learn to ask constructive, penetrating questions. Keep in mind that one great question is worth more than many good answers.

3. Practice breakthrough thinking. Imagine new ways of developing and delivering products and services that could deliver value and performance that far outperforms the competition and or standard measures of expectation! Understand and value the difference between inventing and innovation!

4. Hire a world-class strategy officer, a deep thinker who has the capacity, interest and ability to create a vision that motivates and inspires your company to pursue great efforts to maximize shareholder value.

Endnotes

[lvi] Lippitt, R. (1949). *Training in community relations: A research exploration toward new group skills.* New York: Harper.

[lvii] This difference has been pointed out by Ethernet inventor Bob Metcalfe, columnist Michael Shrage, and others, as discussed by Robert Buderi. See Buderi, R. (2004, May). Reinventing Invention. TechnologyReview.com [On-line serial]. Retrieved April 9, 2005, from: http://www.technologyreview.com/articles/04/05/leading0504.asp?p=1

[lviii] Lippitt, R., 1949, *Training in community relations.*

[lix] Senge, P.M. (1990). The leader's new work: Building learning organizations. *Sloan Management Review.* 32(1)(Fall), 7-23.

[lx] ITT Industries. (2004). Annual Report.

[lxi] DuPont, Inc. (2004). Annual Review. P. 11.

[lxii] On Semiconductor. (2004). Annual Report. Retrieved May 20, 2005. From http://library.corporate-ir.net/library/12/121/121693/items/148552/Annualrpt04-rev0.pdf.

[lxiii] Buderi, R. (2004, May). Reinventing invention. *TechnologyReview.com* [On-line serial]. Retrieved April 9, 2005, from: http://www.technologyreview.com/articles/04/05/leading0504.asp?p=1

[lxiv] Schwartz, P. (1996, April 15). The art of the long view: Planning for the future in an uncertain world. *Currency,* Volume? Page?.

[lxv] Senge, 1990, The leader's new work.

[lxvi] Ibid.

[lxvii] Buderi, R. (2004, May). Reinventing invention.

[lxviii] Ibid.

X-Principle Six: *X-Leaders drive their companies with decisions grounded in facts. They insist on exchanging information with all employees and customers, and they seek opportunities to tell the truth.*

CHAPTER 6

Extracting the Truth

The decisions that X-Leaders use to drive their companies are effective because these decisions are grounded in hard facts. For X-Leaders, good, factual information is the foundation of success, and they insist on exchanging information with their people and their customers. Once an X-Leader has gathered enough data to conclude that a decision is the right one, he or she energetically uses that data to exhort others to implement that decision.

The X-Leader's emphasis on continued learning is, of course, nothing less than a sincere quest for truth, which also shows in the X-Leader's continual search for opportunities to tell the truth and to hear the truth. In other words, when ambiguity exists and clarity is needed. The X-led company's victorious position in the marketplace is driven by factual information shared through informal means, such as conversations, e-mail, and group discussions,[lxix] and through official means, such as notices, meetings, team briefings, and company videos.[lxx] Whatever means of communication are used, the X-Leader makes sure that they are well ordered, because the efficient sharing of information among all members of the company is essential to high performance.

As the X-Leader knows, a company's success or failure in facilitating communication among supervisors, peers, and subordinates is crucial in determining how much trust those people place in each other and in their company, which in turn affects their morale for good or for ill. As a number of studies have shown, failure to communicate information to all employees is likely to result in an atmosphere of low trust, whereas making information easily accessible to all employees at all levels helps to build trust.[lxxi] One reason that trust is important is that employees will not take risks on behalf of a company unless they believe that the people they are dealing with are sincerely concerned about their well-being and, moreover, that these people are competent, honest, and reliable.[lxxii] Without trust, employees assume self-protective, defensive postures that inhibit learning and performance.[lxxiii]

Lack of good communication in a company not only reduces employee trust and morale, it inhibits customer service. Without information, even the most zealous and talented customer-contact employees cannot excel. Employees who want to find solutions to customer needs instead of merely persuading or manipulating customers must communicate with their peers and supervisors about ways of doing so.[lxxiv] Moreover, customers are more likely to feel confident sharing information about their plans with suppliers that are willing to do the same.

> **Employees who feel informed also feel empowered to use the information they receive to contribute more to the company's success.**

Despite the obvious value of establishing good company-wide communications, many companies pay little attention to this aspect of their business.[lxxv] Top managers in most companies don't trust most employees enough to empower them with information and responsibility.[lxxvi] These managers don't want to make themselves vulnerable to loss of control within their organizations.

Without information, however, people cannot act responsibly, even if they want to.[lxxvii] No matter how highly motivated or well trained an employee is, that person cannot contribute to enhancing company performance if he or she doesn't understand the dimensions of that performance.[lxxviii] When senior leaders share information about the company's financial performance, strategy, and operational measures, this action conveys to the company's people that they are trusted.[lxxix] Employees who feel informed also feel empowered to use the information they receive to contribute more to the company's success. Bad news, such as of an impending takeover, loss of competitive advantage, or a threat of redundancies, also must be communicated.[lxxx] Even bad news helps people make rational decisions.

People who feel pride in their jobs and take ownership of their contributions think about what makes sense in their situations and act in ways that serve customers and achieve company goals.[lxxxi] When employees feel that their personal contributions matter to the company, some of them even will take the risk of identifying and challenging procedures that they believe are not in the company's best interests.

The idea that employees can be truly empowered to contribute to the company only when respectful ongoing dialogue is possible for all members of the company was first articulated a hundred years ago by the pioneer management theorist, Mary Parker Follet.[lxxxii] Today, her observations still inspire management theorists, such as Christian Groönroos, who theorize that true dialogue can emerge only away from manipulative, one-way communication.[lxxxiii] Because it is unlikely that any empowerment scheme can work in the absence of trust,[lxxxiv] it is up to leaders to show confidence in employees by accepting their new ideas, providing them with necessary resources, and distributing power to them. Transforming a company requires managers and subordinates alike to accept non-traditional ideas and participate in new types of activities; this transformation can prevail only in a culture of trust.[lxxxv]

The key to establishing a culture of trust is specificity, not ambiguity. The real issues at hand must be fully exposed and fully explored. As X-Leaders understand, managers and subordinates both must "put the moose on the table." Of course, an important way of finding the moose is to respect constructive questions that probe the why, where, how, when, and what of every corporate decision and circumstance, whether those questions come from the mind of the X-Leader, a company employee, or a customer. To help drive the company to its maximum level of performance, both questions and answers must be specific, not vague.

X-Leaders recognize that customers and employees who are deprived of information will attempt to understand situations by fabricating theories based on their own experiences. Some of these people will accept rumors that support their own attitudes, and some will spread rumors that further their own agendas. To maximize a company's effectiveness, innuendos and rumors must be minimized, so X-Leaders must take all necessary steps to make sure that their people have the facts. Fortunately for X-led companies, in a corporate culture that deals with facts and fosters full exchange of information, false rumors are detected easily because both employees and customers immediately challenge them. X-Leaders earn the trust of employees and customers by communicating openly and honestly with them. They earn confidence in the company by presenting the facts as they are.

Aspiring X-Leaders: Use Information to Prepare for Power

How can you, as an ambitious future X-Leader, be transformed into an empowered person? You can empower yourself using truth and facts, and you can help create an atmosphere around yourself that inspires others to behave in empowered ways.

To be an empowered X-Leader, you must start with certain basic understandings. One of these understandings is that, like yourself, most people are willing to do their job well if they are permitted to.[lxxxvi] Allowing people to do their jobs well means, in part, providing them with all the information they need to do their best and to feel competent and secure in their environment. The

> **The key to establishing a culture of trust is specificity, not ambiguity.**

more knowledge you or any worker has, the more you will feel that you own your contributions to the company and the better you can align your efforts with your company's objectives. For these reasons, X-Leaders establish broad-based communication programs that keep their stakeholders informed at all times. To an X-Leader, there is no such thing as over-communicating. If you think you are over-communicating, very likely you are communicating ineffectively and your message is not getting across.

To compete with other future leaders, you must gain knowledge and power. This requires preparation. As an X-Leader-in-the-making, seek opportunities to give people the information they need to do their jobs and to understand the issues at hand so they can deal with those issues accordingly. Learn to deal with ineffective communications by rooting out ambiguities and replacing them with facts. Establish where the information you are receiving is coming from; that information may not be factual. Always, always, always tell the truth. Make your communications as clear as possible, and ask questions until the information you are getting is clear to you. Address rumors and innuendos immediately. Keep your customers well-informed too.

Let people know they can come to you with information, and seek information from other people, especially your supervisors and managers. Even receiving bad news prepares you to make rational decisions and to do your job as well as possible, work toward increased shareholder value, and develop your career to its fullest extent.

Senior Leaders: Stimulate Productivity, Create a Trust-Filled Atmosphere

Conclusive research has established that employees who trust their supervisors like their jobs more, perform them better, and stay at them longer.[lxxxvi] Trusted supervisors also seem to have more influence on their subordinates.[lxxxvii] Trust helps people cooperate, which makes their work more effective and efficient.[lxxxix] As a senior leader of your company, you will do well to spend time promoting trusting relationships with your subordinates and helping managers and supervisors throughout your company do the same. The employees of your company should feel that they can turn to their supervisors to help them solve problems. Establishing trust in today's uncertain, constantly changing business environment is not easy.[xc] As Michael Annison and Dan Wilford have pointed out, "trust does not come with a pay-check, it has to be earned."[xci] Once you establish this trust, your behavior will be imitated. People normally follow the people they trust, and if you earn people's trust by telling the truth to employees and customers and consistently exchanging information with them, the rest of your company will follow suit.

Below, I have listed a number of practical steps you can take to establish trusting relationships in your company.

Look for Opportunities to Tell the Truth

Employees only trust those they feel are telling the truth, [xcii] so obviously, the more often employees perceive you to be telling the truth, the more opportunities they will have to establish trust in you. A good place to start is by giving truthful answers to questions you are asked. Speaking truthfully is a demanding practice, but searching out opportunities to speak the truth is much more difficult. These opportunities exist wherever you encounter ambiguity or lack of awareness of needed information. Make it a practice to replace ambiguity with clarity, and lack of knowledge with information. In such situations, you may have to lead by asking the questions.

Don't distort the truth or hide the facts, and don't permit your subordinates to do so. Your people know more than you think they know. If you and the rest of the senior leadership team don't tell your people what is going on in your company, then your people will fill the gaps in their information with conjecture and rumors. In the absence

> To an X-Leader, there is no such thing as over-communicating. If you think you are over-communicating, very likely you are communicating ineffectively.

of trust, many of these conjectures and rumors will be driven by uncertainty, fear, discontent, and self-interest; these hardly will be in the best interests of the company's shareholders. Telling the truth as often as possible to as many people as possible will help prevent people from mischaracterizing your company.

Successful companies avoid the *mushroom approach* to information dispersal, in which the company keeps employees and customers in the dark and shovels information in their direction in the hope that they will accept it. Instead, successful companies develop a base of shared knowledge on which to compete. In the X-led company, knowledge is the power that leads to the highest possible levels of performance.

Establish Strong Information Technology

Your company should manage information as carefully as other valuable company assets, such as inventory and skills. Without a standardized approach to information technology that includes a common set of platforms, your company's communication system will be incomplete, disorganized, and inept, which is almost as bad as not using information technology at all. You and your fellow senior leaders are responsible for endowing your company with a strong information technology system that will minimize confusion and disruptions.

Hold Company "Town Meetings"

For your company's employees to reach decisions based on facts, you and your fellow senior leaders must give them the necessary facts. Making certain that information is dispersed throughout your entire company is a responsibility too important to delegate. As a basic step in the right direction, you and the rest of your senior leadership team should hold regularly scheduled "town meetings" *and* impromptu employee communication meetings in which you openly communicate with all the people in the company. These forums will set the tone for the company. They should be safe places for candid, constructive dialog among all members of the team.

Open Your Doors to Employees and Customers

You and the rest of your senior leadership team can improve your company's performance by paying attention to the concerns of employees and customers, and seeing to it that those concerns are resolved appropriately. The most direct method of bringing those concerns to light is to establish an open-door policy, in which everyone in the company and all your significant customers feel encouraged to meet with the CEO or any senior leader to speak up about their concerns.

I learned the value of listening to concerns of customers and employees during my experiences decades ago with the open-door policy established by Tom Watson at IBM Corporation. As President and CEO of Lucent Technology Microelectronics Group and, later, as Chairman of the Board and CEO of Zilog, Inc., I established my own open-door policy, which provided me with many occasions to learn and grow. I knew that whenever I took the time to listen, I had a chance to improve my leadership skills, tell the truth, and share important facts.

Establish a CEO E-mail Input System

Another very effective channel of company communication is an e-mail system that permits the CEO to receive unfiltered input from employees and customers. In the companies I headed, I established a "<u>C</u>EO <u>E</u>yes <u>O</u>nly" (CEO) program that provided every person in the company a way to electronically converse with me. Because my correspondents knew who I was, I insisted that they provide me with their identities.

Obviously, for this approach to be effective, I had to earn people's confidence and trust. I kept all the communications I received in absolute confidence, and I didn't share my correspondents' concerns with other members of my staff unless I had permission to do so. I personally read each message. The issues that I didn't personally investigate, I assigned to appropriate and knowledgeable people for review and evaluation. I made certain that every correspondent received a response that closed the issue. Not all correspondents were pleased with their answers, of course, but most were pleased with the thoughtful consideration given to their concerns.

Hire Transformational Leaders

Off the job, people earn trust largely based on their individual characteristics, but on the job, a manager also earns trust by practicing transformational leadership and by ensuring the adoption of fair practices that support their subordinates.[xciii] Transformational leaders, by definition, bring about change, which is a prerequisite of survival for contemporary companies. Whether you are selecting leaders for your company, planning leadership succession, or developing training programs for new or existing jobholders, you should be making sure that the skills of transformational leadership are high on the list of capabilities that you will be looking for and training for.[xciv]

Visit All Company Locations and Meet With Strategic Customers

You and the rest of your company's senior leadership team should frequently visit all company locations. This does not mean visiting mainly senior officers; this means visiting *all* employees at that location, including the people who work in the boiler room and other areas off the beaten path. These people also do work that is vital to the company's success. During each visit, hold a "town meeting" for everyone to attend.

Establish Peer-to-Peer Relationships With Strategic Customers

Establish a peer-to-peer relationship with your customer counterparts. If you are a CEO, you should establish relationships with the CEOs of your major customers; if a CFO, you should have relationships with the CFOs of your major customers; if a sales leader, you should have relationships with the sales leaders of your major customers. All the senior leaders of your company should cultivate these peer relationships, which will provide your company with many opportunities to share professional information and to stitch together a broad coalition of support within your customer base. Establishing this broad coalition of support is undoubtedly very

> **Speaking truthfully is a demanding practice, but searching out opportunities to speak the truth is much more difficult.**

difficult; nevertheless, it should be an objective that is part of your company's effort to establish broad-based communications with your customers.

Each year, your company's CEO and leadership team should meet with your counterparts in your customer companies and, together, review your performance of the prior year. Use what actually happened as the basis for setting expectations for your ongoing relationship with the customer. This appraisal will become something that your customers look forward to every year. This annual meeting provides your company with an excellent opportunity to gain a clear idea of what they expect from you and to tell them what you expect of them. This is a very important step taken by X-Leaders to generate tremendous value from their customer base.

Communicate frequently with your customers. Don't wait for your customers to call you with problems; instead, contact them regularly to find out what is going on and keep them informed. Try to anticipate their concerns before these concerns develop into problems.

Listen for Facts

Your customers will give you all the clues you need in order to sell to them. They will tell you what they need and what they expect. If you listen carefully, you will walk away from every customer communication much smarter and more excited about your opportunity to serve them. Learn to listen well and you will soon learn the facts you need to know.

Tell the Truth

If you want to create a corporate environment in which people feel safe to communicate, you must convince your company that it is each person's responsibility to tell the truth all the time, not just when it is convenient. X-Leaders consider honest speech a core competency and inculcate truth-telling throughout the company.

Of course, it is not easy to tell the truth at all times. The truth can be painful, and sometimes people don't expect to hear the truth or even want to hear the truth. However, in my experience, telling the truth *always* is the right thing to do. A major differentiator between the X-Leader and the typical leader is that the X-Leader is always able and eager to tell the truth, while the typical leader is not.

Challenge Misleaders and Information Hoarders

X-Leaders are reluctant to take anything at face value. They appropriately challenge everything they see and hear. They constantly seek facts and constructively challenge issues.

As a senior leader, you must challenge everyone in your company who is misleading others with communications that lack facts. While you are at it, demonstrate zero tolerance for information-hoarding. Demonstrate that inaccurate communications and uncommunicated information lose value for the company, putting everyone's success in jeopardy.

Don't Let People Suffer in Silence

During my tenure at AT&T and Lucent Microelectronics Group, I realized that many employees were willing to work hard and suffer difficult-to-resolve problems in silence. Instead of seeking help, they struggled with problems until a company product or service was put at considerable risk. Employees were refusing to seek help for several reasons: They feared acknowledging failure, were averse to having someone else help with the problem, or didn't want to share the risk of lost credibility. To change this behavior, we had to develop an appreciation for sharing both victories and failures. By increasing our willingness to share information in an open environment, we all improved our performance.

X-Leaders know that suffering in silence can result in significant damage to the company's overall success because the problem usually is discovered when it is either too late to resolve, or significantly more expensive to do so. Suffering in silence will put your job at risk, along with everyone else's.

Work with your people to ensure that nobody is suffering in silence. People won't reveal their true concerns until they believe that it is safe to do so, so you must not penalize people who come forward and give you news that you do not want to hear. Don't shoot the messenger! Reward the messenger, whether he or she brings you good news or bad. The messenger who bears bad news puts you in a position to turn it into good news.

Corporate Directors: Get the Facts You Need to Exercise Your Fiduciary Responsibility

The board of directors has a fiduciary responsibility to get the facts. If you sit on a board of directors, it is your duty to work with senior management to eliminate internally and externally generated false information that might impact the value of the corporation.

Each director must support the CEO in his or her efforts to communicate honestly with shareholders. To fulfill this duty, you need to be informed by truthful, well-prepared presentations that contain straightforward facts, not layers of positioning and innuendos. To get at the heart of the issue, you must learn how to penetrate topics very quickly. To do so, you must invest time and energy preparing to engage with the management team. You also must insist on being given direct, concise, comprehensive information about the company.

In today's environment, increasing scrutiny by the Securities Exchange Commission, stock-listing companies such as the New York Stock Exchange and NASDAQ, and institutional investors such as CalPers, requires increased disclosure of information to the public. Board members and senior leaders are expected to have greater transparency in their communications to all stakeholders.

To establish transparency, your board must know the facts and ensure that the senior leadership team is communicating the truth to investors. Your board can establish the facts and increase transparency in a number of ways. First, always seek the source of the information you are receiving. Know who said it, who did it, and who believes it. Never base decisions on statements attributed to absent third parties. If you are told, "They said it," ask: "Who is they? Why do they feel this way?"

Second, develop ongoing relationships with a broad base of senior managers. To understand various corporate issues, you will need to communicate regularly with different senior leaders of the company. Readily engage these senior leaders. Ask them constructive questions and listen to learn.

Third, set a tone of open mutual respect that doesn't tolerate surprises. Respectful directors do not surprise the CEO, and they don't expect the CEO to surprise them. Insist on facts and expect the truth.

Fourth, do your homework. The increasing complexity of the competitive business environment requires you and other directors to spend significantly more time than ever preparing for board and committee meetings. Often, you must take it upon yourself to do more than your assignment. X-Leaders always are better prepared than expected and eager to assist senior management in building shareowner value.

Fifth, make sure that you understand what is being said in the boardroom. If you do not understand something that is being said, you obviously cannot be effective in executing your fiduciary responsibility on that topic and related topics. Clarity is the essence of understanding. If something is said that you do not understand, interrupt the discussion to make sure that you are engaged as needed. X-Leaders never fake it.

Professionals and Specialists: Build Your Career on a Foundation of Shared Information and Trust

If you are an accountant or engineer, you already know how essential it is to be informed by clear, non-ambiguous facts. If you are an administrator, sales person, or marketer, you know that clear communications are essential to making informed decisions. In any case, whether you are getting the truth directly impacts your work and career. You need the facts that affect the quality of the work that you do, and you need to know what is expected of you. The better informed you are, the better able you are to do your work. On a more personal level, the success of your career should not be determined by how good you are at decoding hints, subtle suggestions, allusions, indirect references, inferences, insinuations, or innuendos. You should be able to align your efforts with clearly communicated expectations based on well-explained objectives and factual information.

> **X-Leaders consider honest speech a core competency and inculcate truth-telling throughout the company.**

You should always expect to have access to the information that you need to execute your responsibilities.

Throughout your career, you will be competing for personal advancement in your company and profession. If your company bases decisions on facts grounded in truth, you will be competing on a level playing field. To achieve your personal advancement, you can play fair using data, clear communications, and truth. In the process, you will learn a lot about your company, because a company that bases decisions on facts makes sure that information is widely distributed and exchanged. You also will learn a lot about yourself because you will know where the opportunities are and what issues need to be addressed.

However, if you work in a company that is reticent to share information, distributes inaccurate information, or creates an environment that is shrouded in secrecy, it will be very difficult for you to be successful and almost impossible for you to advance. Moreover, getting insufficient or erroneous information will erode trust among the people you work with, including your subordinates, peers, supervisors, managers, and customers.

The process of learning the facts and seeking the truth always results in a more trusting working environment and better relationships with customers. When people have the facts and believe they are being told the truth, they are less likely to hoard information. Better communication leads to more effective working relationships, which in turn lead to better performance and higher productivity. Sharing information with your customers about delivery, pricing, and other factors encourages them to reciprocate in kind, so tell your customers what you are thinking and share your plans with them. If you do, they will be more willing to share their plans with you. Seek their feedback and ask them to critique your ideas in a way that will help you improve your level of customer service. Obviously, the more data you have from your customers, the better prepared you are to serve them, and the better you serve them, the more business you will earn from them. The more business you earn, the better your chances of promotion.

If you work in a company that believes in sharing factual information, you can enrich your career by becoming an effective communicator who builds trust. People want to share information and opinions. If they believe you are willing to share, then they are more likely to share with you. If you create a trust-filled atmosphere, people will be willing to share more with you than you might imagine.

Telling the truth is so important that you must do it *always*, not just some of the time. People may not want to hear the truth, but they will accept it more easily from you if they are sure that you always tell the truth. X-Leaders learn to provide constructive feedback to their peers, supervisors, and customers.

Become a "constructive whistleblower." If you see something that you think is ineffective, inappropriate, or wrong, say what you think in a *constructive way* to the person responsible and to your supervisor. As long as you are constructive in your approach, everybody wins. If the issue is critical, you must not remain silent.

While you are telling the truth, you must also be willing to hear the truth. Finding out what your supervisor expects of you is important to your performance. If you want to be the best in your profession, don't let your boss decide for you in a vacuum what will make you a top performer. Make sure that he or she tells you what you need to know.

If you want your work to be grounded in facts, then share the facts that you know. If you want an open communicative environment, then be communicative yourself. Ask to participate in company-sponsored roundtable discussions. When given the opportunity, be vocal in a positive and aggressive way, but always be a team player. When possible, lead the effort and set the tone. X-Leaders know they earn the right to learn through their willingness to share.

Corporate Customers: Partner With Truth-Telling Suppliers

Your company is not seeking strategic suppliers that over-promise and under-deliver. Your company wants the truth. However, if your company is willing to accept anything less than the whole truth, you are likely to get something less than the whole truth. If you represent a corporate customer, you must be unwilling to accept anything less from a strategic supplier than forthright sharing of factual information, and you must not base your decisions on rumor and innuendo. In short, you must develop open channels of communication with your business partners.[xcv]

If you provide a strategic supplier with incomplete or incorrect information, that company is likely to produce late deliveries of non-competitive products or services. If your company designs a product based on faulty services or non-competitive components provided by a supplier, that product is not likely to be competitive. The better you and your strategic suppliers share information, the more successful you both will be. If your company does not win in the short term, your strategic supplier will not win in the long term.

To maximize the service you receive from your strategic suppliers, you must communicate openly and honestly. Provide your suppliers with the facts they need to deliver outstanding products and services, including realistic expectations for delivery dates and price points. Stress that your company will not tolerate the costs of re-runs, late product deliveries, or any of the other misfortunes that result from poor communication. These costs damage your company and jeopardize your career. To protect both, schedule regular meetings with your strategic suppliers' senior leaders. At these meetings, use data to share your expectations and concerns. Also, meet frequently with suppliers to check on the status of your projects and hear the truth about delivery dates. Last, understand what your suppliers expect from you. Use the truth to manage their expectations.

Seek the truth and communicate the facts: The relationships you build will provide you with competitive products and services that will help you win in your marketplace. If you build trusting, open relationships with your strategic suppliers, your company will reach new heights of service performance.

X-Leaders always tell everyone what they need to know. They speak the truth and reject fiction.

Three Ways to Avoid Ambiguity!

1. Be sincere. Practice full disclosure. Never compromise the truth for convenience.

2. Communicate extensively and habitually. Be willing to tolerate the risk and pain associated with an open exchange of truthful information.

3. Never accept anything less than the truth.

Endnotes

lxix Gardiner, P. D. (1999). Project management. Part of the Heriot-Watt Programme of Management Education by supported Distance Learning.

lxx Pedler, M., Burgoyne, J. & Boydell, J. (1997). *The learning company*, p. 30. New York: McGraw Hill.

lxxi Including studies by Pucik, V., 1988, and Pettitt, 1995, as reported by Gardiner, 1999, Project management.

lxxii Hart, P., & Saunders, C. (1997). Power and trust: Critical factors in the adoption and use of electronic data interchange. *Organization Science*, 1, 23-42; Mayer, R., Davis, J. H., Schoorman, H. D. (1995). An integrative model of organizational trust. *Academy of Management Review*, 20(3), 709-734.

lxxiii Hart & Saunders, 1997, Power and trust; and Mayer, Davis, & Schoorman, 1995, An integrative model.

lxxiv Groönroos, C. (2000). Relationship marketing: The Nordic School perspective. In J. N. Sheth & A. Parvatiyar (Eds.), *Handbook of Relationship Marketing*, pp. 95-118. London: Sage.

lxxv Melhem, Y. (2003). *Employee-customer relationships: An investigation into the impact of customer-contact employees' capabilities on customer satisfaction in Jordan banking sector*. Unpublished doctoral dissertation from the University of Nottingham, Nottingham, England.

lxxvi Randolph, W. A., & Sashkin, M. (2002). Can organizational empowerment work in multinational settings? *Academy of Management Executives*, 16, 102-115.

lxxvii Ibid.

lxxviii Melhem, 2003, *Employee-customer relationships*.

lxxix Pfeffer, J., & Veiga, F. (1999). Putting people first for organizational success. *Academy of Management Executives*, 13(2), 37-48.

lxxx Gardiner, 1999, Project management.

lxxxi Randolph, W. A. (2000). Rethinking empowerment. *Organizational Dynamics*, 29, 94-107.

lxxxii Eylon, D. (1998). Understanding empowerment and resolving its paradox: Lessons from Mary Parker Follett. *Journal of Management History*, 4(1), 16-28.

lxxxiii Groönroos, 2000, Relationship marketing.

[lxxxiv] Rothstein et al., 1995, as discussed by Melhem, 2003, *Employee-customer relationships.*

[lxxxv] Kotter, J. P, 1995, as reported by Melhem, 2003, *Employee-customer relationships.*

[lxxxvi] Melhem, 2003, *Employee-customer relationships.*

[lxxxvii] Goris, J. R., Vaught, B. C., & Pettit, J. D. (2003). Effects of trust in superiors and influence of superiors on the association between individual-job congruence and job performance/satisfaction. *Journal of Business and Psychology,* 17, 327-343; Cunningham, J. B., & MacGregor, J. (2000). Trust and the design of work: Complementary constructs in satisfaction and performance. *Human Relations,* 53, 1575-1591; Gardiner, 1999, Project management; Tan, H. H., & Tan, C. S. F. (2000). Towards the differentiation of trust in supervisor and trust in organization. *Genetic, Social, and General Psychology Monographs,* 126(2), 241-260; Rousseau, D. M., Sitkin, S. B., Burt, R. S., & Camerer, C. (1998). Not so different after all: A cross-discipline view of trust. *Academy of Management Review,* 23(3), 393-404.

[lxxxviii] Goris, Vaught, & Pettit, 2003, Effects of trust.

[lxxxix] Gambetta, D. (Ed.). *Trust: Making and breaking cooperative relations.* New York: Blackwell; Pennings, J. M., & Woiceshyn, J. (1987). A typology of organizational control and its metaphors. In S. B. Bacharach & S. M. Mitchell (Eds.), *Research in the sociology of organizations,* 5, 75-104. Greenwich, CT: JAI; Seabright, M. A., Levinthal, D. A., & Fichman, M. (1992). Role of individual attachments in the dissolution of interorganizational relationships. *Academy of Management Journal,* 35(1), 122-160.

[xc] Annison, M. H., & Wilford, D. S. (1998). *Trust matters: New directions in health care leadership,* p. 34. San Francisco: Jossey-Bass.

[xci] Ibid.

[xcii] Cunningham, J. B., & MacGregor, J. (2000). Trust and the design of work: Complementary constructs in satisfaction. *Human Relations,* 53, 1575-1591.

[xciii] Connell, J., Ferres, N., & Travaglione, T. (2003). Engendering trust in manager-subordinate relationships: Predictors and outcomes. *Personnel Review,* 32(5), 569-587.

[xciv] Davidson, P., & Griffin, R. W. (2000). *Management: Australia in a global context.* Brisbane, Australia: Wiley.

[xcv] Melhem, 2003, *Employee-customer relationships.*

147

X-Principle 7: *X-Leaders have confidence in the abilities of their people. Because X-Leaders are willing to delegate broad responsibilities, they are vulnerable, and they know it.*

CHAPTER 7

Exuding Supreme Confidence

X-Leaders are smart enough to know that they can't achieve great performances by themselves. To perform with exceptional success, X-Leaders must rely on subordinates, to whom they delegate responsibility, authority, and accountability. The same is true of all members of the senior management team. The fact is that senior leaders do not have, and never will have, enough time and information to make all the decisions needed by the company. To execute their responsibilities effectively and efficiently, senior leaders must be willing to delegate broad responsibilities throughout the organization. Although it takes courage on their part, the senior leadership team must create an environment in which their subordinates can earn their trust.

The possibility of earning the company's trust energizes most employees to perform at higher levels; people naturally work harder to achieve a mission when they have the authority to carry out that mission and are held accountable for doing so. When employees have clearly defined responsibilities and accountability, they are able to experience the joy of making good decisions and the pain of making poor decisions. This helps align their concerns with the company's concerns.

Trust in the workplace, of course, is a two-way street; senior leaders also must earn the trust of their subordinates. Employees who trust that the entire company will help them if they encounter difficulties obviously are more willing to take action than those who expect some form of reprimand or reprisal if things go amiss. In trust-filled environments, people reach better, faster decisions because they don't have to spend much time figuring out who is going to be held responsible for making a decision if difficulties crop up.[xcvi]

From the standpoint of the X-Leader, rapid decision-making is an excellent company characteristic for two reasons. First, rapid decisions move projects along more quickly, making the company more nimble in adapting to changes in the business environment.[xcvii] Second, rapid decision-making is a sign that employees are confident enough to pursue their ideas with bold intensity, making the company more innovative.[xcviii] One reason that X-Leaders aren't afraid of employees taking bold initiatives is that this confidence to act boldly goes hand-in-hand with confidence to approach trusted senior leaders for input and advice, which is a likely step for someone who really wants a project to succeed. In fact, an X-Leader values broad delegation of authority so highly that he or she will evaluate other leaders in terms of their ability to delegate. The X-Leader doesn't permit the company's future leaders to wait passively for decisions to flow from the top any more than he or she permits passivity among the company's senior leaders. Instead, the X-Leader focuses on collaborative problem-solving.

The idea that the level of trust existing among managers and workers influences how well people work is not mere theory; a growing body of empirical evidence supports this claim.[xcix] A healthy emotional and social climate inside a company has been shown to spur creativity, speed implementation, and enhance productivity.[c] The most relevant, responsive, and competitive companies are the ones best able to pull their managers and workers together, commit them to the company, and help them transcend narrow personal interests.[ci] The resulting workforces are far more willing to collaborate and also are better at identifying important challenges and opportunities.[cii]

One reason that X-Leaders stand out from the crowd is that they know how to enlist employees' desire to share in accountability for the company's successes and failures. Whatever your leadership responsibilities or aspirations, I believe that you will benefit from following some of the suggestions provided below.

Aspiring X-Leaders: Practice Vulnerability

As an ambitious future X-Leader, the last thing you probably have on your mind is deliberately increasing your vulnerability to risk. However, X-Leaders exude confidence in others because they know that demonstrating some vulnerability helps develop trusting relationships.[ciii] The process of give-and-take helps people feel on equal footing with each other and builds the team's capacity to work together. Don't hide your mistakes from your peers and supervisors; they probably are aware of them anyway!

Instead, use those mistakes as learning experiences and get help, particularly from your supervisor, to make sure that you don't repeat those mistakes. Showing vulnerability gives other people room to demonstrate their skills, which contributes to great solutions and to their confidence as contributors. Being vulnerable, of course, doesn't mean being unsuccessful, so don't neglect to boldly share your successes, too! Give credit where credit is due.

You can offset some of the discomfort you might feel as you practice vulnerability by helping your supervisor and colleagues with projects that increase shareholder value. Ask your supervisor for more responsibility and authority. Without these, your share in rewards for successes will be negligible, and your hard work won't expand your career potential.

If your supervisor is unwilling to delegate more important work to you, your advancement will be seriously impaired because you need to gain skills and become visibly accountable for the success or failure of projects. In that case, practice X-Leadership by helping your supervisor become more effective: Use some of your strengths to fill in some of the gaps left by your supervisor's weaknesses. If you supervisor doesn't need your help or is adamant about not sharing responsibility with you, it's probably time to start looking for another job, perhaps inside your company. If you work in a company where responsibility-hoarding is the norm, though, I recommend looking for a job in an X-led company where your ambition will be recognized and appreciated.

Senior Leaders: Reap the Benefits of Delegation

As a senior leader, you might feel threatened by the idea of delegating some of your authority;[civ] after all, relinquishing control is risky.[cv] If you delegate a decision that goes wrong, the buck will stop at your desk. In fact, the better you and your fellow senior leaders are at spreading responsibility throughout your company and empowering employees to make decisions, the more vulnerable you make yourselves. It is natural that the more you have to lose, the less you'll want to risk losing it.[cvi] However, if you effectively manage the responsibility that you delegate, you won't lose; instead, you will experience substantial gain. In environments where leaders take the risk of delegating responsibility broadly throughout the company to employees who have earned their trust, employees take more risks in pursuit of innovation, which ultimately leads to higher levels of productivity and performance. Happily, you can increase your likelihood of reaping those rewards, while lowering your risk to much more acceptable levels, by following some basic, common-sense measures, which I have outlined below.

Understand What Delegation Does

Whether you think the trend toward delegating power to employees is a positive movement in leadership or suspect that employee empowerment is a dangerous fad, over the last decade you must have noticed that it has become an idea to be reckoned with.[cvii] *Employee empowerment* really means that managers delegate authority to the lowest level at which a competent decision can be reached.[cviii] The chief benefit of this kind of delegation is that people feel more motivated to work because they have a stake in the decisions that flow from that work. The concept of employee empowerment has roots in substantive studies of intrinsic motivation, job design, participative decision-making, social learning theory, and self-management.[cix] Employee empowerment is of great interest to X-Leaders because they create corporate environments that motivate people to pursue greatness.

If you want to motivate your people to be successful, you must want *everyone* in your company to have success and to feel involved in the company. You must desire to feel proud of your people. However, it is important to remember that, when you delegate, you do not abandon your right to hold very strong opinions about the way things should be done. Instead of exercising those opinions by making decisions that other people can make, you exercise them by creating visions that inspire people and missions that challenge them. Don't relinquish your responsibility to develop value statements that will guide people through their decision-making process. It is very important that you, as a senior leader, tell your subordinates what you are thinking and encourage them to use your fledgling dreams and ideas as input in their decision-making.

Minimize Your Risk

Once you consciously acknowledge that the company's success depends on the success of many collective efforts, it becomes evident that you must delegate responsibility to the people involved in those efforts and act to minimize their risk of failure.

Reduce the possibility of failure by making sure that you delegate decision-making at appropriate levels of responsibility. Never delegate to people who are inadequately prepared to accept the responsibility.

After you delegate decision-making responsibility, your work is not over. Be clear in defining the responsibility and what accountability means in that context. Eliminate most opportunities for your subordinates to reach decisions that are not aligned with the best interests of the company by giving them appropriate training and by holding them accountable for doing the right thing. You must provide

> **One reason that X-Leaders stand out from the crowd is that they know how to enlist employees' desire to share in accountability for the company's successes and failures.**

guidelines and establish boundaries that discourage employees from engaging in inappropriate activities outside the spirit of company policies.

An important component of minimizing the risk of failure is challenging subordinates' recommendations. Always, however, present your challenges in a constructive and supportive manner by helping people make the right decisions. Give your subordinates as much leeway as possible, but don't permit them to make serious mistakes. When necessary, don't hesitate to override the authority you have granted to subordinates! They expect you to have more insight into some issues than they do, and they want you to keep them from making truly bad decisions.

Support Your Subordinates' Decisions

As a senior leader, you must stay constructively engaged with your subordinates, and you can't permit them to make catastrophic decisions. However, you must be willing to support their decisions, ideas, and suggestions, even some that you don't like. Let your people know that you understand that the people who make mistakes are the people who make everything else! Encourage them to turn their mistakes into learning opportunities, instead of making the same mistakes again and again.

Guide your subordinates through the decision-making process, but be very careful not to guide them to a specific decision. When you disagree with a subordinate's decision, you should always allow that person an opportunity to articulate his or her point of view. If you consistently override important decisions made by people who have been delegated the authority to make those decisions, you aren't really letting them strengthen their decision-making skills, nor are you developing your own guidance skills. Of course, don't be reluctant to override a decision from time to time. Just don't do it too often!

Solicit Input From Employees

To gain insight and reach good decisions, you must recognize that lots of other people may know more about a problem and its possible solutions than you do. As a senior leader, you should be soliciting information from knowledgeable people. But where will you find them? Very often, they will be employees of your own company. The people best able to contribute to a decision process are those most familiar with the issues and operations under discussion. That is why I strongly believe that consistently soliciting input from employees results in better decisions. Input from people who possess pertinent knowledge enriches the decision-making process and results in a much higher quality decision than might have been reached otherwise.

Build Future Leaders

You cannot develop your company's future leaders unless you provide them with opportunities to learn and to grow! They will gain much more experience and develop much more quickly if you give them broad responsibilities, hold them accountable, and work to develop trusting relationships. Letting them represent you at key industry and media events will help them develop confidence in themselves and help you develop confidence in them as well. Of course, before you move future leaders from behind the scenes, give them the proper support to make sure they are well prepared.

As your subordinates succeed in executing their responsibilities, they will be earning the right to lead, which includes the right to develop their own new individual talent on their own. Developing new talent should be considered an endeavor that enhances their position in the company.

Bring Cultural Imperatives Into the Decision Process

In today's environment, any significant decisions made by the company are likely to be played out across different cultures that have different moral values and norms. For this reason, it makes sense that you first consult people who are familiar with the cultural contexts involved. These cultural contexts will, in large part, determine what actions will engender trust and distrust and stir people's emotions.

For the company to have the capacity to make great decisions when cultural imperatives are at play, the senior leadership team must build a robust collection of experiences that reflect all of the cultures and sub-cultures involved in the company, and in its customer base. This means recruiting a heterogeneous group of leaders. Also, when doing business in a foreign country, decision-making should involve as many foreign nationals of the host country as possible, because they will be sensitive to values and norms unknown to the parent corporation.

Corporate Directors: Govern With Confidence

If you are a corporate director, you often confront the distinction between governing and managing. Because you may have as much experience operating corporations as the senior leaders of the company you serve, you frequently must suppress the urge to take action on problems facing the company.

Not only must you refrain from trying to manage the company, you must counsel your colleagues to do the same when the board seems to be crossing the "bright yellow line" between governance and managing. Directors must transform their urge to manage into a passion for inspecting and supporting.

157

It is not your responsibility to manage the day-to-day operations of the corporation. It is your responsibility to add value to the company by constantly provoking senior leaders to strive for excellence. Concentrate on developing the CEO, not trying to do his or her job. Pursue operational excellence by supporting and inspiring the CEO.

You and the company's other directors enjoy a tremendous opportunity to influence company affairs in a positive way by challenging the status quo. Display a passion for adding value; cherish opportunities to make a difference. Learn to thrive on being seen, heard, and deemed exceptionally valuable to the company. The board's attitude should be "nose in and hands off."

Because the board of directors represents the company's shareholders, you and your fellow directors normally will be guided by the same set of long-term measurements used by shareholders. If, like most directors, you are not an employee of the company, you probably will invest about 250 hours a year working on company business. Even with this time investment, though, you won't be able to thoroughly inspect all the details on which the company's performance

> **Don't hide your mistakes from your peers and supervisors; they probably are aware of them anyway!**

will be measured, particularly if you are an outsider who has never worked for the company. Because it is almost impossible for you and your fellow directors to know everything that you need to know or want to know about the company, you must have confidence in the company's senior leaders. The foundation for an effective working relationship with senior leaders is trust.

Your performance as a board will be evaluated based on management's results, so you and your fellow directors are obligated to give senior leaders the authority they need to fulfill their responsibilities. You need to tell the CEO what you need and, equally important, you must not accept anything less than what is necessary.

The willingness of the board to delegate will be prejudiced by the directors' level of confidence in the senior leaders' ability to deliver outstanding results. The best directors know how to partner with the CEO and earn opportunities to get all the information they need, including as much information about the company and its senior managers, competitors, and customers as possible. You and your fellow directors should talk with senior leaders between board meetings to gain better insight to the company's thinking and behavior. Don't allow yourself to be intimidated by industry jargon; instead, ask the corporation for a primer.

Interestingly, an effective way of causing other people to become vulnerable to your influence is to act in a way that makes you genuinely vulnerable to other people's influence![cx] As you permit other people to influence you, that show of vulnerability causes people to know that your life is open to them and that you are teachable, which conveys your integrity. In turn, people begin to trust you, granting you the privilege of influencing them.[cxi]

The company's performance is inextricably linked to your confidence in the company's senior leadership. If, despite strong efforts to establish respectful trust, the board of directors do not trust your company's leadership, you must change that leadership. The most effective way to execute your responsibility to delegate is to hire the best CEO for the job and make sure that person hires the best talent for the senior leadership team. X-Leaders know that the best people are willing to delegate and that the people who delegate become the best people.

Professionals and Specialists: To Become a Player, Earn Trust

If you contribute to your company through a profession such as accounting, engineering, administration, sales, or marketing, you'll be the last to be officially informed about what is going on in the company. I wouldn't be surprised if you have learned much more about your company's plans than your leaders suspect just to prevent yourself from being kept in the dark. The best way to learn what you need to know is to earn the trust of your supervisor and involve yourself in activities that are strategically important to your company.

If you are not already involved in your company's strategic thinking, your supervisor has not delegated much responsibility to you. Obviously, you will increase your skills faster if your supervisor delegates more important work to you, and you are more likely to be promoted if you are seen as someone who can take on broader responsibilities, successfully complete important projects, and be accountable for a project's success or failure. As your responsibilities increase, so does your value to the company.

Keep in mind that a supervisor who has not shared responsibility with you is unlikely ever to share rewards with you. To earn more, usually you must do more, but that is not enough—you also must have the responsibility of doing more. If you want to be an X-Leader, you will not allow your supervisor to inhibit your learning and earning opportunities by failing to delegate to you the broad responsibilities that will help you to grow in your company.

You may already have learned the hard lesson that a supervisor who is unwilling to share responsibility and rewards will nevertheless be more than happy to share his or her failures. Although you won't enjoy the gains of your work if your supervisor hasn't granted you authority and responsibility, be assured that you will receive a significant piece of the pain if your supervisor fails in his or her job.

Sometimes a supervisor will try to demonstrate authority by trying to convince you that he or she has all the right answers. You both know that is highly unlikely, if not impossible! Nobody has enough skills and knowledge to do everything required for the company's success. If only because your personal success very likely will be linked directly to your supervisor's performance, you should be practicing X-Leadership by helping your supervisor become more effective. Informally look for weak spots in your supervisor's performance (we all have them), and think of them as opportunities to help your supervisor become a better performer. Make your supervisor a better leader, a better planner, or a more effective communicator.

Make sure that your supervisor appreciates your thirst for more responsibility. Ask for it; don't wait for your supervisor to notice that you might be good at taking on broader responsibilities. Demonstrate constructive leadership

> **It is important to remember that, when you delegate, you do not abandon your right to hold very strong opinions about the way things should be done.**

whenever you can by requesting opportunities to work with your colleagues and helping them become successful in their pursuit of shareholder value.

If your supervisor has the skills, time, and willingness to do everything that you do, it should be clear that one of you is superfluous! I suggest you look for another job either inside or outside of your company. You will never be successful working for someone who does your job for you. You will have more opportunity to advance in your company if you work with people who are unselfishly willing to share responsibilities and encourage others. These are the people most likely to share successes and create advancement opportunities.

Be bold, not concerned! Remember that the best solutions don't all have to come from you. Don't suffer in silence—ask for help. Be ready and willing to accept constructive input from your colleagues. Take an inventory of your own skills and capabilities and engage your supervisor in helping you close those gaps. People will want to be on your team if they know you are as eager to ask for help as you are to give it.

Always be willing to share in the give-and-take of teamwork. In your plans and strategies, include ideas from your team members and supervisors, and always acknowledge their input and give them credit for contributing to your success. It's better to give credit when it is not due than to not give credit when it is due. Allow some of your best work to be showcased by others. If you are working on a project where you clearly are the person in charge, the one who developed the majority of the content, allow one of your colleagues who is equally passionate about the topic, but perhaps not as knowledgeable, to get out in front. Help your colleagues to shine and lead and, I assure you, you will receive 10-fold rewards for that effort. Be a team player and you will have broad responsibilities heaped upon you!

Corporate Customers:
Develop Trust Between You and Your Strategic Suppliers

Your company's success is inextricably linked to the quality of your partnerships with your strategic suppliers. Naturally, you want your company's strategic suppliers to assign their best representatives to your account. You want these people to be the kind you can count on to commit themselves to your company's success and look for chances to help you improve your products and services. You will be dependent on them for good advice and knowledgeable answers and, above all, you will need them to have enough authority to get things done. The last thing that you need is to be beaten to the market by your competitors because your strategic supplier's representatives had to keep checking with their supervisors for basic approvals.

To get what you want, you must develop trusting relationships with your strategic suppliers. If your supplier's representatives don't have authority to deliver the prices, terms, and conditions of your relationship, you should ask the supplier to assign people to your account who have the authority to do so.

Working with supplier representatives who have more authority and knowledge is important in other ways, too. People with broader authority can give you better insight into the strategic supplier's culture and plans, which will provide you with better leverage for focusing the supplier's energy on helping you hone your company's competitive edge. People with more knowledge are better able to help you ascertain whether your company is strategically aligned with the supplier. If you discover a misalignment, you can act to reposition the relationship for better results. This is a major advantage.

Never delegate to people who are inadequately prepared to accept the responsibility.

Clearly, if your strategic suppliers delegate broad authority to the people who work with your company, you can be more confident in their willingness to take risks to develop more creative solutions for your company. How can you ensure that your strategic suppliers value broad delegation enough to expose themselves to this kind of vulnerability?

First, demand that the people who service your account are actively involved in setting their company's strategic direction. Although each of these people probably won't be in a position to direct their company's strategy, each of them should be providing input to those who do.

Second, make sure that the representatives who service your company are authorized to make decisions about what you need to have done. They should have the tools and skills needed to deliver the overall design and function of the products and services you need, and they should be able to affect pricing and delivery dates.

Third, before awarding a significant share of your business to a supplier, spend quality time with that company's leadership team and get to know their leadership styles. Those styles should earn your confidence. Award most of your business to strategic suppliers willing to delegate very broad authority to service your company.

Last, as your company develops leading-edge projects, share your plans with your suppliers. When the risks taken by strategic suppliers on your company's behalf significantly help to increase your sales, award your business to those companies. This will heighten the level of trust between your company and those suppliers and will have a long-lasting impact on the relationship.

X-Leaders readily acknowledge that they need help carrying the ball. They know that demonstrating some vulnerability offers tremendous opportunities for success.

Three Ways to Build a Company-Wide Team

1. Encourage everyone around you to pursue masterly performance! Engage with the best and help develop the rest!

2. Resist the urge to play it safe. Never jeopardize success by justifying mediocrity.

3. Display your confidence! Give some deserving person an opportunity to help share your load. Remember to reward them accordingly.

Endnotes

xcvi Child, J. (1977). *Organizations: A guide to problems and practice*. London: Harper & Row; Cohen, S. G., Ledford, G. E., Jr., & Spreitzer, G. M. (1996). A predictive model of self-managing work team effectiveness. *Human Relations*, 49(5), 643-676; Kanter, R. M. (1985). *The change masters: Corporate entrepreneurs at work*. Hempstead, NJ: Unwin; Leana, C. (1986). Predictors and consequences of delegation. *Academy of Management Journal*, 29, 754-774; Leana, C. (1987). Power relinquishment versus power sharing; A theoretical clarification and empirical comparison of delegation and participation. *Journal of Applied Psychology*, 72, 228-233; Spreitzer, G. M., & Mishra, A. K. (1999). Giving up control without losing control: Trust and its substitutes' effects on managers' involving employees in decision making. *Group and Organization Management*, 24(2), 155-187; Yukl, G., & Fu, P.P. (1999). Determinants of delegation and consultation by managers. *Journal of Organizational Behavior*, 20(2), 219-232.

xcvii Ibid.

xcviii Ibid.

xcix Liden, R. C., Wayne, S. J., & Sparrowe, R. T. (2000). An examination of the mediating role of psychological empowerment on the relations between the job, interpersonal relationships, and work outcomes. *Journal of Applied Psychology*, 85, 407-416; Sparrowe, R. T. (1994). Empowerment in the hospitality industry: An exploration of antecedents and outcomes. *Hospitality Research Journal*, 1 17(3), 51-73; Spreitzer, G. M. (1995). Psychological empowerment in the workplace: Dimensions, measurement, and validation. *Academy of Management Journal*, 38(5), 1442-65; Spreitzer, G. M., Kizilos, M. A., & Nason, S. W. (1997). A dimensional analysis of the relationship between psychological empowerment and effectiveness, satisfaction and strain. *Journal of Management*, 23(5), 679-7045; Seibert, S. E., Silver, S. R., & Randolph, W. A. (2004). Taking empowerment to the next level: A multiple-level model of empowerment, performance, and satisfaction. *Academy of Management Journal*, 47(3), 332-349.

c Drucker, P. F. (1993). *Post-capitalist society*. New York: HarperBusiness; Pfeffer, J. (1993). Barriers to the advance of organizational science: Paradigm development as a dependent variable. *Academy of Management Review*,

18(4), 599-620; and Whitney, J. (1994). *The trust factor: Liberating profits and restoring corporate vitality.* New York: McGraw-Hill.

[ci] Ghoshal, S., & Bartlett, C.A. (1995, January-February) Changing the role of top management: Beyond structure to process. *Harvard Business Review,* volume, page

[cii] Miller, D., & Lee, J. (2001). The people make the process: Commitment to employees, decision making, and performance. *Journal of Management,* 27. 163-189.

[ciii] McNicol, B. (1997). Strength in vulnerability. *Leadership Catalyst.* Retrieved on January 15, 2004 at http://www.leadershipcatalyst.org/Publications/Pubs_TC_2.1.htm.

[civ] Hales, C. (1999). Embellishing empowerment: Ideologies of management, managerial ideologies and the rhetoric and reality of empowerment programmes. Paper presented at the 17th Labour Process Conference, March 29-31, Egham, UK.

[cv] Spreitzer, G. M., and Mishra, A. K. (1999). Giving up control.

[cvi] Richardson, H., Amason, A. C., Buchholtz, A. K., & Gerard, J. (2003). CEO willingness to delegate to the top management team: The influence of organizational performance. *International Journal of Organizational Analysis,* 10(2), 134-146.

[cvii] Abrahamson, E. (1996). Management fashion. *Academy of Management Review,* 21, 254–285; Block, P. (1987). The empowered manager. San Francisco: Jossey-Bass.

[cviii] Conger, J. A., & Kanungo, R.N. (1988). The empowerment process: Integrating theory and practice. *Academy of Management Review,* 13, 471-483; Thomas, K. W., & Velthouse, B. A. (1990). Cognitive elements of empowerment: An "interpreted" model of intrinsic task motivation. *Academy of Management Review,* 15(4), 666-81.

[cvix] Liden, R. C., & Tewksbury, T. W. (1995). Empowerment and work teams. In G. R. Ferris, S. D. Rosen, & D. T. Barnum (Eds.), *Handbook of Human Resources Management,* pp. 386-403. Oxford, UK: Blackwell Publishers.

[cx] McNicol, 2004, Strength in vulnerability.

[cxi] Ibid

X-Principle Eight: *X-Leaders convert the energy generated by chaos into better decisions. To avoid precipitating premature closure on major issues, they sometimes conceal their own opinions until other people have had their say.*

CHAPTER 8

Extra Passes Over the Target

There is no question that finding new sources of revenue in today's competitive environment requires outside-the-box thinking. The corporate environments created by X-Leaders encourage people to generate new ideas. Those ideas are then allowed to percolate through the decision process. All this creativity requires a healthy respect for chaos. The confusion, disorganization, irrationality, and lack of control associated with long-term, uncontrolled chaos are organizational disasters that make the word chaos anathema to many leaders and management theorists. However, as X-Leaders know, temporary chaotic situations that are carefully limited by exceptionally strong and confident leaders can produce valuable results without ill effects. In my own leadership experience, I have never observed a temporary, conditional lack of structure to result in a fundamental lack of control within the company, whether it employed hundreds of people or tens of thousands.

When new ideas are explored, a vital, creative disorder ensues. Some disorder also results from the frenzy of activity in a company pushing to accelerate a product's time to market. This disorder must be tolerated and even managed. Fortunately, the conflict between the need for creativity and the demand for quick performance is predictable, and it is a characteristic of X-Leaders that they are able to find some workable balance between these two pressures.

Old-style, command-and-control leadership that puts intense focus on a problem and imposes top-down changes on people might suffice when making simple decisions. But solving today's complex problems requires a leadership style that invites the participation of as many team members as is reasonable. X-Leaders make sure that their important decisions are informed by a large number of relevant facts, ideas, and opinions. Before finalizing their decisions, X-Leaders invest the time and effort needed to consider all reasonable input from their colleagues. Soliciting that input sometimes requires the X-Leader to conceal his or her opinions so as not to intimidate or influence subordinates who may possess important, unexpressed information.

By offering only moderate coordination of the decision process, the X-Leader puts the team at "the edge of chaos," which, behavioral research suggests, substantially reduces the resistance to change that most often complicates management initiatives.[cxii] In addition, tolerating some lack of structure can be a very valuable demonstration of management flexibility, because as long as chaotic elements are restricted within a broad set of moral, legal, and ethical strictures, they imply reasonable control, rather than confinement. Thoughtful and productive problem-solving never should be rushed because it never should be finished. More improved solutions are always available! Although time truly is of the essence, speed should not be allowed to compromise the quality of the end result. No value exists in the on-time delivery of an ineffective service or an ill-conceived product.

X-Leaders are masters of the ability to deliver well-conceived products and services within a competitive timeframe. When X-Leaders put extra time and effort into a decision process, they are not slowing down the process for the sake of procrastination, they are taking care to prevent shareholders from losing value as the result of a poorly informed, quick decision. X-Leaders don't sacrifice a flow of great ideas and creativity just to meet a self-imposed deadline. They know that courageously seeking an answer that is good, rather than quick or convenient, doesn't mean reducing time-to-market or time-to-money. In fact, doing it right usually shortens the period between inception of the new idea and delivery of the exciting new product or competitively enhanced service. Thorough discussion contributes to a good balance between speed and closure.

Today's global business environment certainly can be described as chaotic, but managing in chaotic environments and operating with lack of control are not new business phenomena; in the last decades alone, corporate America has experienced a plethora of out-of-control situations. What is new is that corporate leaders are beginning to explore chaos theory in search of management tools. Although uncontrolled situations frequently exist within the confines of great companies, viewing lack of control as strategically valuable still is considered a rather audacious idea. Merely by acknowledging the presence of an uncontrolled situation in the company, an X-Leader proclaims his or her vulnerability.

Chaos theory attempts to explain the fact that complex and unpredictable results can and will occur, which goes against the traditional scientific view that results are predictable, given sufficient information and understanding. An example commonly used to demonstrate how a small change can produce a major unpredictable result is called the "Butterfly Effect." In theory at least, the fluttering of a butterfly's wings in one location, say Beijing, could ultimately produce a huge weather event halfway around the world in, say, New York. In other words, it is possible that a very small occurrence can produce unpredictable, even drastic, results by triggering a series of increasingly significant events.

One of the basic relationships in nature is that between cause and effect. The belief that everything is caused by something is known as *determinism*, and the linearity of one condition leading to the next and the next, and so on, has been a major assumption in many sciences. The scientific community has long believed in the possibility of making accurate long-term predictions of any physical system so long as the starting conditions were well enough understood and measured. Under this assumption, scientists have used initial conditions to predict later and earlier times and to make deterministic models in engineering and operations management.[cxiii]

The deterministic view in science was substantially altered by the discovery that chaotic systems exist in nature and the realization that no measurement can be made with infinite accuracy. This new information gave rise to the theory of *dynamical instabilities*, which to most physicists is a term synonymous with chaos, the unpredictability that is inherent in a system.[cxiv]

What does all this have to do with finding innovative solutions in a tough, fast-paced market? A little chaos can be a good thing. If you rely on the familiar as your exclusive guide for success, you are going to arrive at similar conclusions over and over again. As I was frequently reminded by one of my colleagues at AT&T, doing things the way you have always done them will never produce different results. If you want to arrive at new conclusions, you need to open the door a crack to let in a little lack of control, a little spontaneity, and a little disorder, which will bring with them lots of new ideas, a few of which might very well be the great ideas you are looking for. The complex needs, wants, ideas, and inventions of human beings are not entirely predictable, nor will your markets be.

X-Leaders of enlightened companies stimulate debate and encourage employees to engage carefully and considerately in decision-making. In the corporate environments created by X-Leaders, debates are required elements in the decision process, and constructive engagement in decision-making is part of every meeting. X-Leaders strongly encourage their people to inspect, understand, appreciate, and challenge all ideas relevant to a solution. They understand that carefully considered attacks of ideas, and suggestions by people with positive attitudes, add great value to the company. Companies that value an active decision-engagement process will have plentiful ideas and creative thoughts flowing from their employees, the best of which will be used to build great products and exciting new services.

Aspiring X-Leaders: Make the Most of Meetings

Most corporate leaders view the presence of chaos in the company as a negative state of confusion and lack of control that implies management failure. Obviously, this is not considered to be the most competitive position from which to operate. In an effort to minimize chaos, companies resort to various control mechanisms to maintain order and to accelerate the decision process. The primary objective becomes to close an open issue as soon as possible, claim victory for that action, and move on to the next issue.

This objective makes most companies much too quick to declare closure. The creativity that is vital to innovation flows freely when people are fully participating in an exciting discussion. As an aspiring X-Leader, you should keep in mind that everyone in a meeting has an obligation to add ideas to the discussion by asking or answering important questions, so make sure that you always contribute your ideas at meetings and encourage your team members to do the same. A discussion of an important topic should not be closed until every person in the meeting has fully expressed his or her views on that topic.

Discussion of an important topic should not end until all reasonable options have been explored and people are satisfied that the conclusions reached will generate the desired outcome. Of course, it is critically important that specific goals, targets, or other specific objectives are defined and accepted at the beginning of each meeting. An important discussion should not be arbitrarily terminated merely because a meeting is scheduled to end; instead, the meeting should be extended or follow-up meetings should be scheduled. Factual data, insightful perspectives, and passion take time to evolve into a great decision. After the decision has been reached, all participants in the decision-making should be totally exhausted from the process and reasonably angry that it took so long—an

> **Although time truly is of the essence, speed should not be allowed to compromise the quality of the end result.**

experience that is relished by an X-Leader. Whenever it is in your power, use your influence to keep a discussion going until a solid solution has been reached. Remember, the objective of any meeting is to thoroughly discuss the topics and make great decisions, not to leave early with less thoughtful solutions. Only after the decision team believes that a superior conclusion has been reached is it time to move on to a new topic.

Your contributions to the meeting (or anyone else's) should not parrot the prevailing view. The value of bringing one's own views to a discussion was brought to my attention when I was recruited from IBM by AT&T. Bob Allen, at that time AT&T's Chairman of the Board and CEO, told me that the last thing AT&T needed was for me to try to be like them; after all, I could never be as good at being like them as they were! As I am sure Bob expected, my arrival at AT&T did sometimes create a bit of chaos because new ideas stir people up.

So do new settings. It is useful to know that the best ideas often are unearthed in unusual settings, which is why operating outside of the norm often feels exciting. When you always do what is expected, you lose the element of surprise and your competitive edge begins to falter.

A few important words of warning: Operating a little out of control is not a strictly harmless methodology for all companies. Only companies led by exceptionally strong and confident leaders are typically up to the challenge. It is vital to keep in mind at all times that a little deviation from strict leadership control *never* can include any compromise whatever in the highest standards of values and ethics. This includes zero tolerance of personal attacks on people. Ideas, but not the authors, should always be open to constructive attack. Personal attacks destroy shareowner value, and the person who follows such a course requires serious training, counseling, disciplining, or dismissal, as appropriate.

Senior Leaders:
Leverage the Strengths of Others Into Shareholder Value

As a senior leader, you constantly deal with the pressure of people's expectations that you will come up with the right answer or get the impossible task done on time. X-Leaders stand head and shoulders above the rest because they are able to function extremely well under this pressure. One reason that they can do so is that they are quite good at leveraging the strengths of others.

If you learn how to leverage other people's strengths, it will be within your power to reduce the pressure of your work while increasing shareholder value. You'll also be encouraging your people to be the best they can be, which will contribute enormously to their happiness, positive energy, and productivity.

Before you argue that getting your people involved in reaching the company's goals can take a lot of time, perhaps too much time, consider the wisdom in the adage, "I don't have time to do it right, but I'll always have time to do it over." Investing significant time in getting it right in the first place is a wise decision. If you do so, in the end you will discover that you have made an investment in efficient, effective action. X-Leaders find ways to get the job done both right and on time by thoroughly discussing their next course of action to solve problems before they occur.

In a nutshell, the best way to turn your company into an innovation-generating community that will churn out value to shareholders is to make all your people feel welcome. Offer them the extraordinary opportunity to express what they think and how they feel, as well as instilling in them an obligation to contribute their thoughts and ideas to the entire company's success. Ask your people constructive, penetrating questions. Listen well. Don't purport to have all the answers all the time, and don't arbitrarily shut down discussions to meet deadlines. Take time to ensure that all your people are doing their level best to help the company reach good decisions. If they do, they will feel more valued by the company and accept more ownership of decisions. The people that you make welcome in this way will reward you and the rest of your senior leadership team with much more robust solutions.

At first, leading by lessoning your control and seeking value in somewhat chaotic discussions might seem oxymoronic to you. After all, leaders are taught to engage in structured activities like controlling, planning, organizing, and directing, not in becoming more adaptable and flexible! However, by limiting your controlling influence on your colleagues and subordinates, you will be encour-

> **X-Leaders don't sacrifice a flow of great ideas and creativity just to meet a self-imposed deadline.**

aging them to think and act more boldly. You also will be preparing them to start making some less important decisions so that you can spend more time thinking through the weightier ones.

To build a successful company, you and your fellow senior leaders must be surrounded and supported by great people. Although identifying and developing these people is one of your most important responsibilities, these are only initial steps. The highly energized and very talented people you are surrounding yourself with will have great ideas and demand opportunities to fully express them. If you are clinging to an exceedingly structured bureaucracy, you will be limiting their creativity and discouraging their diversity of thought, which eventually will jeopardize your company's future. The best ideas surface in a helpful environment that engages people in decision-making. And don't forget that even the best ideas need refinement through constant processing. To increase the odds of finding better answers, you must be willing to tolerate some chaos and limited control.

The pursuit of competitive advantage requires creating a new future by disrupting what we have done in the past. As psychologists tell us, pain is most likely to cause us to change when we re-conceptualize it as a means by which significant learning occurs. Physicists inform us that, in the realm near chaos, an isolated, relatively small variation can produce huge effects. They also tell us that nothing novel can emerge from highly ordered and stable systems, such as crystals, incestuous communities, or regulated industries. On the other hand, completely chaotic systems, such as stampedes, riots, and rage, are too formless to coalesce.[cxvi] As the corporate transformation architect, Richard T. Pascal, correctly asserted, generative complexity takes place in the boundary between rigidity and randomness.[cxvii] "Equilibrium," he pointed out, "is a precursor to death." A company in equilibrium is at risk.[cxviii]

How can you harness the abundant energy found in chaotic situations? Like most people, you and your subordinates probably feel intimidated by the very thought of encountering chaotic energy. Not without reason. However, encountering well-managed chaotic energy need not be a frightening experience. If you and your fellow senior leaders follow the suggestions outlined below, you can engage your people's interest and participation in solving the problems that your company faces, including finding new sources of revenue.

Share the Ownership of Solutions

Out of chaos arise originality, imagination, inspiration, and vision, so it is a good idea to raise the energy level of a strongly led company by encouraging healthy discussions of possible solutions to problems. Obviously, engaging your people in a decision process does not mean turning key decisions over to the entire company. Your people know that you are paid to hold the responsibility for key decisions, but they will be thrilled to participate in helping you find the best solution. Invite as many people as prudently possible to share in the development and ownership of your company's solutions. Everyone in a position to have something to say should be given the opportunity to say it, and everyone having some responsibility to contribute should be given the opportunity to contribute. Always provide enough time for various points of view to be reasonably discussed. Be patient and develop a tolerance for debate. Engage all of your colleagues using this approach and clearly communicate that you expect everyone in your company to use this approach at all times.

176

Lead Constructive Debate

Most successful solutions aren't the result of serendipity, they are the result of thorough discussions of the challenges being faced and potential ways of meeting those challenges. Surround yourself with confident people who are eager to learn and willing to listen to new ideas, and encourage them to thoughtfully and helpfully question each other's ideas. Teach them how to ask effective, open-ended questions and to make carefully considered comments that encourage further dialog, instead of shutting down the discussion.

When someone offers an idea that has been considered previously, don't simply discard it. Use the suggestion as a springboard for encouraging its author to continue contributing to the discussion. First, clearly state that the suggestion was already considered and deemed to be an inappropriate option. Next, question the individual who made the suggestion to determine whether that person has a different perspective or additional information that justifies reconsidering the idea. This kind of careful listening demonstrates to the team that you are open to fresh ideas and helps everyone in the room to feel comfortable. When your problem-solving team feels safe, they will give you superior performance.

Never Accept the First Answer as the Best Answer

When exploring complex issues, you should never accept the first answer as the best answer. I have found that this practice is helpful even when discussing simple matters. To really understand why one solution is better than another, it pays to be as interested in the wrong answer as the right one. The more thorough your understanding of the less attractive course, the better you will understand the best course.

Conceal Your Opinion

You and the rest of the senior leadership team should often conceal what you regard as the best answer to a question until a reasonable number of alternatives have been explored. Doing so will encourage others to articulate their points of view without fearing misalignment with their leaders. All of your own new ideas won't be great ideas anyway. Everyone already knows this is the case, but a sincere demonstration that you are willing to put yourself in a somewhat vulnerable position will substantially strengthen the decision team. Although you and your fellow senior leaders are expected to have more insight into many issues, you must demonstrate that you don't think you have a lock on intellect. By creating a situation in which other people become more engaged in solving a problem, you will be increasing the likelihood that a better solution will surface.

You should take time to listen, even when you are certain that your answer is the best one. Once you and your fellow senior leaders have earned other people's trust and confidence, those people will be willing to explore more imaginative solutions to the problems at hand. Effective solutions flow more freely from the collective thinking of an entire team than from the isolated thinking of a leader.

Manage Chaos, Don't Let Chaos Manage You

Managing in an environment in which some level of chaos is acceptable is quite difficult, so don't let tolerance of chaos become a standard operating principle of the company. Occasionally accepting a certain lack of structure with a specific purpose in mind does not mean leading a lawless society. Use your thorough discussions to help balance quality and speed. Resist the urge to close issues without considerable thoughtful discussion, but don't encourage delays. Being sincerely engaged in finding the best solution doesn't justify missing important deadlines, or being late to market with new products and services. Qualitative decisions must be made without unreasonable delay. Your company must always maintain a sense of purpose, which requires you and the rest of the senior leadership team to maintain uncompromising focus.

Be Vigilant for Misaligned Behavior

Encouraging debate does not mean encouraging a free-for-all; it means demanding that all members of the team participate fully in searching for a good decision. Don't allow anyone to opt out of the process or deter others from participating. Don't accept one person's view as the best or only view. Never allow people to be personally attacked for their ideas. Be vigilant for misaligned behavior and show very little tolerance for it.

Create a Variety of Communication Platforms

It is up to the senior leadership team to create an environment in which everyone's views are valued. To engage people more fully in problem-solving, you must expose them to a complete range of ideas. In today's company, this requires creating multiple platforms for open dialog. One such platform is the group think-tank session, in which employees from different areas of the business are challenged to discuss better ways of developing products and services. This is a great method for collectively identifying alternative solutions for organizational challenges. Another platform is the round table meeting, in which subordinates discuss corporate directions and policies with the CEO or other senior leaders. Round table meetings allow senior leaders to be intellectually honest with subordinates in a setting that is conducive to two-way dialog. It is very important to create open forums that permit accurate information to flow. If your senior leadership team does not use a variety of platforms to communicate with your people, you probably will fail to communicate altogether.

Tell the Truth

Remember, if you do not tell your people what is going on, they will rely on conjecture. When people who lack information paint a picture to fill in missing information, that picture usually is designed to meet their own needs. Your senior leadership team cannot afford to have employees conjecturing about your company's strategic intent and operational performance. Tell people the truth and engage them in identifying problems, finding potential solutions, and deciding on the best course to follow in solving those problems.

Delegate Easy Decisions

Quality decisions always require deep thought. Free up time to concentrate on thorny issues by delegating decisions that do not require intense analysis to someone with lesser skills and experience. Companies flourish when they leverage all of the creative brainpower within their reach. After you have hired and trained the best people you can find, be willing to follow their decisions when appropriate. There is no shame in following a great idea that is not your own!

179

Make Room for Discussion

To position your company to generate great returns for shareowners, you and your fellow senior leaders must help all the people in your company pursue maximum performance at all times. It is up to you to create an atmosphere that challenges everyone's intellect and interest. Be extreme and insist that debates and constructive engagement are the norm in your company, not the exception. Stress to all employees that rushing to closure can be a costly mistake. When your people start actively looking for the best possible solutions, expect meeting agendas to change frequently. Reviews of possible solutions will also take longer because your people will be generating more ideas and reducing them down to the most attractive solutions. In the new corporate world order, you and your fellow senior leaders may no longer be able to demand greatness, but if your leadership is extreme, you will create an environment in which greatness will flourish.

Corporate Directors: Initiate Disruptive Thinking

If you are a corporate director, you know that board meetings typically are well-planned, highly structured events featuring carefully rehearsed presentations by experts on various topics. The meeting's operating principles are provided by *Robert's Rules of Order*, and time allowances are tightly measured. This careful order results in a dignified setting in which to conduct very serious work, but it doesn't leave much room for getting to the heart of a pressing issue by asking penetrating questions and receiving knowledgeable answers.

It is time to shake things up a bit. At the cost of disrupting a tight board schedule, dig deep for the information that you need. Although such intervention is at odds with the way boards have been run during the past three decades, effectively engaging the problems faced by the company is the key to enlightened corporate governance today.

Understandably, creating an environment that facilitates effective engagement in problem-solving is not easy, but it is necessary. The potential rewards for serving on a board never have been greater, but neither have the risks and exposure. Board decisions are becoming much more complex and risky, and their impacts more profound than ever before. If you are serving as a director, you'd better be prepared to serve well and to go beyond mere duty of care. You must anticipate the thinking of the senior leadership team.

It takes time for every member of the board to join a debate about a problem and then evaluate the alternative solutions presented by the senior leadership team, but this effort is less costly to shareholders than failing to consider all the issues and missing opportunities.

Don't suffer in silence because you don't want to slow down a board meeting. Your questions are important to the company because you (and most of the company's other directors) need to acquire knowledge about the topic at hand from the presenter of that topic, who probably was chosen specifically for his or her expertise in that field. Although you can't hope to acquire expertise in a topic during a single board meeting, you do need enough understanding of important topics to exercise your fiduciary responsibilities. Today, "hair-shirt directors" who challenge the status quo through thoughtful and reasonable questions are highly valued in the boardroom.

Be willing to create a bit of chaos in the boardroom by breaking down a heavily structured agenda in pursuit of the truth. If necessary, force the agenda by commanding the opportunities you need to ask penetrating questions, gain an understanding of an issue under discussion, and articulate your points of view. With the proper spirit and good planning and preparation, both understanding and efficiency can be achieved.

To satisfy your growing thirst for information and understanding of strategic

> **If you rely on the familiar as your exclusive guide for success, you are going to arrive at similar conclusions over and over again.**

issues, you and your fellow directors must make sure that board agendas allow ample time for you to engage in thoughtful problem-solving. Longer, more intense discussions will require longer, more frequent board meetings, a price that both directors and senior leaders must pay in your pursuit of outstanding corporate governance. You can help conserve the board's precious time by doing your homework and showing up at the meetings on time prepared to lead.

The board also should sincerely tolerate, and even encourage, constructive intervention by directors who want to prevent new ideas from being excluded from discussion by conventional thinking. Being original, inspired, and imaginative enough to create a vision requires embracing some level of chaos. As an X-Leader in the boardroom, you must always find a way to influence the board agenda to ensure that issues that you consider important are addressed. In reality, of course, board meetings never will be long enough or frequent enough to satisfy all of your questions, so you will need to stay in contact with other directors between board meetings. And, you will need to supplement your board attendance with one-on-one meetings with the CEO and other senior leaders.

The bold initiatives of the company's senior leaders must be met with X-Leadership from the company's board of directors. You and your fellow directors have collective responsibility to regard the initiation of disruptive thinking as a positive value in the boardroom.

Professionals and Specialists: Create a Little Chaos

Whatever your contributions to the company, your success is related directly to the company's success. If you are highly motivated, you will thrive in a corporate environment that tolerates a little chaos to actively engage all employees in addressing the company's concerns. This is the kind of environment created by companies that lead their industries and attract the best talent and the brightest stars—the kind of company in which a person with high aspirations wants to work.

As an accountant, administrator, engineer, sales representative, or marketer, your comfort in your workplace and confidence in your job depend on your leaders exerting a reasonable amount of control. However, you also want your company to tolerate a little chaos because some loosening of control generates new opportunities for you and your colleagues to get personally involved, perform well, get recognized, and get ahead. Sometimes, too, the best ideas are the direct result of spontaneous action and thought.

X-Leaders are not inspired by calm and status quo! If you want to become an X-Leader in your field, you'll need ample opportunity to run outside of the company's traditional boundaries. As a creative person, you naturally want to explore current issues and make meaningful contributions. And as an ambitious professional, you obviously want to work in an environment that encourages people to maximize their learning and demonstrate leadership. For you, tremendous benefit lies in keeping topics open and issues on the table.

If your company values spontaneity and new ideas, it probably is a competitive force in its industry. However, if your company doesn't thoroughly explore alternatives, you are working for a company that limits your opportunities to be engaged in decision-making. This will make it very difficult for you to distinguish yourself from your colleagues and to be successful in your company. The hard fact is that limited exposure means limited visibility, which means limited advancement opportunities. Another negative aspect of working for a company whose senior leaders make business decisions without exploring all the facts is that, sooner or later, they will judge you without exploring all the facts. Premature closure on important issues limits the success of everyone in the company.

Nevertheless, you can turn chaotic energy into synchronization. Start by recognizing that you and your colleagues are the heart and soul of your company because you operate in the areas where all of the company's real work gets done. You should be guided by three values: 1) an obsession with serving customers, 2) a commitment to business excellence, and 3) a deep respect for each person's contribution to the success of the team. If you adhere to these three basic values, you will be well on your way to great achievement in your career.

You may be an expert in your field, but you probably have not had much opportunity to develop leadership skills. Your company will value you more highly if you take charge and become a formal—or even informal—leader. One way to demonstrate leadership and earn critically important recognition is to fully engage yourself in several aspects of the business. When analyzing business problems, be willing to investigate and understand all reasonable points of view.

Be bold in your initiatives. Instead of being intimidated by someone else's knowledge of a subject under discussion, ask questions to gain insight. Let your ideas flow, and let other people in the meeting know that you expect an opportunity to be involved because you have something to contribute. Having a lot to learn and having a lot to contribute both are fantastic sources of dynamic energy. If you are in a meeting and have not had a chance to ask your most interesting questions, let it be known. If you find yourself in the minority and others don't need further discussion, then schedule some private time with the leader to seek answers to your questions. Keep in mind, however, that if you are not satisfied with your understanding, you probably are not alone. Other people are likely to need clarification too.

If you succeed in becoming an X-Leader in your field, you will be expected to develop outstandingly quick and efficient solutions. No matter what kind of pressure is being exerted on you, however, you must be reluctant to accept any major decision at face value. You must subject all major decisions to a reasonable level of chaotic review. Your approach to problem-solving will be more effective if you time your questions carefully, because the timing of an observation can be just as important as its profundity. Be careful not to use up all of your best ideas too early in the discussion. To maximize the impact of your observations, always reserve one or two of your best questions for the latter part of the

> **There is no shame in following a great idea that is not your own!**

discussion, when you will be able to leverage what you have learned from listening to other participants. The result will be a richer and more valuable inquiry.

X-Leaders are bold and ask tough questions. They don't permit an important meeting to end until all participants have added their views. This extreme approach may be the X-Leader's most important tool for developing the best possible solutions for customers. You, too, must not allow structure to inhibit your ability to learn and grow.

Corporate Customers: Capture the Value in Chaotic Energy

The success of most companies is greatly dependent on the quality of their strategic suppliers. No company should expect less from a strategic supplier than it expects from its own people, because strategic suppliers really are members of the company's extended team. If you represent your company in a relationship with a strategic supplier, you should expect an honest, customer-centric business engagement that benefits both parties. A strategic supplier that intends to deliver the most creative and competitive products and services to you should be including many appropriate people in their decision-making about those products and services.

If your strategic suppliers are unwilling to listen to their own people, they are probably unlikely to listen to you either. If they offer you quick answers to complex problems, those answers frequently are wrong answers. Leaders who are intolerant of chaos do not encourage the in-depth analysis needed to develop break-through products and services, nor do they look for fresh approaches to the market. You should expect X-Leadership, not mediocrity, from your strategic suppliers.

Because a strategic supplier's approaches to problem-solving and decision-making are so important to your company's success, you should evaluate that company's leadership as rigorously as you would the leadership of any competitor. You should be as interested in and committed to your relationship with those leaders as you are to your relationships with your own colleagues. Hold frequent strategic meetings with the suppliers' key leaders and engage them in your company's development process and account planning. Obviously, by doing so, you will be demonstrating vulnerability, but you simultaneously will be demonstrating a confident awareness that you must be candid with them to achieve the best solutions. For most projects, the key to success is shared expectations.

Some corporate customers are masters at placing unrealistic demands on their strategic suppliers. Don't let your company be one of those customers! In your strategic meetings with your suppliers' leaders, always set audacious goals and objectives, but don't impose unrealistic demands just to keep the heat on. If you don't trust a strategic supplier, find a replacement for that supplier. Your objective should be to help the supplier develop the products and services that you need, not to force them to rush to develop ineffective products and services. If you place unrealistic demands, an overly aggressive supplier might initially jump through hoops to meet your expectations, but in the long term your relationship with this supplier will wither.

You will receive consistently better products and services if you partner with your strategic suppliers and allow them to develop timely and thoroughly thought-out solutions. However, don't allow these partners to use lack of structure to justify a failure to perform. Be resolute in accepting nothing less than the pursuit of world-class performance excellence.

X-Leaders thrive on intense engagements with problem-solving and are eager to consider all reasonable solutions. They welcome challenges, both internal and external. When making fundamental business decisions, X-Leaders refuse to sacrifice excellence for speed.

Three Tips for Encouraging Diligence Without Compromising Velocity

1. Ask questions. Accept nothing at face value. Craft a style that helps you to constructively challenge everything.

2. Be curious. Invest time considering new options.

3. Resist the urge to rush to a quick fix. Thoroughly discuss all reasonable options and use what you learn to anticipate and solve problems before they cause delays.

Endnotes

[cxii] Carrol, T., & Burton, R. M. (2000). Organizations and complexity: Searching for the edge of chaos. Computational and Mathematical Organizational Theory, 6, 319-337.

[cxiii] Pascale, R. (2000). Surfing the edge of chaos: The laws of nature and the new laws of business, pg. 3. New York: Leader to Leader Institute; Carrol & Burton, 2000, Organizations and complexity; Burns, J. S. (2002). Chaos theory and leadership studies: Exploring uncharted seas. Journal of Leadership and Organizational Studies, 9, Part 2.

[cxiv] Cambel, A. B. (1993). Applied chaos theory: A paradigm for complexity. San Diego, CA: Academic.

[cxv] Vroom, V. H. (1993, Spring). Two decades of research on participation: Beyond buzzwords and management fads. Yale Review of Management, volume, 22-32.

[cxvi] Pascale, 2000, Surfing the edge of chaos.

[cxvii] Ibid.

[cxviii] Ibid.

[cxix] Lear, R. W. (1995, July/August). Re-engineering the board. Chief Executive, 105, p. 12.

X-Principle Nine: *X-Leaders believe that the company comes first, and they insist on teamwork. They do not tolerate divisional or functional departmental boundaries in the corporate culture.*

CHAPTER 9

Excalibur Level Cooperation

X-Leaders firmly believe that the company's overall performance comes first. They develop themselves for the purpose of maximizing their contributions to the company's success, and they seek phenomenal customer service for the sheer pleasure of earning as much of the customer's business as possible.

For X-Leaders, the chief ingredient of sustainable success is teamwork. X-led employees come to understand that, for them to win as individuals, the entire company has to win. Consequently, these employees tend to focus on common goals and to voluntarily share their resources. This is exactly what X-Leaders want, and they view anything less as weakening the company's foundation. They refuse to tolerate any activities, such as internal political differences and personal innuendos, that undermine excellence and fair play, and discourage cooperation. X-Leaders abhor internal bickering because it makes companies dysfunctional.

X-Leaders are not naïve. They understand that various functional departments and divisions within the company will develop different opinions and strategic ideologies, each building protective barriers around their spheres of influence. X-Leaders, therefore, motivate the leadership team to put the company first, and to thoughtfully and constructively resolve differences between departments and divisions, and to bring down barriers. Before taking conclusive action on requests from individuals, departments, or divisions, X-Leaders examine those requests in light of the company's broader corporate perspectives. Their aim is to dismantle the company's political bastions, because quests for personal power in the company, through political means, are the antithesis of cooperative effort.

X-Leaders have good reasons to want to minimize the extraneous, internal clutter of *workplace politics*, the never-ending struggle for power, authority, and influence in the company. Political wrangling in the workplace consumes time, restricts information sharing, and creates barriers to communication, obviously reducing people's effectiveness and efficiency.[cxx] Many people whose workplaces are rife with politics feel so much stress and have such a difficult time developing positive job attitudes that they move out of the company as soon as they can. [cxxi] Unfortunately for the shareholders of companies that tolerate such internal strife, the people who are made most uncomfortable by workplace politics tend to be the creative, hard workers who fear that credit for their effort, determination, and emotional labor will be falsely claimed by backroom "wranglers and saboteurs."[cxxii cxiii] The people least threatened by workplace politics are those who have the least at stake, the people who don't expect rewards, perhaps because they are less able to earn them.[cxxiv]

Wrangling for power and influence takes place in every organization, but environments characterized by lack of trust, uncertainty, and limited resources tend to bring out people's insecurities. Under these circumstances, individuals and groups are more likely to pursue their own interests through flattery, conforming to other people's viewpoints, and developing power coalitions.[cxxv] On the other hand, when a company makes clear that all of its resources are directed toward its business goals and employees understand and share their supervisor's priorities, workers feel more in control and are better able to assess their fit with the company.[cxxvi] Employees know that they fit with the company they work for when they can use the company's name with pride and describe its virtues to other employees and to customers. The senior leadership team can feel confident that that they have galvanized their people to the company's goals when employees refer to the company as "we," not "they."

Aspiring X-Leaders: Widen Your Horizon

In your present job, you do your best to contribute to the success of your division. But if you want to lead your company someday, it is not a good idea to make yourself indispensable in your present location. If you become stuck in your current division, the amount of influence you will be able to earn will be severely limited. To rise to the top of your company, you need to develop a broad view of its workings and a broad base of support.

For help in planning how you will make vital contacts and gain opportunities to earn recognition of your leadership skills, seek out a personal mentor in a different functional department or division of the company. This person should help you understand your company's organizational dynamics. Become very familiar with your company's organizational charts and the backgrounds and approaches of its leaders. If your investigations reveal that your company's inter-divisional efforts are driven by teamwork, your career efforts will gain you the best results.

To further broaden your view of the company and make important contacts, meet and work with people in other functional departments or divisions. Volunteer for assignments that include such people. As you are working, learning and meeting people, always be guided by ethical business values. Remember that teamwork makes the dream work. Be honest, fair, respectful, and kind. These values will smooth the way as you make difficult decisions and negotiate deals. cxxvii If you have enough knowledge, experience and interest, offer to serve as a mentor for someone in a different division.

It is crucial that you connect your personal development to the success of the company, not merely your department or division. Everything you do should have a link to building shareholder value. Your mentor should be able to help you link your comprehensive performance plan directly to company performance. Start thinking of yourself as a member of the entire company, not just of your department or division.

Senior Leaders: Promote Teamwork

Considering that the different functional departments and divisions of your company almost inevitably will develop different ideologies and erect boundaries around their spheres of influence, you might be asking yourself why you should spend your valuable leadership resources trying to eradicate those boundaries. The answer goes back to your responsibility to protect shareholder value. Your company's overall operating costs will be substantially less if all of your company's people are operating efficiently as one team, instead of duplicating costs in their efforts to build individual empires. Your company's people—especially your best people—will be much more productive as well. The company's overall productivity is negatively impacted when divisional or functional departments operate in a divisive mode. Intellectual properties (such as patents) and assets (such as employees) are resources that belong to the company, not to the different functional departments and divisions responsible for their management. Sharing ownership throughout the company is an excellent way of greatly lowering operating costs, but using company resources to further individual political agendas greatly increases those costs.

> The senior leadership team can feel confident that that they have galvanized their people to the company's goals when employees refer to the company as "we," not "they."

Political maneuvering, especially at high levels, is thought to reduce individual performance in two ways: by de-motivating workers and by inhibiting cooperation.[cxxviii] According to the *expectancy theory*, people feel motivated to perform well if they expect a reward for that good performance. However, in politically charged environments, the level of reward is determined by factors other than performance.[cxxix] When people suspect that they are working in a highly politicized workplace, they also suspect that performing well won't earn them the rewards they normally would expect for that performance. According to *equity theory*, when rewards are distributed to members of a favored clique who "go along to get ahead," people tend to do the minimum required to keep their jobs.[cxxx] Political maneuvering in itself is distinctly non-cooperative, and people who work in highly politicized environments tend to view cooperation as both out of the norm and risky.[cxxxi] Moreover, to avoid scrutiny in politically charged workplaces, people are likely to "keep their heads down" by immersing themselves in their work, which makes them largely unavailable to help their co-workers.[cxxxii]

Teamwork and keeping people's focus on the company as a whole make it more difficult for company politics to flourish. It is more difficult to build political bastions when employees focus on a common goal than when separate entities are developing their own agendas. Below, I have outlined suggestions to help you build the kind of ethos that embraces company-wide teamwork.

Recognize and Reward the Creation of Shareholder Value

Reduce people's motivation to create self-interested political domains in the company by establishing a corporate culture that pays for performance and rewards risk. All employee recognition and compensation should be based on value created for the shareowners. Motivate every person in the company to be a team player by using a financial reward linked directly to the company's success.

I recommend that, for very senior managers (those reporting directly to the chief executive officer or the chief operating officer), at least 75% of total compensation (including salary, bonuses, stock grants, stock options, etc,) should be linked directly to the overall success of the *entire* company. For divisional and functional departmental leaders, this percentage should be at least 50%. For all other managers and supervisors, this percentage should be at least 25%. For everyone else in the company, this percentage should be 5%, or more. In my leadership experience, this schedule will enable the board of directors and CEO to leverage the company's focus on maximizing shareowner value. However, these percentages are not cast in stone; they should be adjusted according to the circumstances of each company.

Whatever schedule is used, the important thing is that each and every employee of the company arrives at work every day knowing that his or her contribution to the company's success will be measured, and that those measurements will affect the size of that person's paycheck.

Articulate the Company's Plans, Activities, and Goals

If you and your fellow senior leaders link each employee's pay to the company's overall success, you also must create opportunities for employees to impact that success and give them a very clear idea of how to do that. You and the rest of the senior leadership team must clearly communicate to every employee your company's plans, activities, and goals. In addition, you must make certain that each employee is given carefully considered, helpful feedback about his or her individual performance and the collective performance of the entire company.

Lead by Example

If you want your people to believe in teamwork, you should believe in it, expect it, and display it. Using teamwork as the company benchmark will help keep political baggage to a minimum.[cxxxiii] The real competition is outside the company, so don't contribute energy to political bickering inside your company. When you encounter obstacles to cooperation, eliminate them. When you become aware of barriers between functional departments or divisions, constructively reduce them. Don't allow departmental isolation, divisional bickering, or internal competition to get in the way of delivering outstanding products and services to customers.

Treat the Company as a Whole

After you and your fellow senior leaders build common goals for the company, you must motivate all of your company's employees to work to achieve these common goals. To establish in employee's minds that the company is one unit whose success affects each of them, treat the company as a whole. Frequently visit all of your company's locations to articulate this very important point. Stress that the company's success as a whole is a more important measurement of performance than the success of any one division or functional department.[cxxxiv] Establish global employee communication meetings in which you broadly communicate the company's expectations and the status of its performance. These meetings should be the norm, not the exception.

The results produced by the whole always will be greater than the results produced by the sum of its parts. X-Leaders take advantage of synergy by building on the strengths of the entire team.

Corporate Directors: Keep Everyone's Eye on the Ball

Every corporate director understands that shareholder value is most often derived from the valuation of the collective company, not from the valuation of individual divisions or functional departments.[cxxxv] If you are a corporate director, you are well aware that fulfilling the company's mission, focusing the company on serving its customers, and monitoring the company's competition leaves no time for wasted motion. The more time and resources spent making peace within the company, the less time and resources are available for fulfilling vital external responsibilities. This puts the expected shareowner return on invested capital at risk. The board must work with the CEO to ensure that the leadership team does not tolerate infighting that results in divisional and functional departmental disruption.

How can the board of directors ensure that the senior leadership team puts the company first and refuses to tolerate divisional and functional departmental infighting? Begin by keeping in mind that the company is a living entity whose value outweighs that of any of its parts. Over time, many of the company's people will come and go, but the company will stand if it is well managed. The key to keeping everyone's eye on the ball is tying compensation to corporate performance. Therefore, the board needs to understand the reward process that the CEO has implemented for his or her team.

This understanding demands that the board assess the company's culture, which will be greatly aided by holding an annual board review of the company's employee satisfaction survey. Occasionally getting a different point of view through independent organizational effectiveness assessment can also be very helpful.

The company's success depends on action, so work with the CEO to understand what he or she is doing to maximize the synergy of the entire company. Don't regard yourself and your fellow board members as separate from the company. Be inclusive. Speak in terms of we and us, not you. Invoke a team spirit.

Professionals and Specialists:
Link Your Contributions to the Company's Success

Your company views your professional skills, and those of other professionals within it, as resources. If your company views your professional skills as tied to the specific functional department or division in which you work, your opportunities to learn, earn, and advance will be considerably less than if the company views your skills as tied to the entire company.

For example, if you are working for a company that believes in eliminating unnecessary boundaries between divisions and functional departments, you will have greater access to a broader array of tools and skills than otherwise. This alone will increase your opportunities for career advancement. Your relationship with the company will be more enduring than with a functional department or division. Divisions and functional departments come and go, but successful companies continue on. In the broader sense, any company whose employees work as a team has an improved chance of beating the competition. Of course, if you work for a company that beats the competition, you will have a much better chance of sustaining a long-term career in your company. Moreover, your company has only one stock, and your customers and potential employers will judge you on the values and culture of your corporation, not on those of your division or functional department. You should be working to influence the outcome of the whole corporation, not just your little corner of it.

Of course, you must make sure that you contribute to the success of your functional department or division, but you can profit much more handsomely if you simultaneously tie your future to the success of the company as a whole. By following the four recommendations below, you can maximize your personal wealth.

Build a Broad Base of Experiences Throughout the Company

If you want to become a corporate leader, then you must build a broad base of support throughout the company. A good way to meet people in other divisions is by volunteering for cross-functional and cross-divisional assignments. To gain insight into other parts of the company, seek out a personal mentor, preferably from another division, or if you are qualified to do so, offer to serve as a mentor for someone in another division. These cross-divisional or cross-functional experiences will help broaden your knowledge about the company, thereby enhancing your advancement opportunities. A word of warning: To gain most cross-divisional or cross-functional experiences, you will need some mobility and the support of others throughout the company. Do not allow yourself to get locked into your current functional department or division without that support, and never allow yourself to become indispensable to your division or to your functional department.

Link Your Performance Plan to the Success of the Company

Link your comprehensive performance plan directly to the success of the company. If your performance measurements are connected only to the success of your functional department or division, and you cannot see a link to the overall success of your company, you are working on the wrong goals. Everything done within a department or division should be linked to building shareowner value.

Understand How Companies Work

It is extremely important that you understand how companies in general work, and specifically the company in which you work. This might require taking a course on organizational dynamics. It is vital that you know where your company's leadership comes from and what the leadership does. Become a student of your company's

> **If you want your people to believe in teamwork, you should believe in it, expect it, and display it.**

organizational charts, both formal and informal. Don't allow yourself to be captured by a company whose leadership you do not understand. If you want the best shot at success, you should be working in a company in which the relationships between the functional departments and operating divisions are driven by teamwork.

199

Follow Ethical Standards and Use Business Diplomacy

Whatever you do, your work should be guided by ethical business values, including honesty, fairness, mutual respect, kindness, and goodness. This does not mean that you can or should ignore the tough realities of business. You will still need to make difficult decisions, resolve conflicts, and negotiate deals. This is where business diplomacy comes in.[cxxxvi]

To get things done, you need to work with people, and the tools of diplomacy will help you and the people you need to work with understand each other's points of view and reach common ground. You can use these tools to deter people from circumventing each other's work and needs and to avoid and dissipate hostilities. These tools are respect, honesty, and tact. Using these tools helps people recognize and value the differences among them, voice appropriate agreement, build trust, and develop relationships. Diplomacy is useful nearly always, but particularly when action is bogging down in turf battles, resource wars, and dysfunctional departmental competitions.[cxxxvii]

Corporate Customers: Partner With Companies, not Divisions or Departments

Corporate customers want relationships with their strategic suppliers that make it easy to do business. If you are representing a corporate customer, you will have much more confidence in a strategic supplier if that supplier's people operate from a perspective of their entire company's broad interests, instead of the much narrower interests of their specific functional division or department. To get the best possible service from your strategic suppliers, you need to work with people who know how to leverage the strength and value of their entire company for your benefit, not just the strength of one division or department.

You should expect your strategic supplier's people to be united within their own company. If your supplier's people are not united in their efforts to deliver exceptional products and services to you, their focus will be blurred, their energy too widely dispersed, and the quality of their service uneven. They will frequently burden you with inaccurate, inconsistent, and incomplete information. This dysfunctional behavior will negatively impact your timeline and costs.

Before you build a relationship with a strategic supplier, do your homework. Make sure that the supplier's people present a consistent picture of their company's goals and commitments. Understand the supplier's organizational structure, and investigate the supplier's business model, objectives, and strategies.

Once you are satisfied that you can build a good relationship with the supplier, use your corporate interactions to build relationships with the company as a whole. Make sure that multiple people of your company at all levels engage with their counterparts in the supplier company. If appropriate, these contact points should include the board of directors, senior leaders, and community associates, all of whom can

> **Become a student of your company's organizational charts, both formal and informal.**

significantly help leverage an effective relationship between you and the supplier. Never build any relationship around a personal agenda or divisional strategy that is not linked directly to the supplier's overall corporate direction and expectations. Expect the supplier's people to acknowledge all of your concerns as corporate issues; don't permit any of the supplier's people to blame one of their functional departments or divisions for a failure to perform.

If you insist on working with strategic suppliers who know how to focus on the larger picture, you will streamline your efforts to build great products, which will speed up your company's success.

X-Leaders expect cooperation throughout the company. They champion the corporate culture and its core values. X-Leaders believe that corporate teamwork brings dreams into reality.

Three Ways to Maximize Shareowner Value

1. Keep your eye on the prize. Don't permit internal boundaries in your company to obscure your view of the bigger picture.

2. Think and act as though boundaries do not exist in your company. Don't limit your horizon to the people you know; instead, be eager to partner with other functional departments or divisions within your company.

3. Always think and act inclusively. Use the pronouns *we, us,* and *ours,* instead of *they, them,* and *theirs,* or *I, me,* and *mine.*

Endnotes

cxx Eisenhardt, K. M., & Bourgeois, L. J., III. (1988). Politics of strategic decision making in high-velocity environments. *Academy of Management Journal*, 31(4), 737-770.

cxxi Poon, J. M. L. (2003). Situational antecedents and outcomes of organizational politics perceptions. *Journal of Managerial Psychology*, 18(2), 138-135.

cxxii Hochwarter, W. A., & Treadway, D. C. (2003). The interactive effects of negative and positive affect on the politics perceptions-job satisfaction relationship. *Journal of Management*, 29(4), 551-567.

cxxiii Biberman, G. (1985). Personality and characteristic work attitudes of persons with high, moderate, and low political tendencies. *Psychological Reports*, 57, 1303-1310; Hochwarter & Treadway, The interactive effects of negative and positive affect.

cxxiv Hochwarter & Treadway, The interactive effects of negative and positive affect.

cxxv Prasad, (1993). The etiology of organizational politics: Implications for the intrapreneur. *SAM Advanced Management Journal*, 58(3), 35-41.

cxxvi Witt, L. A. (1998). Enhancing organizational goal congruence: A solution to organizational politics. *Journal of Applied Psychology*, 83(4), 666-674.

cxxvii London, M. (1999). Principled leadership and business diplomacy: A practical, values-based direction for management development. *Journal of Management Development*, 18(2), 17-19.

cxxviii Randall, M. L., Cropanzano, R., Bormann, C. A., & Birjulin, A. (1999). Organizational politics and organizational support as predictors of work attitudes, job performance, and organizational citizenship behaviors. *Journal of Organizational Behavior*, 20, 159-174.

cxxix Kacmar, K. M., & Ferris, G. R. (1991). Perceptions of organizational politics scale (POP) development and construct validation. *Educational and Psychological Measurement*, 51, 193-205.

cxxx Moorman, R. H. (1991). Relationship between organizational justice and organizational citizenship behaviors: Do fairness perceptions influence employee citizenship? *Journal of Applied Psychology*, 76, 845-855.

cxxxi Witt, L. A. (1998). Enhancing organizational goal congruence.

cxxxii Ferris, G. R., & Kacmar, K. M. (1992). Perceptions of organizational politics. *Journal of Management*, 18, 93-116.

cxxxiii Biberman, G. (1985). Personality and characteristic work attitudes of persons with high, moderate, and low political tendencies. *Psychological Reports*, 57, 1303-1310; Hochwarter & Treadway, The interactive effects of negative and positive affect; Poon, 2003, Situational antecedents; Witt, 1998, Enhancing organizational goal congruence.

cxxxiv Witt, 1998, Enhancing organizational goal congruence; Hochwarter & Treadway, The interactive effects of negative and positive affect.

cxxxv Most corporations have only one stock. In instances where corporations also have tracking stocks, the entities that have the tracking stocks are viewed as separate companies, and not separate divisions or functional departments.

cxxxvi London, 1999, Principled leadership.

cxxxvii Ibid.

X-Principle Ten: *X-Leaders expect greatness. They are results-oriented, honest, and personally accountable.*

CHAPTER 10

Expect What You Get

X-Leaders audaciously expect to produce exemplary results, and they expend the necessary resources to achieve these results. They make excellence their benchmark and then plan to exceed it. In the corporate environments they create, people so strongly expect to achieve excellence that they are surprised when occasional failures occur. In this atmosphere of continual learning, even failures are regarded as opportunities to learn how to win the next engagement. High expectations also help the X-led company to stay a considerable distance ahead of its competitors. This is important because high-performing companies are targeted by their competitors.

Interestingly, X-Leaders and their followers usually deliver more than is expected of them precisely because they have high expectations. Research suggests that setting specific, hard-to-reach goals indeed does lead to increased performance. Regarding the difficult goal as important, believing that one has the capacity to reach the goal, committing oneself to reaching it, and receiving constant feedback from one's supervisor all can contribute to that increased performance.[cxxxviii]

One of the most striking characteristics of X-Leaders is their truthfulness and sense of personal responsibility. The X-Leader's honesty and personal accountability are ethically commendable, but they also make valuable contributions to the X-led company's competitive position. For example, in an atmosphere of honesty and accountability, the company's senior leaders feel safe enough to acknowledge areas that need substantial improvement so that these can be addressed.

As a direct result of the company's excellence in developing outstanding products and services, the corporate customers of the X-led company become the winners in their own markets and the leaders in their own industries. When the X-led company delivers superior performance, it earns larger shares of customer dollars.

In an X-led environment, employees tend to set audacious goals not only for the company, but for themselves as individuals. They strive to be the best of the best, to perform much better than average, and to expect high compensation for outstanding performance. In return, these audacious goal-setters earn frequent rewards and salaries in the top quartile of their profession. This is the fulfillment of a psychological contract with the X-led company that drives exceptional performances.

> **High expectations also help the X-led company to stay a considerable distance ahead of its competitors.**

Incentives have been shown to increase people's commitment to reaching goals.[cxxxix] Incentive pay in particular significantly strengthens people's tendencies to commit to goals; moreover, their commitment increases as the payout and frequency of payout increases.[cxl]

No matter how great the company performs, that performance can never quite meet the expectations of the X-Leader because that leader enjoys the journey toward higher and higher goals. As soon as one level of high performance is reached, the X-Leader raises the bar to an even higher level of performance. X-Leaders truly expect greatness.

In this environment, everyone believes that it is important to understand why and how they win and lose, so people tend to analyze their successes and failures. The results of these analyses are shared appropriately throughout the company and are celebrated as continued learning. Every improvement in the company's overall performance increases shareholder value.

Aspiring X-Leaders: Become Honestly Great!

If you genuinely want to become an X-Leader, you must believe in your ability to do great things. If you don't yet have that conviction, it is time to develop it. You also must overcome any resistance you feel to being honest with other people, including being honest about your own successes and failures.

To become great, expect to become great. Great performance normally follows high expectations. In fact, the strong relationship between high expectations and great performance has been demonstrated over and over again in a variety of cultures. You probably will achieve no more than you expect to achieve, so expect a lot! One reason that X-Leader's keep raising the bar for the company is that they understand that people tend to achieve only what they expect to achieve.

Use honesty to drive out your co-worker's fear of the unknown and to increase their confidence in the company. Use personal accountability and fear of failure as highly effective motivators. Honest people who hold themselves personally accountable will strive to maximize their contributions, because they do not want to fail or put the company in jeopardy. Of course, recognizing people's achievements and tying their compensation to the company's overall success also increases people's performance. So does giving subordinates honest, direct feedback about the value of their contributions and helping them design personal roadmaps to improved performance. Helping people strive toward personal improvement will increase their contributions to the company's success. All these actions will leverage honesty and personal accountability to motivate those you work with to deliver outstanding contributions to the company.

Great talent always is very difficult to find, so the more you improve your ability to make the most of your natural gifts, the better chance you will have to succeed in your quest to earn X-Leadership.

Senior Leaders: Inspire Honesty and Accountability

How can you, as a senior leader, help create a corporate environment that motivates people to be results-oriented, honest, and in constant pursuit of greatness? Following the suggestions below can help you capture and convey the excitement of creating excellence.

Point the Way to Greatness

Your company's people will find their way to greatness much more quickly if they know where greatness lies. You and your fellow senior leaders must decide what greatness means to senior leaders, customers, and shareholders, and then use that definition to devise a set of clearly defined goals for your people to target. Distribute copies of those goals throughout the entire company and make sure they are discussed thoroughly in all your communications. Consistently let everyone in the company know what kind of progress the company is making in meeting these goals.

Set Inspiring New Benchmarks

Motivate each of the company's divisions or functional departments to use the best performance in its class as its benchmark. In other words, the finance department should aim to collect its accounts receivables more efficiently than its most efficient competitor, the engineering division should aim to design and deliver its new products to the market in shorter cycles than its most nimble competitor, the sales team should aim to close customers more quickly than their toughest competitors, etc. In short, the senior leadership team should be encouraging the entire company, division by division and department by department, to set the standard by which quality is judged.

Communicate Lessons Learned

Institute "best practices" and "lessons learned" communications through which employees make recommendations based on their actual experiences. Make sure these vehicles reach everyone in the company.

Idiot-Proof Company Operations

Minimizing waste is an efficient way to increase profits, so concentrate on tightening processes so that downtime is reduced and errors are eliminated. Aim to make the manufacturing of bad products impossible by "idiot-proofing" operations and processes, that is, designing them to have zero failures.

Link Quality With Value

Quality is inexpensive if you always deliver outstanding products. In fact, quality only becomes expensive when you fail to expect greatness. However, quality does not win without the value generated by delivering great products to customers, on time, at world-class, competitive prices!

Get a clear understanding of the customer's expectations and make sure that your company is committed to exceeding those expectations. If your people entertain low expectations, their performance also will be low, bringing down shareowner value and risking employees' jobs. Always expect great results.

Leverage Accountability Into Greatness

When you demonstrate vulnerability by delegating broadly, expect greatness in return. Expect greatness from your leaders, your colleagues, your subordinates, and (perhaps most of all) from yourself. In the long run, what matters to the company are positive results, and the company's senior leaders are fully responsible and accountable for whatever results the company produces. Don't risk results you won't be proud of by accepting anything less than the full pursuit of excellence.

Inspire Honesty and Accountability

To build an environment that leverages honesty and personal accountability to produce outstanding results for shareholders, you must set audacious goals for the company. In fact, you should expect performance levels higher than any other company in your industry. Then you must convince your people that they will achieve great things if they have outstanding teamwork and a passion for serving customers.

To do so, you must set an example by expecting great things of yourself. You also must surround yourself with great people who help you sustain your exemplary performance. This means not being afraid to hire people smarter than you who are willing to work at least as hard, and then investing in training them to be the best in their professions.

If you want other people to conduct themselves with honesty and integrity, you must let them see that you never compromise your honesty and integrity. You'll set an excellent example to emulate when you are seen as always seeking the truth and never passing the buck. Of course, your reward for doing your great work will be more great work to do!

Corporate Directors: Enforce Honesty as the Best Policy

Directors have a very personal stake in expecting greatness in the company they govern because their reputations are aligned with that company. For this reason alone, you should not want to be associated with a company that doesn't at least expect to deliver great results to its shareholders.

You and your fellow directors are not accountable for the company's performance, but you are responsible for the selection and supervision of the company's CEO, who bears direct responsibility for that performance. You also are responsible for ensuring that all of the company's results are candidly and accurately reported,

> **Quality is inexpensive if you always deliver outstanding products.**

which means that you must ensure that the CEO is delivering truthful, factual reports to you.

Usually the board will get what it expects and inspects, which means that you should expect greatness from the leadership team and then verify the results of their performance using factual measurements. Before you set goals for the CEO and the company, do your research and make sure that the goals you contemplate are grounded in factual data. When the results come in, the board must aggressively inspect the supporting data before the results are recorded and reported. Next, the board must invest the time necessary to

212

understand the company's performance. Thanks to the Sarbanes-Oxley Act, new disclosure requirements exist to help the board ensure that required data are reported in an accurate and timely fashion.

Each director should demonstrate true leadership by constructively encouraging the company's senior leaders to achieve greatness in every aspect of the company's business. To be effective, directors must work with the CEO and the senior leadership team to earn mutual trust and respect.

Professionals and Specialists: To Become the Best, Work for the Best

If you want to be great at your profession, take the quick route and work for a company that demands greatness. A company that expects you to do great things also will expect to invest in you, encourage you, and support your efforts. In its striving for excellence, it probably is serving its customers well, and thus is earning value and generating shareholder returns. For these reasons, the company that demands greatness also is likely to win in the marketplace, which (if you work for it) will help to preserve your career opportunities.

In a results-oriented company that insists on honesty, the environment will be less politically charged, and therefore your path to personal success will be less strewn with roadblocks placed there by people busy amassing unearned personal power in the workplace. Your performance will be measured on the results of your work and not on your personal popularity, increasing the likelihood that your genuine contributions to the company's success will be recognized and valued.

A company that values and invests in employees also is much more likely to create opportunities for those employees to gain responsibility and accountability. If you prove yourself in such a company, you will earn opportunities to learn, advance, and increase your earnings.

You can become the best if you expect to be the best, prepare well, and work smart in a company that will help you every step of the way. Before you decide that delivering greatness is what you really want to do, find out whether you are ready for the task. To deliver greatness, you will need physical stamina, mental toughness, interest in your work, and compassion for other people. If you want to devote your physical, intellectual, and emotional energies to this challenge, it's time to get in shape!

First, develop a plan to become the best at what you do. Expect to become a leader in your field. Average performance will gain you an average career. Next, evaluate your company to determine whether it will support your efforts at greatness. If you are working at a company that doesn't expect greatness, then you aren't likely to achieve it there. Find employment at an X-led company that targets greatness. (On the other hand, if you look into your heart and find that you really don't want to pursue greatness, but the company that you work for expects greatness, you'll be happier working in a company that won't be expecting so much of you.)

Learn to appreciate your journey to greatness, which will be filled with wins and losses. You will live a much happier life if you enjoy your small victories and achievements as you progress toward your goal. X-Leaders don't wait until they reach the top to enjoy themselves, they enjoy every step of the way. You will

> **Expect greatness from your leaders, your colleagues, your subordinates, and (perhaps most of all) from yourself.**

have losses along the way; analyze why you failed and don't repeat your mistakes the next time you attempt to win! Many lessons can be learned only through experience. When you experience a success, use the energy boost you gain from that success to power you to the next project. Prepare your launching pad for your upcoming successes by sharing your experiences, learning, and successes with your colleagues. Become known as a willing partner and teacher. Helping other members of your team make great achievements will enhance your opportunity to become a major contributor to your company's success. Together, you will build the foundation for many future successes.

When in doubt, don't waste time and energy suffering in silence. Seek help from your supervisor, colleagues, and customers. If you are to be great, you must learn how to ask for help. Keep in mind that you must learn to leverage all of your resources in your pursuit of greatness. You can't do it alone!

Stay current in corporate affairs. Learn how your company works. Understand the formal and informal organization of your company. If you are in pursuit of greatness in the corporate world, you must become a student of your company and learn to understand what happens within it. An X-Leader uses his or her knowledge of how the company works to leverage success.

Ask for tough assignments. Always be willing to take on the task that seems to be most difficult. Never underestimate the challenge, but be willing to reach for the stars!

Corporate Customers: Demand Greatness

Your company has nothing to lose and everything to gain by demanding greatness from your strategic suppliers. If your suppliers expect greatness of themselves, your company will be rewarded with on-time delivery of higher quality products and improved customer services at competitive prices. Having a results-oriented strategic supplier will enhance your confidence, but if your customer-supplier relationship is based on honest facts and the pursuit of greatness, your confidence will soar.

When a strategic supplier's people base their actions on factual data and their company's commitments to you, respond in kind by being open with them. A relationship built on honesty is a relationship that is likely to last. However, just as you would not deliberately choose to do business with a dishonest supplier, avoid doing business with a supplier with marginal performance or weak goals. The products and services they deliver will translate into marginal satisfaction for your own customers. Work only with suppliers who expect, demand, and deliver greatness.

Always award your company's business to companies whose behavior

> **You probably will achieve no more than you expect to achieve, so expect a lot!**

and attitudes are well aligned with your expectations, and who demonstrate a commitment to achieving performance that meets or exceeds your expectations.

How can you ensure that your strategic partners are in pursuit of greatness? At the first opportunity, review their strategic plans. Encourage them to share their expectations with you, and reciprocate by sharing your expectations with them. If you expect them to pursue greatness, they will expect you to do the same. Understand your strategic supplier's corporate history. Look for a track record of delivering outstanding results; if they don't have high levels of past performance, find out whether they have a plan to change their corporate environment.

Before you and your company's other leaders place a significant component of the company's success (and its leaders' personal success) into the trust of a strategic supplier, your company's leadership team should get to know your supplier's leadership team very well. You should know them on a personal level, and you should know their management histories, performance track records, and success at achieving greatness. Establish shared expectations with the supplier, and base these expectations on honest, open communication of information based on facts. Don't mislead their people with false or unreasonable expectations. Remember, customers who demand great products and service from their strategic suppliers are more likely to get them than customers who don't.

X-Leaders expect to win. They know that, in business, winning is what really counts. By winning in business, the X-Leader earns opportunities to pursue all the other things that, outside of the business world, are more important than winning.

Three Ways to Raise Expectations

1. Stretch yourself. Although excellence can be an elusive goal, learn to enjoy the constant pursuit of it. Establish audacious personal goals that can be achieved only through great performance.

2. Define audacious benchmarks. Find out what makes the difference between good performance and great performance, then aim to outdo your strongest competitors.

3. Redefine acceptable performance. Never consider good performance a victory. Celebrate progress, but expect to achieve great performance often.

Endnotes

[cxxxviii] Locke, E. A., & Latham, G. P. (2002). Building a practically useful theory of goal setting and task motivation: A 35-year odyssey. *American Psychologist*, 57(9), 705-17.

[cxxxix] Locke & Latham, 2002. Building a practically useful theory of goal setting; Yukl, G. A., & Latham, G. P. Consequences of reinforcement schedules and incentive magnitudes for employee performance. Problems encountered in an industrial setting. *Journal of Applied Psychology*, 1976, 60, 294-298.

[cxl] Riedel, J. A., Nebeker, D. M., & Cooper, B. L. (1988). The influence of monetary incentives on goal choice, goal commitment, and task performance. *Organizational Behavior and Human Decision Processes*, 42(2), 155-180; Locke & Latham, 2002. Building a practically useful theory of goal setting; Hollensbe, E. C., & Guthrie, J. P. (2000). Group pay-for-performance plans: The role of spontaneous goal setting. *Academy of Management Review*, 25(4), 864-872.

X-Principle Eleven: *X-Leaders are role models.*
They set the example.

CHAPTER 11

Exemplify the Standard

The X-Leader is a role model who doesn't wait for others to set the tone for the rest of the company. The X-Leader's behavior is widely emulated because he or she practices outstanding professionalism. This individual knows that great performance usually is a direct result of great leadership, so he or she develops great leadership skills to set an example for everyone else in the company to follow. This accelerates the performance of the company and helps deliver sustainable increases in shareowner value.[cxli]

Leadership, the ability to guide and direct people, is different from authority, the right to enforce rules. So far, however, no one has adequately answered one of the most basic questions about leadership: How do leaders induce people to follow them?[cxlii] Clearly, followers must conclude that they do better to follow than not; but why do they conclude this? And how does the leader lead them to this conclusion? One possible answer has been put forth by researcher Benjamin Hermalin, who has hypothesized that people follow because they believe that their leader has superior information and is not misleading them. The leader's signals are convincing because he or she sets an example or makes a sacrifice.[cxliii]

Some high-level corporate role models set the standard for appropriate behavior for most situations highly evident throughout the company. Under the influence of some trusted corporate role models, employees exude a winning attitude and great loyalty to the company. Effective role modeling has been shown to lead to increases in job satisfaction and overall performance. Remarkably, even customers emulate many of the characteristics of senior leaders who are great role models. More importantly to the company, customers want to do business with great leaders. Investment analysts reward successful corporate role models with high evaluations because they view their behaviors as benchmarks, and the directors of company's led by outstanding role models also are held in high esteem in their industries.

> **Leadership, the ability to guide and direct people, is different from authority, the right to enforce rules.**

The X-Leader walks the talk. All of the X-led company's behaviors are linked to the X-Leader's example. The results of leading by example (if the example is an exceptional one) are remarkable, but what compels the X-Leader to set the example in the first place? Why does this individual need to be a role model? One possible explanation is that great people want to work with other great people. They want opportunities to learn and to emulate the performance and behaviors of other exceptional people.

If you learn the power of setting a great example, you will find yourself doing your best every day of your life. Below, I've presented some specific suggestions for people who want to lead more effectively or do business with leaders.

Aspiring X-Leaders: Lead by Example, Learn by Example

Your aspirations are high, but your position might not be—yet. Even if you are standing on the first rung of your career ladder, it is not too early to practice leadership. If you already are a supervisor or a manager, you should be expanding your management skills by learning and practicing leadership skills.

You should learn the difference between managing and leading, if you don't know it already. Managers organize and direct other people's work. Leaders guide people by showing the way. To be an X-Leader, you must value both sets of skills, with the understanding that leadership takes management to new levels. If you do not yet have the skills or authority to organize other people's activities, you can lead by example, guide by sharing your views, and inspire with your vision and enthusiasm.

What you cannot responsibly do, if you want to be an outstanding leader, is compromise the duties of leadership for the sake of popularity or convenience. Once you take on the responsibility of leading, you should demonstrate your leadership with every decision, every day. Of course, you won't reach that high level of leadership overnight, but you can try. Responsible leadership takes practice and discipline.

It also takes study. You will be leading by example, and you should also learn through example. Examine the leadership practices of people you respect and try them on for size. If they fit, put them into practice in your own life. This is how you eventually will develop your own unique leadership style, which will become one of your most important assets in life. Study, practice, implement; then study, practice, and implement again. If you want to make a commitment to becoming a corporate leader, start now to model behavior that leads to good performance and increased shareholder value. When you do so, you may be surprised to find that your behavior will influence people around you, without you saying a word.

X-Leaders surround themselves with people who can help them be great leaders. These people have great skills, a passion for the company, and they are eager to practice X-Leadership themselves. They also are team players. Whenever you participate in a hiring decision or the selection of a new team member, look for these characteristics in the people being considered.

Help the people around you to feel more confident in their abilities to make contributions that will serve customers or otherwise add value to the company. As you continue down your road to X-Leadership, you will reach a point where you will be expected to create an environment that encourages your subordinates to perform at their highest levels. Everyone has the responsibility to lead, so encourage others to inspire and guide other people. When the people you work with act confidently, display good teamwork skills, or try to make contributions to the company, reinforce their behavior with some kind of reward, even if it is only a kind word of recognition of their efforts. However, if you are in a position of authority, make sure that your subordinates are rewarded appropriately and frequently for work that furthers the company's goals. Include leadership principles in all your technical, financial, and marketing presentations. Business leaders don't lead only from podiums, in meetings, and in conversations. Make leadership part of everything you do.

When you do so, you will increase your value to your company and gain the support of the people you work with. The support of your supervisor will be especially vital to your advancement, so involve him or her in your leadership development as much as you can. Always be on the lookout for new opportunities to learn and contribute. Be very sensitive to your supervisor's attitude toward receiving feedback from subordinates. If your supervisor welcomes your suggestions and shares increasing responsibility with you, you are lucky and will advance rapidly under that person's tutelage. But if your supervisor is averse to suggestions or offers by subordinates to demonstrate responsibility and leadership, tread carefully! Aim to work in an environment where management is considered merely acceptable but leadership is expected. Whatever you do, find someone in a position of leadership, either inside or outside your company, whose leadership skills you respect and who can mentor you in leadership skills and advise you what steps to take to advance your career. Then listen carefully to the advice that person has to offer.

Senior Leaders: Raise Your Followers to New Heights

The best leaders are emotionally committed to the purpose of leadership. You should be working to make your company become known throughout your industry for outstanding products and services that directly result from your superior leadership. When you are regarded as a leader whose behaviors and performance strongly influence your followers to reach great heights of achievement, your career opportunities will increase exponentially and your market value will be enhanced in your company and your industry. How can you become a role model who raises your followers to new heights?

Set High Expectations for Your Company

If you want people to perform at a high level, you must set the benchmark at a high level. Always encourage success, but be willing to tolerate failure when it happens in the pursuit of excellence.

Ensure that all of your company's employees have a documented personal development plan that emphasizes individual leadership responsibility. Of course, not everyone in the company will develop into a great leader, but everyone in the company should be expected to improve his or her leadership skills.

Make sure that your company's philosophy, vision, and mission are taught to every person in the company, along with ways to implement them. A good way to do so is through train-the-trainer programs. Although these guiding principles won't change, their implementation must be flexible enough to reflect the various cultures and subcultures within your company, as well as your company's changing goals and circumstances. Solicit employees' feedback on your company's guiding principles and training programs. Remember, as a role model, it is your job always to show respect for other people's ideas and opinions.

Your behavior always should mirror your company's values and set an example for your company's employees. Depend on it—your people will imitate you in whatever you do.

Align Senior Leaders to a Common Set of Goals

Your team of senior leaders must implement a common set of leadership principles that represent your company's style, values, and expectations. You will need help to align yourselves to those common values. Hire a leadership coach (who will work with your human resources people) to develop and implement a comprehensive leadership program for the senior leadership team.

As part of your alignment to a set of common values, senior leaders compensation should be inextricably linked with leadership results. In addition, when a senior leader develops a leadership style that is particularly effective, that person should be rewarded for setting an outstanding example. X-Leaders never stop learning, and they never stop leading.[cxlv]

Hire People With High Aspirations

High performance companies are staffed by people who want to achieve high performance. Your company should hire people who possess a blend of skills, talent, behavior, and attitudes that reflect your customer base and the type of company you and your fellow senior leaders want to build. Your company also must make huge investments to train and develop those people. Although they already possess the specific innate talents you look for, enhancing those talents will enormously benefit your company, especially if you make sure that your people are also taught how to align their progress with company expectations.

Make Leadership Skills a Core Competency in Your Company

The quality of a company's leadership is a critical factor in the company's success, and you can make uncompromising leadership a competitive advantage. Regard the ability to effectively model positive behaviors as a core competency for the company. Inspire your subordinates to become role models for the rest of

> **Examine the leadership practices of people you respect and try them on for size.**

the company. Reward them for successful role modeling, but do not tolerate any modeling of negative behaviors that don't promote cooperation, teamwork, and high ethics.

Make employee leadership development a collaborative responsibility of individual leaders, line managers, and your human resources department. Your human resources people should be responsible for company training and general people-development, but not for developing your company's leaders. Sharing the responsibility of leadership development benefits both the company and the individual.

Effective leadership is the result of effort and discipline. Good role modeling behavior should be recognized and rewarded throughout the company, but it must begin at the top. Your company's leaders should be highly skilled, both in their professions and in their leadership.

Remember, People Imitate What They See

Whatever example you and other senior leaders set, many people in the company will emulate your behavior. That is one reason why it is of considerable importance that your actions conform to the highest standards of honesty and integrity. If any of the company's leaders or managers engage in dishonest or unethical behavior, that behavior will be replicated in the workforce. To clarify what the company expects, senior leaders should develop a binding code of ethics that clearly articulates how your company expects employees to behave and perform. Publish and distribute that set of definitive values and make sure everyone in the company understands that they must adhere to them. To guide people, you must clearly define your expectations.

Use Visible Reinforcements

Leadership should be a core competency in your company, not just a program of the month, or a slogan posted on the wall. However, using visible reinforcements like posters, articles, and speeches will help your people understand that the company really does expect all employees to sharpen their leadership skills. Use visual reinforcements to remind each person in the company that effective leadership is everyone's responsibility.

Corporate Directors: Developing a Model Company Makes Shareholders Happy

As a corporate director, you should care very deeply about whether the leaders of the company you represent are superior role models. In today's accelerating, competitive environment, product and service differentiation are very difficult to establish, and exceptional leadership is essential to gain an edge in the marketplace.

The company's future success, or lack of it, will be heavily influenced by the leadership characteristics of the company's CEO and senior leadership team. One reason is that people buy from people they like, the people who are fair and who treat them like they want to be treated. Another reason is that leaders who are trusted by their employees bring out the best in those employees, including great performance and high employee satisfaction. [cxlvi]

The most important asset of most companies is their people. To deliver great performances, those people must be inspired and led. As a director, you understand that great shareholder return is directly correlated with great performance. Moreover, given the increasing scrutiny on corporations, the leaders are more than ever required to do so with a style and values that are aligned with the shareholder and customer expectations. You should expect the company's senior leaders to be role models for the company.

To achieve role-model performance by the CEO and the senior leadership team, the board must hire a great CEO who understands and values the practice of great leadership. The board must inspect the senior leadership team to see if they understand the difference between good management and great leadership and are leading accordingly. Great leaders always create advantages for the company in their pursuit of outstanding results. The board should observe the company to determine whether senior leaders are exhibiting role-model behavior and performance. A review of leadership should be a major segment of the board's review process. The board should monitor leadership performance like they monitor other key measurements of the company's performance. What gets measured gets done.

Of course, the board of directors should pay the CEO for demonstrating the model behavior that is so essential to building a model company that enhances shareholder value. Make leadership a major component of the CEO's compensation plan.

Last, the board should demonstrate their personal commitment to X-Leadership by practicing what they preach: The company's directors should be role models for the company too.

Professionals and Specialists: Lead in Your Field

Leaders are not necessarily managers. Managers direct. Leaders guide. Even if you are not a manager in your company, but someone who contributes essential professional skills to the company's success, you can make yourself more valuable to your co-workers and your company by becoming a role-model to your peers. Of course, doing so will provide you with yet another asset on which to build your career.

The best place to learn how to be a great role model is in a company where leadership is practiced to the maximum extent. If you are lucky enough (or smart enough) to work in a company led by an X-leader, emulate that leader's behavior. Great leaders make the best corporate role models because they know what kinds of behaviors cause great results. Of course, those great results will provide you and your co-workers with more and better opportunities for long-term career advancement.

In an X-led company, if your colleagues regard you as a good role model and an effective leader, they will be more likely to support your efforts and your career aspirations. If your supervisor thinks that you demonstrate a capacity for leadership and want to lead, he or she will be more willing to increase your responsibilities and help you advance your career because; in X-led companies, supervisors considered to be people developers are more likely to be promoted. (Interestingly, promotions for supervisors mean promotional opportunities for their subordinates!) If your supervisor's leaders are X-Leaders, your supervisor will have their support in investing in your personal development and giving you chances to develop and demonstrate your skills.

To become a great role model, you must learn everything you can about the principles of X-Leadership. It is worth investing time, money, and effort to build an effective working relationship with someone who can help you become a great leader. Find a highly effective leader to mentor you, either inside or outside your company. Establish a candid relationship with that person.

Always be on the lookout for new opportunities to learn and contribute. Inform your supervisor that you are willing to invest the time and energy required to become a great leader. If you succeed in encouraging your supervisor to help you gain

Leadership should be a core competency in your company, not just a program of the month, or a slogan posted on the wall.

leadership knowledge and experience, you will generate tremendous personal opportunities. Provide carefully considered, helpful feedback to your supervisor to help improve his or her effectiveness in leading you. Both positive and negative feedback can be useful, but you must provide your feedback in a professional, non-threatening manner. Be careful! As discussed earlier, some

229

supervisors do not appreciate any kind of feedback from their employees, let alone negative feedback! Quietly investigating whether your supervisor is likely to be willing to accept feedback from you definitely is worth doing. You might discover that your supervisor is averse to feedback from subordinates, but you might discover that your supervisor is a confident leader who enjoys feedback and is eager to improve his or her leadership skills. The better prepared your supervisor is to lead you, the better your chances of advancement in the company.

Let it be known throughout your company that you want to learn how to become a great leader, and that you understand the difference between good management and great leadership. Let it be known that you desire to manage and to lead. Aim to work in an environment where good management is considered merely acceptable performance and great leadership is always expected.

Whenever you observe someone demonstrating great leadership practices, emulate those practices. Don't be afraid to imitate positive behavior or experiences that you found valuable. Look for opportunities to set a good example. As you learn role-model behaviors and performance skills, you will be selected with increasing frequency to participate in leading-edge development projects and committee assignments. Seek to become a spokesperson for your profession or your discipline. Develop a role in the industry to demonstrate your leadership. Strive to make your leadership capabilities the benchmark from which all of your contemporaries are compared.

Corporate Customers:
Use Model Behavior to Enhance Your Company's Value

There are a number of good reasons why your company should choose to partner with strategic suppliers that practice X-Leadership, but one of the most compelling is that partnering with a supplier known for model behavior and performance will substantially enhance your company's reputation and value. I know from experience that, when I was working for IBM, many of my customers were as proud of being my partner as I was of being their supplier. Model behavior and performance is what they expected, and model behavior and performance is exactly what they got.

If your company expects your strategic suppliers to adopt model behavior, you should do the same. When customers treat their suppliers like valued partners, they are very likely to receive great performance in return. You should be teaching your suppliers and, at the same time, learning from them. Teach your suppliers by telling them exactly what you expect. Don't be afraid to ask them to align their performance with your expectations. Learn from them by practicing the leadership qualities that you expect from them. Both customer and supplier should encourage each other to walk the talk. Reward your model suppliers with most of your business, and always be willing to discontinue your relationships with companies that don't live up to your expectations. Work with people and companies who want to share the excitement and rewards of producing the best products and services.

X-Leaders are much more than what most people expect them to be: They are what many people dream of being. They are the role models for their companies and their industry.

Four Steps to Becoming a Model Leader

1. Conduct a personal assessment. Define the personal and professional behaviors that are aligned with your values. Review your corporation's code of conduct.

2. Observe. Study the personal and professional behaviors of individuals in your company and industry that you deem to be successful.

3. Emulate. If successful people in your corporation demonstrate personal and professional behavior that is consistent with your values, emulate them.

4. Change. If successful people in your corporation demonstrate personal and professional behavior that is inconsistent with your values and is unacceptable to you, become an agent of change. If you do not believe you can change your company, then you should change ... to a new company.

Endnotes

cxli Rich, G. A. (1997). The sales manager as a role model: Effects on trust, job satisfaction, and performance of salespeople. *Journal of Academy of Marketing Science*, 25(4), 319-328.

cxlii Hermalin, B. E. (1998). Toward an Economic Theory of Leadership: Leading by Example. *American Economic Review*, 88, 1188-1206.

cxliii Hermalin, 1998, Toward an Economic Theory; Stata, 1989, Spring, Organizational learning; Rich, 1997, The sales manager as a role model.

cxliv Rich, 1997, The sales manager as a role model.

cxlv See Stata, 1989, Spring, Organizational learning; also Senge, P. M. (1990, Spring). The leader's new work; Building learning organizations. *Sloan Management Review*, 32(1), 7-23.

cxlvi Rich, 1997, The sales manager as a role model.

CHAPTER 12

Summary

X-Leadership is about individuals taking bold initiatives to manage their activities and behaviors in a manner that significantly enhances career advancement and company value. People who follow the X-Leadership Principles discussed in this book certainly will create substantially broader career opportunities for themselves, and deliver exceptional results to their companies.

Clearly, X-Leadership is a concept that can only be achieved by those who are enlightened enough to see its long-term value. If you wish to become an X-Leader, you must recognize that X-Leadership provides the only sustainable method of winning. X-Leadership cannot provide a quick fix for a career that has been inadequately prepared by a poorly motivated person, or easy answers for a business that is in trouble.

X-Leadership is a complex concept based on a simple design. Although accepting the merits of X-Leadership is relatively easy, effectively implementing X-Leadership principles simultaneously, is not.

Aspiring X-Leaders: Plan Your Route to the Summit

X-Leadership cannot fix a career that is in shambles. Practicing X-Leadership requires long-term dedication and a passion to succeed. X-Leadership cannot be practiced by anyone unwilling to commit substantial time, effort, and energy to advancing his or her career. However, if you follow the X-Principles thoughtfully and passionately, you will produce phenomenal results and will significantly advance your career.

You can and should enlist the aid of your company's human resources department as you execute your plan to become a powerful X-Leader at the top of your corporation. Human resource specialists cannot answer all of your questions, but they are likely to be very helpful. Nevertheless, it will be your responsibility to plan your route to the summit.

Senior Leaders: Implement the X-Principles in Any Situation

Embedding the concept of X-Leadership into your corporation's environment will increase shareholder value, but it is not an easy task. This effort will require a significant commitment from you and the other members of your senior leadership team. You must be willing to invest the time needed to study the principles of X-Leadership discussed in this book, implement them with passion, and consistently practice them. If your company's employees suspect that you are insincere in your support of X-Leadership, your company could suffer long-term damage. Likewise, if your board of directors and shareowners regard you as an ineffective leader, your career will suffer.

Most people are motivated to aim for higher levels of performance by their thirst for recognition, reward, and the satisfaction they receive for doing great things. The principles of X-Leadership can be implemented in almost any situation to help create an environment that encourages high performance.

Although X-Leadership will work in almost any situation, it cannot be practiced by every person. Successfully following the principles of X-Leadership is possible only for people who are committed to lead and who are eager to take on more responsibility. Practicing X-Leadership is not for people who are quite content to be led.

If you are interested in accelerating your career advancement, practicing the X-Leadership Principles in earnest will complement your other efforts to achieve more. To be successful in X-Leadership, you must develop the skills needed to communicate and to deploy resources effectively. If you follow the principles outlined in this book, you will improve your overall ability to develop yourself and lead the rest of your company.

Corporate Directors:
Establish a Link Between Governing and Leading

It is not difficult for corporate directors to affect a company's leadership. The most effective way for you to impact leadership initiatives is to practice the principles of X-Leadership. In my opinion, enlightened corporate governance and X-Leadership are a perfect match.

I am sure that most corporate directors will be able to align themselves intellectually with the principles of X-Leadership, but aligning themselves emotionally may be more difficult. Leading a company's development process requires establishing a passionate link between governing and leading. You and your fellow directors must desire to lead, not inspect. Not surprisingly, if the board on which you serve allocates significantly more time to supporting corporate leadership development, you and your fellow directors will be required to spend less time inspecting the day-to-day operations of the company.

Corporate directors should be leadership role models for the company they serve. Obviously, implementing the principles of X-Leadership is a major undertaking that might seem daunting. Nonetheless, the board of directors holds primary responsibility for ensuring that the company's leadership delivers value to the shareowners, which is undoubtedly a daunting task. However, you and your fellow directors should not allow the inevitable frustrations of governance to discourage you from pursuing the values of X-Leadership. A board of directors must work with the company's senior leadership team to maintain a steadfast focus on leadership development.

Professionals and Specialists: Take the Lead

People who contribute specialized services to the company, such as accounting, administration, engineering, sales, or marketing, typically have much less control than their company's senior leaders and directors and, at times, they even have less control than their customers. With little control to exercise, they are likely to encounter the most difficulty implementing the principles of X-Leadership. However, they also have the most to gain from the experience.

If you are a professional working in a company, developing X-Leadership should be your top priority. Following the principles of X-Leadership will maximize your personal contributions to your company and your benefit from making those contributions. Before you begin to use X-Principles, however, you need to assess your working environment to determine whether it is a safe place to pursue X-Leadership. Most companies will be energized by your efforts to take on more leadership within the company, but some companies will only tolerate those efforts, not support them, and a few companies will summarily dismiss the idea of an in-house professional engaging in any company leadership activities.

In situations where a supportive leadership team practices the principles of X-Leadership, a specialist like yourself can substantially improve your professional effectiveness, and obviously advance your career, too. In such an environment, if you effectively practice the principles of X-Leadership outlined in this book, you will move more easily from your current status into a leadership role. Take the lead and become a role model for your company.

Corporate Customers: Get Substantial Improvement From Your Strategic Suppliers

Corporate customers who practice X-Leadership allocate significant time to building strong, long-lasting relationships with the senior leaders of their strategic suppliers. They invest time in educating their suppliers and learning from them. If your company takes the road to X-Leadership, you will see substantial improvement in the overall quality of the products and services delivered by your strategic suppliers.

When your company sets high expectations for your strategic suppliers, some of them may be unable or unwilling to do what it takes to meet those expectations. In that case, you may need to replace those suppliers with capable business partners who share your expectations and are willing to develop higher levels of performance. If the relationship is worth repairing, it might be a good idea for your company to act as an X-Principle role model for that supplier.

Are You Ready?

Genuine leadership development is self-directed. Whether you are a senior leader, a corporate director, a specialist working in a corporation, or a corporate customer, you should carefully assess whether you are prepared to pursue the principles of X-Leadership. The road to X-Leadership is paved with golden opportunities and flowered with special rewards all along the way, but the journey is fraught with some very rigorous challenges and requirements.

To succeed in following the X-Principles, you must be extremely motivated. Although you would not have achieved your current status without substantial commitment and dedication, you will find that following the X-Principles will challenge even the most highly motivated individual. Leading significant change will require you to maintain a burning desire to make a difference in your company and

> **Although accepting the merits of X-Leadership is relatively easy, effectively implementing X-Leadership principles simultaneously, is not.**

to develop exceptional boldness and confidence in your pursuit of excellence, while at the same time earning the praise and support of your colleagues. You will need enough internal fortitude and intellectual honesty to appraise your own performance, acknowledge your own weaknesses, and build on your own strengths. You must be willing to accept change. You must make pursuing your career an integral part of your lifestyle. To implement the 11 X-Principles outlined in this book, you must have a sharp focus on each of them.

Pursuing X-Leadership is so taxing that you will find it difficult to maintain a balance between your career goals and your family goals. Early on in the process of achieving X-Leadership, you must learn how to integrate the two.

Your personal goals and your family goals cannot survive without each other in the long term.

The major test of your capability of pursing X-Leadership is whether you can be objective enough to match the Principles with your own needs. Believing that you are aligned with the principles of X-Leadership is one thing, but committing to practicing these principles is another. X-Leadership requires taking chances every day and making bold moves often. Answer honestly: Are you willing to risk taking on the ever-increasing levels of responsibility demanded by X-Leadership?

If you are willing to take on heavy burdens of responsibility, you must next assess how effective you are likely to be at implementing X-Leadership in your company. Reaching this assessment is a process that will require you to spend time understanding the implications of your efforts. You should scan your company to see whether it will tolerate an enlightened contributor such as yourself. You might discover that your company as a whole is unwilling to tolerate X-Leadership, or that the chairman of the board may want to implement it, but not the senior manager, or vice versa.

If you conclude that your efforts ultimately can be successful, but you nonetheless encounter negative views of your pursuit of X-Leadership among your managers, peers, and customers, you must tolerate these negative views. And, of course, you must continue to deliver outstanding performance in your current role to earn the right to pursue X-Leadership.

Make bold moves. I guarantee that you will start to receive immediate feedback and, most likely, immediate payback. Be willing to ignite the company, improve your productivity, and be willing to stick with it for the long haul.

Select a few X-Principles that fit your current situation and pursue those. Although you eventually will need to integrate all of the X-Principles into your leadership, you do not have to master all 11 principles at once. Don't procrastinate. Start now. Get on the path of fulfilling your long-held dream of becoming the best that you can be. If you truly want to be a great leader, then start building your leadership skills today. Learn. Practice. Take charge.

CHAPTER 13

Conclusion

I wrote *Corporate Rise* to share my views on the subject of extreme personal leadership, what I call X-Leadership. It was my intention to outline the leadership principles that I have practiced throughout my career.

These X-Principles have proven to be very effective. Each one is strongly grounded in my own practical experience, and a number of them have been substantiated by scholarly research and supported by other leadership practitioners.

Some readers will be able to adapt these principles to their situations quickly, whereas other readers will have difficulty aligning their current environments with them. Some readers, of course, will not even attempt to implement these principles, either because they don't believe they will work, or because they use other strategies that seem more appropriate for their situations. Whatever leadership approach you currently use, I believe that attempting to implement these X-Principles will enhance your chances of continuing on the path of success. These principles work! They have worked for me and they will work for you.

I encourage you to read as much as you can about the practice of leadership. It is enormously important that leaders find some set of guiding principles that inspire and encourage them to do their best. Of course, I am confident that if you compare my principles of X-Leadership with any other programs or concepts that you choose, you will value mine!

I have advised you over and over again in these chapters to be fearless in your pursuit of excellence. If you want to make it to the top, there are more opportunities than you can imagine! Sadly, there are more opportunities to win through passion, planning, and performance than there are people who have the courage and willingness to get in the game and stay in the game.

You won't be able to wish your way to the top of the corporate ladder, although you might get lucky enough to be advanced to the top without practicing X-Leadership. Nevertheless, your chances of getting to the top will be enhanced substantially if you implement the X-Principles discussed in this book.

Share the thoughts and principles in *Corporate Rise* with your colleagues and friends. Challenge them to tell you why they believe these principles will or won't work for you or for them. Engage them in the process of assessing whether you believe yourself to have the courage, the interest, and the passion to become an X-Leader.

If you are a person with high aspirations, the principles of X-Leadership were designed specifically for you! I wrote *Corporate Rise* to help high achievers think through what is most important to them. I trust that you will come back to this book from time to time and reflect on each principle for inspiration to continue your pursuit of greatness.

These X-Principles are not designed for everyone. Some people are not prepared to make the commitment and sacrifices necessary to achieve a high level of responsibility in business. This should be expected, especially considering that there is room for only a few at the very top of the corporate world. Those few come from the very small group willing to do what is necessary to make it to the top.

Interestingly, though, the farther up the ladder you climb, the greater your chances of continuing in your ascent because, as you approach the apex of your climb, the competition, while more intense, takes place among a smaller and smaller group of competitors. If you believe you have a true calling to leadership, take heart! Establish a plan and execute it.

Remember that X-Leadership cannot and will not be accomplished by any person working alone. You must establish partnerships with your colleagues to earn opportunities to pursue your X-Leadership goals. Your pursuit must be constructive and your approach compassionate. These characteristics will encourage others to support you on your way to the top, and to follow you once you get there.

So gather your passion, your energy, and your courage. Prepare yourself for the journey! Always remember that preparation is the key to success! Without preparation, you will lack knowledge. Without knowledge, you will lack power. Without power, you will lack a base from which to compete. Build a solid foundation. Go for the gold, and I will look for you at the top!

Three Myths to Reject

Myth #1: It's never too late.

It is always later than you think! Act with a sense of urgency. Remember, it is your career, and you are the only one who really cares about it. You don't have time for wasted motion! No matter how good you are or how hard you work, you will have great difficulty trying to make up for lost time.

Myth #2: It's better to be lucky than good.

Luck is a random occurrence, but preparation is the key to success. Being lucky always will be helpful, but you should not leave your career to chance!

Myth #3: Winning isn't everything!

Of course you shouldn't attempt to win at any cost! However, you must remain mindful that, in corporate America, consistent winning is the only thing that counts!

CHAPTER 14

The X-Principles at a Glance

I have always believed in the pursuit of excellence. My belief that success is the result of hard work and outstanding preparation has continually reinforced my confidence. The harder I work, the better prepared I am for the task at hand. The better prepared I am, the better results I produce.

The X-Principles I have set forth in *Corporate Rise* are grounded in world-class practical experience. I developed this set of personal leadership principles over a period of 30 years, and they have guided my leadership approach in very large global companies, as well as in small start-up companies. They have consistently produced outstanding results for me and the companies I have led. On the surface, these principles may seem deceptively simple, but deploying them—simultaneously and effectively—requires knowledge and passion.

This section is provided as a reference tool. It will assist in your *extreme personal leadership* development and implementation program. Use this segment regularly and it will serve as a constant refresher for you! Reference it frequently to measure and monitor your progress toward success! Below, each *X-Principle* is summarized for quick review. (The X-Principles at a Glance are also available at corporaterise.com).

X-Principle One

X-Leaders have a passion for developing people. They are in constant pursuit of every employee's success. X-Leaders do not declare total victory until all the people around them have succeeded.

What are the features of a corporate environment in which people are constantly being developed?
- People are measured by the greatness of their accomplishments, not by the number of hours they work on a given day, or to whom they report.
- Employees develop an insatiable appetite for learning.
- The corporate environment is not politically charged because leaders are truly passionate about developing all of the people around them.
- Work has become a pleasant experience, and people really enjoy being in the workplace. They can't wait to get to work in the morning to contribute to the company's success!
- Although competitors are constantly recruiting the company's best people, the company has a very low involuntary attrition rate.
- People's personal development and the company's business development are inextricably linked.

Why does the leader constantly pursue everyone's success?
- The workforce is retained.
- Increased individual performance translates into superior collective performance.
- The broadest set of talents available in the marketplace are recruited.
- Politics are replaced by performance.

How does the company help everyone in the company succeed?
- Senior leaders determine how much money is currently invested in people development, then ...
- Senior leaders create a budgetary formula, based on annual revenue, for establishing the company's planned people-development investment. This formula is similar to the one used when establishing the expense percentage used for product development.

- Senior leaders track people-development performance in the same way that they track other major categories in the budget.
- Senior leaders establish an appropriate correlation between people-development investments and the company's bottom-line performance.
- The board of directors measures management's people-development performance and holds managers more accountable for achieving people-development objectives than other objectives, including product-development and revenue objectives.
- Every person in the company follows a personal development plan that has been jointly created by that person and his or her immediate supervisor.
- Senior leaders establish a personal development day that each employee uses every quarter.
- The results of frequent employee-opinion surveys are shared with the entire company and used to inform a company-wide action plan.
- Leaders develop a comprehensive coaching program and an appropriate mentoring program.

X-Principle Two

X-Leaders find imaginative ways to inspire people to transform themselves for the better. They motivate themselves and others to reach higher levels of performance by linking great ideas to exhilarating images of success.

What happens when the leader inspires people to transform themselves for the better?
- People who make mistakes admit them and correct them.
- The pace of conversations, meetings, interactions, and even foot traffic seems much faster and more kinetic than in most business environments.
- The company develops more intellectual property (patents, know-how, technology, copyrights) than its top-performing competitors.
- The company is perpetually reinventing itself.
- The company's leader is viewed as the industry spokesperson.
- The company regularly receives awards for new products or service designs.

247

Why do X-Leaders motivate themselves and others to reach higher levels of performance?

- People want to share their ideas in an environment that encourages, not rejects, radical thinking.
- Many a great idea has emanated from a litany of bad ideas.
- Companies face greater difficulties differentiating themselves from their competition.
- Increasing demand for the company's products and services raises shareholder value.

How do X-Leaders link great ideas to visions of success?

- People's courage in bringing new ideas to the table is acknowledged and rewarded.
- Brainstorming sessions are made a regular part of each workday.
- Leaders take bets on a few long shots (low-odds opportunities).
- Scenario-planning is made an integral part of the planning process.
- Leaders who are not great communicators seek help from colleagues and consultants to learn better communication skills.
- Leaders and subordinates are expected to work at the limits of boundaries that are way out of their comfort zones.

X-Principle Three

X-Leaders cultivate creativity by looking at common things in uncommon ways. They expose old issues to new options and develop fresh approaches to long-standing problems.

What happens when X-Leaders expose old issues to new options?

- People acquire the boldness to stop the CEO in the hallway to tell him/her about great new ideas the company should be developing, and they develop the audacity to follow up with the CEO if they do not see the idea being addressed.
- People constantly develop innovations that surprise the company, most often in a pleasant way.

- Taking inventions to higher levels (innovation) becomes a core competency of the company.

Why do X-Leaders promote looking at common things in uncommon ways?
- The best and the brightest want to join companies that give them the freedom to use the full spectrum of their abilities to break new ground.
- Competition is based on available knowledge, which is being exchanged at an exponentially increasing rate. Differentiation therefore is difficult to maintain, dictating the ever-present need for innovation.
- The basic needs and wants of most customers already are being met by existing products and services. It requires creativity to address those needs and wants in different ways.
- Road maps to new products provide guidance and confidence to the investment community and all stakeholders.

How does the company develop fresh approaches to old problems?
- People receive rewards and recognition for developing new products and services.
- Every product and every procedure is viewed as a work in progress and subject to continual improvement. Good is not considered good enough; the expectation is for greatness!
- What already exists is not allowed to get into the way of what could exist.
- Suggestions gathered through a company-wide suggestion program are used as progress points as the suggestions are addressed.
- A minimum of 10% of the non-management workday, 20% of a manager's workday and 30% of an executive's workday is spent in developing innovations in products, services, or procedures. Innovation goals are included in the employee's personal performance plan and adherence to that plan is reflected in the employee's performance appraisal.
- Creativity workshops are offered to all employees.

X-Principle Four

X-Leaders are customer-centric; they realize that unless someone buys something from their company, everything they do is totally irrelevant.

What are the features of a customer-centric company?
- The company has a majority share of customers' business.
- The company is consistently gaining share from competitors, who are already behind the company.
- Through frequent business interactions, customers actively seek the company's counsel and advice about their strategic plans.
- The company and its customer-partners desire the same results.

Why does the X-Leader insist on customer-centric behavior?
- Product differentiation isn't enough for consistent revenue generation.
- Customers rarely do business with people they don't like and trust.
- Generally, customers understand their markets better than their suppliers.
- Many customers will choose to do business with suppliers they think value and appreciate them more than other suppliers.
- Customers are the only partners that actually bring revenue to the company.

How does the company achieve customer-centricity?
- Every meeting starts with a focus on the customer.
- A documented sales plan is developed for every major customer and sales channel.
- A corporate customer-relationship manager is appointed to build on the idea of sharing expectations with the customer.
- The company has numerous customer contacts with people throughout the customers' company.
- Because a company's tone is set at the top, a CEO partnership program connects the company to its strategic customers.
- The company asks customers to fill out report cards on the company's activities. Leaders and employees throughout the company establish "listening posts" in customer companies that channel information back into the company.

- The company's design and sales goals are audacious.
- Creativity is used to make customers into industry heroes.
- Leaders clearly articulate to customers how much of their business the company expects to earn.
- A training engine is built to drive customer-centricity throughout the company.

X-Principle Five

X-Leaders are visionaries who anticipate the future and identify marketplace opportunities before they become trends. X-Leaders often know what customers will need before the customers do.

What happens to company's that anticipate marketplace opportunities?
- The company becomes the benchmark to which all others are compared.
- Many of its leaders become industry luminaries whose opinions about market direction are sought by analysts.
- The company spawns entrepreneurs.
- The company's strategic intent forms the basis of competitors' plans.

Why do X-Leaders work to anticipate future trends?
- Customers' lead-time for product development is continually getting shorter.
- Visionaries prevail; followers endure.
- It is important to be the first to introduce new consumer-technology products, because 60% of gross margins in this area are earned in the first six months after introduction.
- Enlightened customers expect customer-centric service.
- People want to work for leading-edge companies.

How does the company know what customers will want before the customers do?
- The company requires its people to acquire knowledge about the industry, marketplace, technology, and trends.
- Leaders create opportunities for people to gain that knowledge.

- The CEO champions the process of predicting future events.
- Defining the future is made part of everyone's job.
- Relationships and partnerships with appropriate stakeholders are forged to collaboratively generate ideas about the future.

X-Principle Six

X-Leaders drive their companies with decisions grounded in facts. They insist on exchanging information with all employees and customers, and they seek opportunities to tell the truth.

What happens when the X-Leader seeks the truth?
- Employees and customers feel free to constructively question the why, where, how, when, and what of every circumstance and decision.
- Real issues are fully exposed and explored. The "moose" is put on the table.
- Specificity, not vagueness, is the hallmark of all answers.
- Every employee and customer immediately challenges false rumors.
- Employees and customers feel confident in the company and themselves because they believe they are fully informed and aligned with the company's leadership.

Why do X-Leaders drive their companies with decisions grounded in facts?
- Customers value relationships built on openness and honesty.
- Customers are more likely to share the direction of their company with suppliers who do the same.
- Knowledgeable employees feel more empowered, which results in higher levels of performance.
- A company that is intolerant of rumors and innuendoes is a more productive company.
- Customers and employees who lack information will fill in the blanks with conjecture and rumor.
- Companies and people that don't over-communicate tend to under-communicate.

How does the company communicate factual information to guide employees and customers?

- The company invests in a strong information technology (IT) system.
- The entire company uses a common set of information and communication platforms.
- Senior leaders openly discuss the current status of the business at frequent, regularly scheduled employee communications meetings.
- The CEO and senior leaders establish open-door communications.
- A CEO (Chief's Eyes Only) e-mail program solicits suggestions from employees. These suggestions are accessed by the CEO and no one else.
- Senior leaders frequently visit all locations of the company.
- Senior leaders frequently visit all strategic customers.
- Senior leaders establish peer-to-peer relationships with their counterparts in strategic customer companies.
- The company and its strategic customers conduct annual CEO-to-CEO performance and expectation reviews.
- Leaders and customer contact people listen well because most customers provide all the clues needed to sell to them.

X-Principle Seven

X-Leaders have confidence in the abilities of their people. Because X-Leaders are willing to delegate broad responsibilities, they are vulnerable, and they know it.

What happens when the X-Leader feels confidence in the company's people?

- Employees take ownership in the company's performance and share accountability for that performance.
- Speed characterizes the decision-making process.
- Employees experience the joy of making good decisions and the pain of making wrong decisions, which aligns their behaviors to the company's best interests.
- Employees seek the CEO's or senior management's input for ideas or suggestions more often than for direction or decisions.

Why do X-Leaders delegate broad responsibility throughout the company?
- Employees are energized when authority is delegated broadly and aligned with responsibility and accountability.
- Senior leaders do not have the time, knowledge, or information to make all key decisions required by the company.
- Better decisions are made when senior leaders recognize the value of soliciting input from the employees most familiar with the issues under discussion.
- Decision-making authority is shared with people who understand cultural imperatives at play within and outside the company.

How does the company accomplish shared responsibility?
- The company recruits a heterogeneous group of managers.
- The ability of each senior leader to delegate authority is appraised by the CEO; other leaders and managers are similarly appraised.
- Each level of management clearly understands which decisions they are responsible for.
- When managers disagree with decisions reached by their subordinates, they constructively challenge those decisions.
- Vision, mission, and value statements guide the decision-making process throughout the company.

X-Principle Eight

X-Leaders convert the energy generated by chaos into better decisions.
To avoid precipitating premature closure on major issues, they sometimes conceal their own opinions until other people have had their say.

What happens when the X-Leader encourages thorough problem-solving?
- Debate and constructive engagement are the norm.
- Thorough discussion is considered to be as important as finality in the decision process.
- Employees' ideas and thoughts are plentiful, and inappropriate potential solutions usually can be discarded without offense to employees.
- Meeting agendas change frequently, and discussions and reviews take longer.

- Problem-solving sessions typically are exhausting, but exhilarating and successful.

Why do senior leaders encourage people to participate in decision-making?
- Great ideas require nurturing by collaborative thinking.
- Many people do not recognize their ability to contribute ideas and thoughts until they are involved in an iterative thinking process with others.
- Most of the time there is more than one right answer.
- It is important not to allow the process to become more important than the ideas you are trying to generate.
- Creating chaos helps to redefine boundaries for people's thinking.

How does the company help people generate ideas and solve problems?
- Regularly scheduled meetings are held at all levels of the company.
- The issues to be resolved are defined for every meeting or discussion.
- Problem-solvers clearly understand how much time they have to make the decision.
- All of the decision participants actively engage in the discussion and decision-making process.
- Some humor in the discussion keeps the creativity level high.
- The group leader offers more questions than answers.
- All ideas and suggestions are explored thoroughly, but the people offering ideas are not attacked.
- Problem-solvers stay focused on the issue and do not allow chaos and lack of structure to obviate the need for speed. Group leaders bring tangential thinking back to the issue at hand.

X-Principle Nine

X-Leaders believe that the company comes first, and they insist on teamwork. They do not tolerate divisional or functional departmental boundaries in the corporate culture.

What happens when the people act like the company comes first?
- Resources are aligned with corporate business needs.

- Employees refer to the company as we instead of they.
- The company's name is used in most employee and customer discussions.
- People voluntarily share resources in pursuit of common goals.
- When divisional or company issues arise, there is an immediate tendency to examine them in light of broader corporate perspectives before taking action.
- Individual, departmental, or divisional successes are highly valued, but are always secondary to the overall success of the company.
- Customers view the company as easy to do business with.

Why do X-Leaders insist on teamwork?
- Productivity is maximized.
- Overall operating costs are reduced.
- Political bastions are weakened.
- People's desire and willingness to share information increases.

How does the company foster teamwork?
- A minimum of 50% of senior leaders' compensation is tied to the company's success.
- Senior leaders share company goals, plans, activities, and results with everyone in the company.
- The CEO clearly articulates how he or she expects the company to act as a team.
- The company exhibits zero tolerance for breaches of trust and dishonest or unethical activities, and issues immediate public responses directed to the appropriate employee or department.
- Global employee communications meetings are the norm, not the exception.
- Senior leaders frequently visit all locations of the company.

X-Principle Ten

X-Leaders expect greatness. They are results-oriented, honest, and personally accountable.

What happens when X-Leaders expect greatness of their company?
- Excellence is considered the standard, and people are surprised by failures.
- The company's results set the benchmark for the industry.
- The company's people readily acknowledge their strengths and weaknesses.
- As a result of the company's outstanding products and services, the company's customers maintain leadership in their own industries.
- Employees' salaries rise to the top quartile of all salaries in their profession.
- The results of employee satisfaction surveys continually exceed the norms of high performance companies.
- The results of the company's customer satisfaction surveys consistently far exceed those of the company's competitors.
- Without the need for management direction, all successes and failures are analyzed, and the results of these analyses are shared appropriately throughout the company.

Why are X-Leaders results-oriented, honest, and accountable?
- Great performance normally follows great expectations.
- Honesty drives out fear of the unknown and creates a more confident, aggressive company.
- For people who are personally accountable, fear of failure is one of the strongest motivators.
- Direct, honest feedback on the value of each employee's contributions provides road maps for individual and corporate success.
- Great talent often is attracted to great companies.

How does the company encourage honesty and accountability?
- Senior leaders define the company's goals, document the company's performance results, and distribute both to everyone in the company.
- The company is audacious in its expectations.
- Benchmarking becomes a standard method of evaluating the performance of the company.
- "Best practices" and "lessons learned" communications distribute needed information throughout the company.

- Leaders attempt to minimizing waste and downtime by idiot-proofing operations and processes.
- The company refuses to compromise quality.
- The company does not design beyond the point of value.
- Board members link employees' compensation directly to the company's performance.

X-Principle Eleven

X-Leaders are role models. They lead by example.

What happens when X-Leaders set a highly visible example for the company?

- Appropriate behavior for most situations is highly evident throughout the company.
- A winning attitude permeates the corporate culture.
- Customers emulate many of the characteristics of senior leaders.
- Employees are extremely loyal to the company.
- The investment community references the company's leadership in its business or industry analyses.
- The board of directors includes highly respected leaders in their industries.

Why do X-Leaders become role models?

- Great people want to work for great people.
- People produce more for great leaders.
- Customers want to do business with great leaders.
- The investment community rewards great leadership with higher valuations.

How does the company produce role models?

- The company hires the best people.
- The company makes huge investments in training and developing employees.
- The company sets high expectations.
- The company tolerates mistakes and learns from them.

258

- Each employee has a personal development plan that emphasizes individual leadership responsibility.
- Senior leaders are assisted by a leadership coach.
- Leaders' compensation is tied, in part, to leadership success.
- Leadership is treated as a separate discipline.
- Leadership is regarded as a core competency.
- Leadership development is viewed as a shared management responsibility, not solely a human resources responsibility.

Bibliography

Albrecht, K. (1983). *Organizational development: A total systems approach to a positive change in any business organization*. New Jersey: Prentice Hall.

Amabile, T. M. (1988). A model of creativity and innovation in organizations. In L. L. Cummings and B. M. Staw (Eds.), *Research in Organizational Behavior*, 10, 123-167.

Amabile, T. M. (1993). Motivational synergy: Toward new conceptualizations of intrinsic and extrinsic motivation in the workforce. *Human Resource Management Review*, 3, 185-201.

Annison, M. H., & Wilford, D. S. (1998). *Trust matters: New directions in health care leadership*. San Francisco: Jossey-Bass.

Baker, M. (1999). GWEC: A white paper. *The Global Wireless Education Consortium overview document*. Retrieved April 27, 2004, from the GWEC Web site at http://www.gwec.org/about4.cfm

Bandura, A. (1977). *Social learning theory*. Englewood Cliffs, New Jersey: Prentice Hall.

Basadur, M. (1964). Organizational development interventions for enhancing creativity in the workplace. [Working Paper #43]. Available from Management of Innovation and New Technology (MINT) Research Centre, Michael G. DeGroote School of Business, McMaster University, Ontario, Canada.

Bass, B. M., & Avolio, B. J. (1990). *The implications of transactional and transformational leadership for individuals, teams, and organizational development.* Greenwich: JAI Press.

Bassi, L. J. et al. (1997). *Position Yourself for the Future: The Top Ten Trends.* Alexandria, VA: American Society for Training and Development.

Bassi, L. J. & Van Buren, M. E. (1998). The 1998 ASTD State of the Industry Report. *Training and Development,* 52(1), January, 21-43.

Bennis, W., & Beiderman, P. I. (1997). *Organizing genius: The secrets of creative collaboration.* Boston: Addison-Wesley.

Biberman, G. (1985). Personality and characteristic work attitudes of persons with high, moderate, and low political tendencies. *Psychological Reports,* 57, 1303-1310.

Buderi, R. (2004, May). Reinventing Invention. *TechnologyReview.com* [Online serial]. Retrieved April 9, 2005, from http://www.technologyreview.com/articles/04/05/leading0504.asp?p=1

Burns, J. M. (1978). *Leadership,* p. 226. New York: Harper & Row.

Burns, J. S. (2002). Chaos theory and leadership studies: Exploring uncharted seas. *Journal of Leadership and Organizational Studies,* 9, Part 2.

Cambel, A. B. (1993). *Applied chaos theory: A paradigm for complexity.* San Diego, CA: Academic.

Carnevale, Anthony P. (1991). *America and the New Economy*. San Francisco, CA: Jossey-Bass.

Carrol, T., & Burton, R. M. (2000). Organizations and complexity: Searching for the edge of chaos. *Computational and Mathematical Organizational Theory*, 6, 319-337.

Chartier, C. T. (1998). *Strategic leadership: Product and technology innovation in high-technology companies*. Unpublished doctoral dissertation, Alliant International University.

Colvin, G., & Selden, L. (2002, November). Profitable customers: Organizing your company around them. Discussion conducted at the meeting of the Fortune Global Forum, The Power of Leadership: Mastering the New Realities, Washington, DC.

Connell, J., Ferres, N., Travaglione, T. (2003). Engendering trust in manager-subordinate relationships: Predictors and outcomes. *Personnel Review*, 32(5), 569-587.

Csikszentmihalyi, M. (1996). Creativity: *Flow and the psychology of discovery and invention*. New York: HarperCollins.

Cunningham, J. B., & MacGregor, J. (2000). Trust and the design of work: Complementary constructs in satisfaction. *Human Relations*, 53, 1575-1591.

Dauphinais, G. W., & Price, C. (1999). *Straight from the CEO: The world's top business leaders reveal ideas that every manager can use*. New York: Simon & Schuster.

Davidson, P. & Griffin, R. W. (2000). *Management: Australia in a global context*. Brisbane, Australia: Wiley.

De Dreu, C. K. W., & Van de Vliert, E. (Eds.). (1997). *Using conflict in organizations*. London: Sage.

Eisenhardt, K. M., & Bourgeois, L. J., III. (1988). Politics of strategic decision making in high-velocity environments. *Academy of Management Journal*, 31(4), 737-770.

Eylon, D. (1998). Understanding empowerment and resolving its paradox: Lessons from Mary Parker Follett. *Journal of Management History*, 4(1), 16-28.

Fastcompany. (2004, April). Things leaders do: GE's Jeff Immelt on the ten keys to great leadership. *Fastcompany.com* [On-line serial]. Retrieved May 3, 2004, from http://www.fastcompany.com/magazine/81/

Ferris, G. R., & Kacmar, K. M. (1992). Perceptions of organizational politics. *Journal of Management*, 18, 93-116.

Gambetta, D. (Ed.). *Trust: Making and breaking cooperative relations*. New York: Blackwell.

Gardiner, P. D. (1999). Project management. Part of the Heriot-Watt Programme of Management Education by supported Distance Learning.

Gist, M. E., & Mitchell, T. R. (1992). Self-efficacy: A theoretical analysis of its determinants and malleability. *Academy of Management Review*, 17(2), 183-211.

Global Wireless Education Consortium. (2004). *Stronger wireless curriculum for higher education*. [Brochure]. Available from 1501 Lee Highway, Suite 110, Arlington, VA 22209-1109.

Goldstein, I. L., & Ford, J. K. (2002). Training in organizations. (4th ed.) Belmont, CA: Wadsworth Group.

Goris, J. R., Vaught, B. C., & Pettit, J. D. (2003). Effects of trust in superiors and influence of superiors on the association between individual-job congruence and job performance/satisfaction. *Journal of Business and Psychology*, 17, 327-343.

Groönroos, C. (2000). Relationship marketing: The Nordic School perspective. In J. N. Sheth & A. Parvatiyar (Eds.), *Handbook of Relationship Marketing*. London: Sage.

Hansen, D. A. *Total Quality Management (TQM) Tutorial/Help Page*. Retrieved May 4, 2005, at http://home.att.net/-iso9kl/tqm/tqm.html - Principles%20of%20TQM

Hart, P., & Saunders, C. (1997). Power and trust: Critical factors in the adoption and use of electronic data interchange. *Organization Science*, 1, 23-42.

Hermalin, B. E. (1998). Toward an Economic Theory of Leadership: Leading by Example. *American Economic Review*, 88, 1188-1206.

Herzberg, F. (1966). *Work and the nature of man*. Cleveland, OH: World.

Hochwarter, W. A., & Treadway, D. C. (2003). The interactive effects of negative and positive affect on the politics perceptions-job satisfaction relationship. *Journal of Management*, 29(4), 551-567.

Holl, J. M., & Frost, P. J. 1989. A laboratory study of charismatic leadership. *Organizational Behavior and Human Decision Process*, 43, 243-269.

Hollensbe, E. C., & Guthrie, J. P. (2000). Group pay-for-performance plans: The role of spontaneous goal setting. *Academy of Management Review*, 25(4), 864-872.

Howell, J. M., & Frost, P. J. 1989. A laboratory study of charismatic leadership. *Organizational Behavior and Human Decision Process*, 43, 243-269.

Kacmar, K. M., & Ferris, G. R. (1991). Perceptions of organizational politics scale (POP) development and construct validation. *Educational and Psychological Measurement*, 51, 193-205.

Kirkpatrick, S. A., & Locke, E. A. (1996). Direct and indirect effects of three core charismatic leadership components on performance and attitudes. *Journal of Applied Psychology*, 81(1), 36-61.

Lear, R. W. (1995, July/August). Re-engineering the board. *Chief Executive*, 105, 12.

Li, T. Y., & Yorke, J. A. (1975). Period three implies chaos. *American Mathematical Monthly*, 82, 995-992.

Lippitt, R. (1949). *Training in community relations: A research exploration toward new group skills*. New York: Harper.

Locke, E. A., & Latham, G. P. (2002). Building a practically useful theory of goal setting and task motivation: A 35-year odyssey. *American Psychologist*, 57(9), 705-17.

London, M. (1999). Principled leadership and business diplomacy: A practical, values-based direction for management development. *Journal of Management Development*, 18(2), 17-19.

Maidique, M. A., & Hayes, R. H. (1984). The art of high-technology management. *Sloan Management Review*, 25(2)(Winter), 29.

Marshall, R. (1994). Organizations and learning systems for a high wage economy. In Clark Kerr and Paul D. Stadohar (eds.) *Labor economics and industrial relations*. Cambridge, MA: Harvard University Press.

Maslow, A. H. (1954). *Motivation and personality*. New York: Harper.

Mayer, R., Davis, J. H., Schoorman, H. D. (1995). An integrative model of organizational trust. *Academy of Management Review*, 20(3), 709-734.

McClelland, D. C., & Boyatzis, R. E. (1982). Leadership motive pattern and long-term success in management. *Journal of Applied Psychology*, 67:737-743.

Melhem, Y. (2003). *Employee-customer relationships: An investigation into the impact of customer-contact employees' capabilities on customer satisfaction in Jordan banking sector.* Unpublished doctoral dissertation from the University of Nottingham, Nottingham, England.

Moorman, R. H. (1991). Relationship between organizational justice and organizational citizenship behaviors: Do fairness perceptions influence employee citizenship? *Journal of Applied Psychology,* 76, 845-855.

Pascale, R. (2000). *Surfing the edge of chaos: The laws of nature and the new laws of business.* New York: Leader to Leader Institute.

Pedler, M., Burgoyne, J. & Boydell, J. (1997). *The learning company.* New York: McGraw Hill.

Pennings, J. M., & Woiceshyn, J. (1987). A typology of organizational control and its metaphors. In S. B. Bacharach & S. M. Mitchell (Eds.), *Research in the sociology of organizations,* 5, 75-104. Greenwich, CTP JAI.

Peterson, I. (1993). *Newton's clock: Chaos in the solar system.* New York: Macmillan.

Pfeffer, J., & Veiga, F. (1999). Putting people first for organizational success. *Academy of Management Executives,* 13(2), 37-48.

Porter, M. E. (1990). *The competitiveness of nations.* New York: Free Press.

Prasad, (1993). The etiology of organizational politics: Implications for the intrapreneur. SAM *advanced management journal,* 58(3), 35-41.

Pyzdek, T. (2003). *The Six Sigma handbook, revised and expanded: The complete guide for greenbelts, blackbelts, and managers at all levels.* New York: McGraw Hill.

Ralphs, L. T., & Stephan, E. (1986). HRD in the Fortune 500. *Training and Development Journal,* 40, 69-76.

Randall, M. L., Cropanzano, R., Bormann, C. A., & Birjulin, A. (1999). Organizational politics and organizational support as predictors of work attitudes, job performance, and organizational citizenship behaviors. *Journal of Organizational Behavior, 20,* 159-174.

Randolph, W. A. (2000). Rethinking empowerment. *Organizational Dynamics, 29,* 94-107.

Randolph, W. A., & Sashkin, M. (2002). Can organizational empowerment work in multinational settings? *Academy of Management Executives, 16,* 102-115.

Poon, J. M. L. (2003). Situational antecedents and outcomes of organizational politics perceptions. *Journal of Managerial Psychology, 18*(2), 138-135.

Reichheld, F., & Detrick, C. (2002, September 19). Want to know how to keep expenses low? Think loyalty. *American Banker.*

Rich, G. A. (1997). The sales manager as a role model: Effects on trust, job satisfaction, and performance of salespeople. *Journal of Academy of Marketing Science, 25*(4), 319-328.

Riedel, J. A., Nebeker, D. M., & Cooper, B. L. (1988). The influence of monetary incentives on goal choice, goal commitment, and task performance. *Organizational Behavior and Human Decision Processes, 42*(2), 155-180.

Rousseau, D. M., Sitkin, S. B., Burt, R. S., & Camerer, C. (1998). Not so different after all: A cross-discipline view of trust. *Academy of Management Review, 23*(3), 393-404.

Schneider, S. M. (1997). Learning to be creative [A response to Sternberg et al., 1996]. *American Psychologist, 52,* 745.

Schwartz, P. (1996, April 15). The Art of the long view: Planning for the future in an uncertain world. *Currency.*

Seabright, M. A., Levinthal, D. A., & Fichman, M. (1992). Role of individual attachments in the dissolution of interorganizational relationships. *Academy of Management Journal*, 35(1), 122-160.

Senge, P.M. (1990). The leader's new work: Building learning organizations. *Sloan Management Review*, 32(1)(Fall), 7-23.

Stahl, M. J. (1986). *Managerial and technical motivation: Assessing needs for achievement, power, and affiliation.* New York: Praeger.

Stata, R. (1989). Organizational learning: The key to management innovation. *Sloan Management Review*, 30(3), 63-74.

Stein, D. L. (Ed.). (1989). *Lectures in the sciences of complexity.* Redwood City, CA: Addison-Wesley.

Sternberg, R. J. (1999). The theory of successful intelligence. *Review of General Psychology*, 3, 292-316.

Sternberg, R. J. (2000). Identifying and developing creative giftedness. *Roeper Review*, 23(2), 60-64.

Sternberg, R. J., & Lubart, T. I. (1995). *Defying the crowd: Cultivating creativity in a culture of conformity.* New York: Free Press.

Tan, H. H., & Tan, C. S. F. (2000). Towards the differentiation of trust in supervisor and trust in organization. *Genetic, Social, and General Psychology Monographs*, 126(2), 241-260.

The National Center for the Educational Quality of the Workforce, The other shoe: Education's contribution to the productivity of establishments. 1995, EQW, RE02, p. 2. Note: Productivity is measured by output.

Tierney, P., & Farmer, S. M. (2002). Creative self-efficacy: Its potential antecedents and relationship to creative performance. *Academy of Management Journal*, 45, 1137-1148.

Tierney, P., Farmer, S. M., & Graen, G. B. (1999). An examination of leadership and employee creativity: The relevance of traits and relations. *Personnel Psychology*, 52, 591-620.

Uhl-Bien, M., & Graen, G. B. (1992). Self-management and team-making in cross-functional work teams: Discovering the keys to becoming an integrated team. *Journal of High Technology Management Research*, 3(2), 228.

U.S. Department of Labor. *Employee Tenure in 2002. September 19, 2002.* Retrieved January 15, 2005 from the USDL Web site: ftp://ftp.bls.gov/pub/news.release/History/tenure.09192002.news

Vroom, V. H. (1993, Spring). Two decades of research on participation: Beyond buzzwords and management fads. *Yale Review of Management*, volume?,22-32.

Wall, T. D., Jackson, P. R., Mullarky, S., & Parker, S. K. (1996). The demand-control model of job-strain: A more specific test. *Journal of Occupational & Organizational Psychology*, 69, 153-167.

weLEAD, Inc. (2003, January). Leadership tip of the month, January, 2003. *leadingtoday.org*. Retrieved February 21, 2005 from http://www.leadingtoday.org/Onmag/jan03/transaction12003.html

weLEAD, Inc. (2003, February). Leadership tip of the month, February, 2003. *leadingtoday.org*. Retrieved February 21, 2005 from http://www.leadingtoday.org/Onmag/feb03/transform22003.html

Witt, L. A. (1998). Enhancing organizational goal congruence: A solution to organizational politics. *Journal of Applied Psychology*, 83(4), 666-674.

Yukl, G., Gordon, A., and Taber, T. (2002). A hierarchical taxonomy of leadership behavior: Integrating a half century of behavior research. *Journal of Leadership and Organizational Studies*, 9(1), 15-31.

Yukl, G. A., & Latham, G. P. (1976). Consequences of reinforcement schedules and incentive magnitudes for employee performance. Problems encountered in an industrial setting. *Journal of Applied Psychology, 60,* 294-298.

Zien, K. A., & Buckler, S. A. (1997). From experience dreams to market: Crafting a culture of innovation. *Journal of Product Innovation Management, 14,* 274–287.

Index

*The letter b following a page number denotes a box on that page.